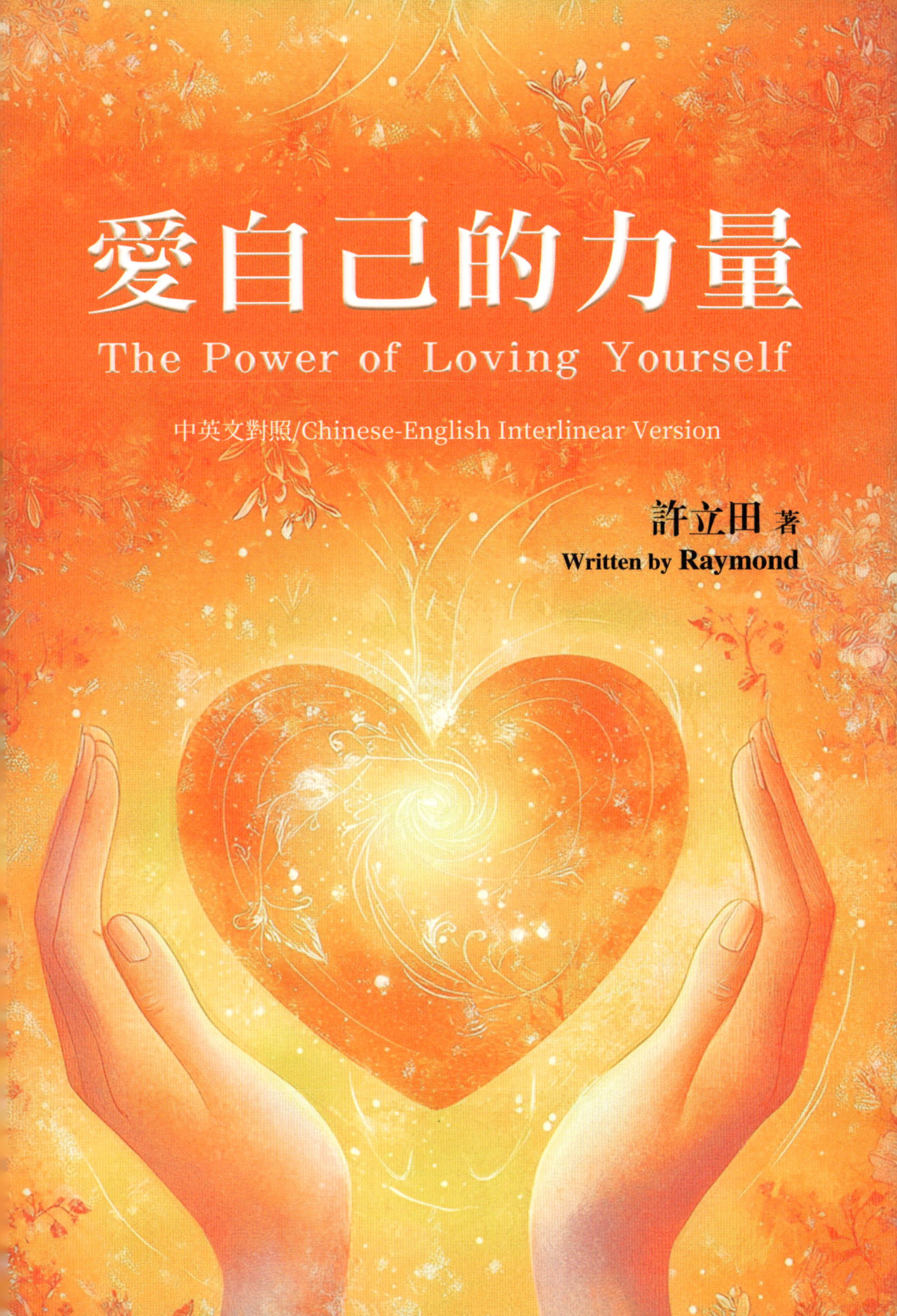

自序：心的成長與分享

　　這是一本充滿正向能量和思考方向的書！看這本書時，其實有兩個人在看，哪兩個人呢？現在的我，還有內在心靈深處的「我」，這是本與「我」共讀的書，必須靜下心來慢慢的讀，在靜心慢讀中，細細斟酌文章裡的一句話或一段文字，其間，隱藏了不少深層又廣泛的喻義，第一次、第二次、每一次讀它，都會有不同的感受和體會，看越多次，會越明白文字間的涵義，細心領會與「我」共讀的感受，體會「彼此（我與我）」呼應、認同的境界。我們都想真正的做到愛自己，因此，文章內容次數看得越多，很多想法會自然而然成為生活習慣的一部份，自然而然愛自己。

　　真的瞭解自己？喜歡自己？信任自己？全部接納自己嗎？我會不斷反覆、經常習慣的做這樣的動作：「我是不是真的能夠閉眼靜心下來，與自己內心深處的『我』對話？是不是能夠確實的問一問那位隱藏在我內在心靈的『我』：『你（我）』懂我嗎？」

　　如果連最基本的，只是「自己跟我」，才「兩個人」都相處不來，都互相不瞭解「我」，那怎麼跟身邊的人好好相處？只有清楚自己，才能清楚別人。能夠真心全部接納自己，相對的就可以接納其他的人、事、物。喜好、厭惡人人都有，就看用什麼態度和方式去面對。

　　觀念影響一生，任何人都想快樂、自在，然而，如果觀念一直不變，任何的改變都只是曇花一現。觀念的改變不容易，而什麼才是真的變了呢？就是在不知不覺中，經過了一段時間，周遭的人發現我變了，而不是自己說自己變了，那才是真正的改變。

　　改變自己，是從自我內在完全的改變，包括了思想、觀念、態度、習慣和行為，而非只是表層或壓抑內在的暫時性改變。

　　簡單、愉快、自在、溫和、陽光，我的生活態度多少也影響了周遭的人，他們會感受到輕鬆的氣息和氛圍，感覺到單純、積極，也感受到我激勵和客觀分析的理性，我漸漸發現，無論是好或壞的思維，人都是會相互影響的。

　　多年來，有朋友問過我類似的問題：知道某某人嗎？看過某

Preface: The Growth and Sharing of the Heart

This is a book filled with positive energy and guidance for thoughtful reflection! When reading this book, it feels like there are two readers present. Who are they? The current "me," and the deeper, inner "me." This book is a shared experience with my inner self, requiring calm and careful reading. During this mindful reading, I often pause to reflect on a phrase or passage, as they carry deeper and broader meanings. Each time I read it—whether it's the first, second, or even the hundredth time—I discover new insights and feelings. The more I read, the clearer the hidden meanings become, and I gradually reach a state of mutual understanding and recognition between "me" and my inner self.

We all strive to truly love ourselves. The more I read the content of this book, the more these ideas become a natural part of daily life, effortlessly leading to self-love.

Do I really understand myself? Do I truly like myself? Trust myself? Accept myself fully? I frequently ask myself, "Can I truly close my eyes, calm my mind, and have a conversation with my inner self? Can I ask that hidden part of me, do you understand me?"

If I can't even get along with "myself"—just two people—how can I build meaningful relationships with others around me? Only by understanding myself can I understand others. Accepting myself completely enables me to accept others as well. Preferences and dislikes are natural, but it's all about the attitude and approach in dealing with them.

Our mindset shapes our life. Everyone wants to be happy and free, but if we don't change our mindset, any change in life will only be temporary. Real change doesn't come easily. True transformation occurs when those around us notice the change, not when we declare it ourselves.

Changing oneself starts from a complete internal shift, including thoughts, perspectives, attitudes, habits, and behaviors—it's not just a surface-level adjustment or a temporary suppression of feelings.

My simple, joyful, and positive attitude toward life influences those around me. They sense the lightness in the atmosphere, the simplicity, and

某書嗎？做過某某活動嗎？而我的回答幾乎都是：沒有啊。朋友說：那剛才說的那些話和觀念，怎麼跟某某某幾乎一樣？

這些事只是想讓大家知道，只要願意，我們都可以找出適合的方法，以自己的方式一樣可以達到自我成長的境界，讓生命因此充滿陽光、正向，在平淡中可以擁有無限喜悅。

近年來，朋友希望我把沒有經過任何書本理論框限的思維，以及自己如何一路走來的感覺和想法寫下來，可以留下文字也可以分享經驗。

然而，講的比較快，寫的比較慢，將語言轉變成文字，需要更有系統的排列才能一目了然、顯而易懂。不過還好，「寫作」這位「朋友」，已經陪伴我數十年了，對我來說，和這位「朋友」一邊遊戲一邊完成工作，是多麼快樂的事。

我把過去到現在的一些想法彙集成冊，然而我們都會成長，想法會不斷改變，未來一定會產生不同的思維，而無論是什麼變化，只要是好的想法和做法能夠成為習慣，從那一刻起，我們就已經擁有簡單、陽光、自信、喜悅的人生。

本書用中英文對照，並非想練就中英文能力，而是希望中文的朋友看了之後送給英文的朋友，也可以讓英文的朋友看了之後送給中文的朋友，即使我的英文不好需要請人翻譯內容，這也表示語言只是過程，陽光自信的人生觀是無國界的。

我們擁有了正向的想法，好的思維就會如泉湧般不斷的激勵自己，擁有了好的思維，當然就能夠與我和「我」共同成長，真（珍）愛自己！

許立田
2025/01/15

the positivity I embody. Over time, I've realized that both good and bad thoughts have a ripple effect, influencing those around us.

For years, friends have asked me, "Do you know this person? Have you read that book? Have you tried this activity?" My answer is often, "No." They respond, "Then why do the things you say sound so much like what those people say?"

I share this to show that if we are willing, we can all find our own ways to grow and reach a state of self-improvement, making our lives brighter, more positive, and filled with joy even in the simplest moments.

In recent years, friends have encouraged me to write down my thoughts and experiences—thoughts not confined by any theories from books—so they could be shared with others.

While it's easier to speak than write, I find joy in the process of writing. Writing has been my companion for decades, and completing this work alongside this "friend" has been a source of happiness.

This book is a collection of thoughts from past to present. However, as we grow, our ideas will continue to evolve. No matter how things change, as long as positive ideas and practices become habits, we will already have a simple, confident, and joyful life from that moment onward.

When we embrace positive thinking, good thoughts will flow like a fountain, constantly encouraging ourselves. With the right mindset, we can grow alongside our inner self and truly love ourselves.

Raymond
15/JAN./2025

自序：心的成長與分享	4
壹、愛自己	16
1. 認識自己優缺點	20
2. 照顧自己健康	26
3. 內心充滿自信	32
4. 規劃自己人生	38
5. 擁有愉快心情	44
6. 與我共舞、享受單獨的喜悅	50
7. 觸動心靈	56
8. 為自己、為所愛的人而活！	60
貳、愛的傳達	66
9. 有質感的擁抱	68
10. 文字的憾動	72
11. 用行動的表示	76
12. 心靈感應的傳遞	80
參、自我修煉與成長	86
13. 我是三歲小孩	88
14. 我是溫室花朵？	94
15. 音樂滋潤心靈	100
16. 哭、蛻變與成長	104
17. 聆聽、回應、同理心	110
18. 鼓勵別人、說服自己？	114
19. 生命處處是溫暖	118
20. 觀念和習慣	124
21. 擁抱心靈淨土	128

Preface: The Growth and Sharing of the Heart	5
Part One: Loving Yourself	17
1. Understanding Your Strengths and Weaknesses	21
2. Taking Care of Your Health	27
3. Confidence from Within	33
4. Planning Your Life	39
5. Having a Happy Mood	45
6. Dance with Me, Enjoy the Joy of Solitude	51
7. Touching the Soul	57
8. Live for Yourself, Live for Your Loved Ones!	61
Part Two: The Transmission of Love	67
9. The Embrace of Quality	69
10. The Resonance of Words	73
11. Expressing Through Actions	77
12. Telepathic Communication	81
Part Three: Self-Cultivation and Growth	87
13. I Am a Three-Year-Old Child	89
14. Am I a Greenhouse Flower?	95
15. Music Nourishes the Soul	101
16. Crying, Transformation and Growth	105
17. Listening, Responding, and Empathy	111
18. Encouraging Others, Persuading Oneself?	115
19. Everywhere in Life is Warmth	119
20. Concepts and Habits	125
21. Embracing the Spiritual Sanctuary	129
22. Personification of Emotional Expression	133
23. Seizing the Opportunity	139

22. 擬人化的情感抒發	**132**
23. 掌握先機	**138**
24. 易受感動的心	**142**
25. 善解人意	**146**
26. 成功有效能的態度	**148**
27. 家	**152**
28. 貴人	**156**
29. 忍耐？不在意！	**160**
30. 時差	**164**

肆、反向思考、無限寬廣　　　　　　　170

31. 我老了？	**172**
32. 一代不如一代？	**176**
33. 增廣見聞	**180**
34. 善良	**184**
35. 不如意，十之八九？	**188**
36. 學歷？經歷？	**192**
37. 幽默回應	**196**
38. 沒空的醒思	**200**
39. 美食、豪宅	**204**
40. 認知層次	**208**
41. 不自覺的負面激勵	**212**
42. 開心「當下這一秒」	**216**
43. 生存韌性	**220**
44. 相信的迷思	**224**
45. 沒有困難只有方法	**230**
46. 所有生命	**236**

24. An Easily Moved Heart	143
25. Understanding and Empathy	147
26. Attitudes for Success and Effectiveness	149
27. Home	153
28. Benefactors	157
29. Endurance? Not a Concern!	161
30. Time Difference	165

Part Four: Reverse Thinking, Infinite Broadness	171
31. Am I Old?	173
32. Each Generation is Better Than the Last?	177
33. Expanding Knowledge	181
34. Kindness	185
35. Unfulfilled Expectations	189
36. Education? Experience?	193
37. Humorous Responses	197
38. Time Management Reflections	201
39. Food and Luxury Homes	205
40. Cognitive Levels	209
41. Unintentional Negative Reinforcement	213
42. Happiness in the "Present Moment"	217
43. Resilience in Survival	221
44. The Myth of Belief	225
45. No Difficulty, Only Methods	231
46. All Life	237
47. A Journey of the Mind	241
48. Are We Treating Them Well?	245
49. Success	251
50. Perfect Imperfection	255

47. 心情的旅行　　　　　　　240

48. 對牠好嗎？　　　　　　　244

49. 成功　　　　　　　　　　250

50. 不完美的完美　　　　　　254

51. 生命存在　　　　　　　　258

伍、認識自己、提昇內在　　264

52. 我是誰？　　　　　　　　268

53. 前世？今生！來世？　　　274

54. 我和人的關係　　　　　　282

55. 人和人的關係　　　　　　286

56. 人和自然、宇宙的關係　　292

57. 如何愛人、愛我？　　　　298

陸、大自然心靈之旅　　　　304

58. 煙靄繚繞的湖泊　　　　　306

59. 溪谷的迴響　　　　　　　308

60. 雲的變幻　　　　　　　　310

61. 石頭　　　　　　　　　　312

62. 遠眺的感動　　　　　　　314

63. 大海的聲音　　　　　　　316

64. 雪　　　　　　　　　　　318

65. 世界輕旅行　　　　　　　320

51. Existence of Life   259

Part Five: Knowing Yourself, Elevating the Inner Self   265

52. Who Am I?   269
53. Past Life? Present Life! Future Life?   275
54. My Relationship with People   283
55. The Relationship Between People   287
56. The Relationship Between Humans, Nature and the Universe   293
57. How to Love Others, Love Myself?   299

A Journey of the Spirit in Nature   305

58. The Misty Lake   307
59. Echoes of the Stream   309
60. The Transformation of Clouds   311
61. Stones   313
62. The Emotion of a Distant View   315
63. The Sound of the Ocean   317
64. Snow   319
65. Light Travel Around the World   321

愛自己

Loving Yourself

愛自己的感覺是：心靈上完全接納，自我擁有；情感上滿心，肯定溫暖；情緒上平靜，自在與無為。把那些感覺全部融入自我內在心靈深處，就會愛自己。

Loving yourself means fully accepting, embracing, and possessing yourself on a spiritual level, and feeling joy, satisfaction, and warmth emotionally.

壹、愛自己

　　能夠先真正做到愛自己，才能真正懂得愛別人。很多人想要愛別人，卻很少人先做到愛自己。自己不瞭解自己、不會照顧自己，卻想要照顧別人、愛別人，這會流於空洞和不切合別人真實的需要，因為，那都不是自己發自內心的真實感受後自然流露的愛。

　　就好像，我是小孩子，我要的是父母、大人陪我玩，而不是大人所想的一堆玩具、零食，我就會快樂。我年老獨居，我要的是有人或家人陪我聊天，而不是別人所想的三餐無虞、找個傭人照顧。我心情鬱悶，我要的是有人靜靜的傾聽我心裡的話，而不是一堆的建議或吃喝玩樂。

　　要如何愛？怎樣才算愛？就是在身體及精神層面都能體會自己、照顧自己，那就是自然流露的「愛自己」，是發自內心自信以及對自己外在肯定的一種感覺，且無形中會散發出一股正向能量。或許曾經有這樣的經驗：關愛別人卻遭到拒絕。這是因為如果沒有先真正懂得愛自己，那麼一切的付出會流於形式和表層，當然很難讓對方有實際的感受，如果真的懂得愛自己，內心自然會散發出愛的感覺，外在行為自然會流露出愛的表現，就會知道應該如何對別人付出愛，即使遭到回絕，也不會在意。

　　愛自己的感覺是：心靈上完全接納、包容與擁有；情感上愉悅、滿足與溫暖；情緒上平靜、自在與無為。把那些感覺全部融入自我內在心靈深處，就會愛自己。

　　「愛自己」這句話，我靜心感受其中的意境：

- 真的清楚明白「我―是―誰―嗎」？「我是誰？」是的，我瞭解自己有多深？
- 會因為發生某些不如意或不愉快的事情而討厭自己嗎？
- 會覺得別人優秀而認為不如別人和盲目崇拜人事物嗎？
- 會因為和別人的財富做比較而洩氣嗎？
- 瞭解自己身體健康狀況，而且確實做到保養健康嗎？
- 瞭解自己的行為及個性，而且清楚知道自己的喜怒、愛好

Part One: Loving Yourself

To truly love others, you must first genuinely love yourself. Many people want to love others, but few start by loving themselves. If you don't understand yourself or know how to take care of yourself, how can you care for or love others? Love that isn't rooted in true inner understanding is shallow and disconnected from the real needs of others.

It's like being a child. What I really want is for my parents or other adults to play with me, not a pile of toys or snacks they think will make me happy. Or as an elderly person living alone, what I truly need is someone to talk to, not just having my meals taken care of or being assigned a caretaker. When I'm feeling down, what I want is for someone to quietly listen to me, not a barrage of suggestions or distractions.

How do we love? What counts as love? It's when you can fully understand and care for both your body and spirit—that's the natural expression of self-love. It's an inner confidence and acceptance that radiates a positive energy. You may have experienced trying to care for someone, only to have them reject it. This happens when love is superficial, without a foundation of self-love. If you truly understand how to love yourself, your actions will naturally convey love, and even if rejected, it won't bother you.

Loving yourself means fully accepting, embracing, and possessing yourself on a spiritual level, and feeling joy, satisfaction, and warmth emotionally. It also means feeling calm, free, and at peace. When all these feelings merge deeply into your inner being, that is when you truly love yourself.

When I reflect on the phrase "love yourself," I ponder its deeper meaning:

- Do I truly understand who I am?
- Do I dislike myself when things don't go as planned or when I'm unhappy?
- Do I feel inferior and idolize others just because they seem better than me?

嗎？

- 能夠每天心情輕鬆愉快嗎？無論再大的煩瑣事情，都可以沉穩面對讓自己快樂嗎？能夠凡事客觀理性思考嗎？
- 能夠確實規劃自己的生涯、時間、工作、財富、生活圈，非不得已，不麻煩不依賴別人，不讓家人、親朋好友擔心嗎？

凡此種種，其實就是真的做到「愛自己」。

「我愛自己」是最重要的，願意愛自己就會愛自己更多，知道如何愛自己，也會明白要用什麼適當的方法去愛別人，那種由內在自然而然所散發的肢體語言，是最純真也最被接受的，這樣的「愛自己」，當然可以愛別人。

- Do I get discouraged when I compare myself to others' wealth?
- Do I truly understand my health status and take care of it?
- Am I aware of my actions and personality, knowing what makes me happy or angry?
- Can I face each day with ease and joy, calmly handling even the most troublesome matters? Can I objectively and rationally think through things?

To truly love yourself is to cultivate these qualities, allowing yourself to grow and naturally radiate love to others.

1. 認識自己優缺點

　　什麼是優點？什麼是缺點？是不是充分瞭解自己的優缺點？其實，多數的優缺點是沒有標準的。自己認為的優點，在旁人眼中可能是缺點；自己認為的缺點，在旁人眼裡也可能成為優點，所以，優點未必是優點，缺點未必是缺點；優點可能是缺點，缺點可能是優點，也有時候它是一體兩面。

　　重點在於能夠瞭解自己的人格本質，認識、承認、接受自己的優缺點，才能改造自己、建立自信，那麼，即使看起來可能是缺點的習性，也可以在盡量不影響、妨礙別人的原則下做自己。

　　我常會思考一些觀念，來審視自己：

- 在溫和、衝動；內向、外向；熱忱、冷漠；迷糊、機靈的特質裡，我有哪些？喜歡和不喜歡的人、事、物又有哪些？在工作、求學、生活、人際關係、家庭生活中，清楚別人的觀感和想法嗎？自己和別人之間的相處，可以盡量做到平衡嗎？認識、清楚自己的優缺點嗎？

　　例如：我覺得沒自信，然而目前似乎無法改變。其實，只要認清這個事實然後接受它，不強迫自己設定什麼目標、改變的時間或做什麼個性上的修正，這樣反而沒有壓力，只要願意，在經過一段長時間的自我成長和磨練後，就會漸漸變得有自信。

- 清楚知道自己喜歡和不喜歡的人、事、物嗎？而且無論喜歡或不喜歡，都會用平靜的心去面對，不會有情緒波動起伏很大的反應（例如：喜歡的事興奮異常；討厭的事嗤之以鼻），遇到開心的事能夠一抹微笑；不開心的事可以一笑置之嗎？

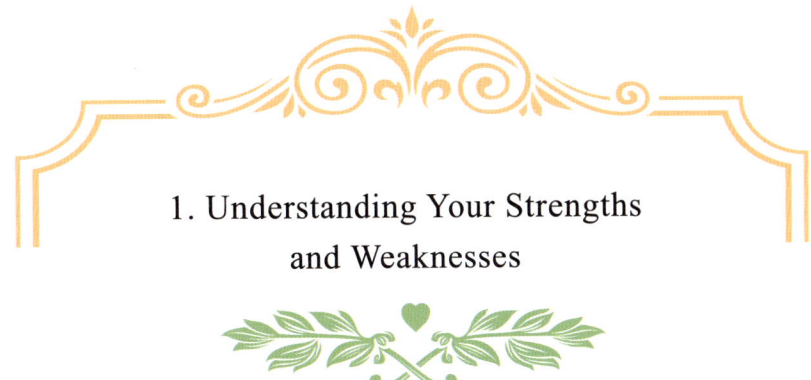

1. Understanding Your Strengths and Weaknesses

What are strengths? What are weaknesses? Do you truly understand your own strengths and weaknesses? In fact, most strengths and weaknesses don't have a fixed standard. What you see as a strength might be viewed as a weakness by others, and what you consider a weakness might be seen as a strength by someone else. Therefore, a strength may not always be a strength, and a weakness may not always be a weakness. They can sometimes be two sides of the same coin.

The key lies in understanding your true nature, recognizing, admitting, and accepting your strengths and weaknesses. Only then can you transform yourself and build self-confidence. Even what appears to be a weakness can be embraced, as long as it doesn't interfere with or harm others, allowing you to be yourself.

I often reflect on certain concepts to examine myself:

- In traits like being gentle or impulsive, introverted or extroverted, passionate or indifferent, confused or sharp, which ones apply to me? What are the things, people, or situations I like or dislike? In work, study, life, relationships, and family life, am I clear about others' perspectives and thoughts? Can I balance my interactions with others? Do I truly understand my own strengths and weaknesses?

For example, I feel insecure, but I can't seem to change that at the moment. Actually, once I recognize and accept this fact, without forcing myself to set any goals, timelines, or personality adjustments, I'll feel less

再仔細想想，別人喜歡的，是我喜歡的嗎？例如：別人喜歡我跟著他們四處交友、應酬，我真的喜歡嗎？

別人討厭的，真的不好嗎？例如：別人不喜歡我的穿著或打扮，那真的會妨礙到別人嗎？

別人眼中對我的任何觀點，除非是傷害到他人，那當然要修正，如果只是個人的喜好或觀感，那麼，只要在盡量不去妨礙別人的原則下，當然可以開心做自己。

例如：朋友說我很少參加聚餐。如果個性不喜歡應酬，而且也不會影響人際關係和工作效率，朋友也能瞭解、接受，那麼，不喜歡應酬交際，它是優點還是缺點呢？

我的工作包括了業務推廣，觀念中，業務工作必須主動出擊和拜訪陌生客戶。然而我很清楚我的缺點在於不知道如何和陌生人打開話題、交際應酬；優點是專精於分析判斷、解答客戶所有疑惑和提供最適當的建議，對於每一項銷售的產品，有非常透徹的專業知識。

然而，不主動推銷、客戶不上門、不建立人際網絡，那些優點根本沒用，專精於分析的企劃能力，如果沒有經過市場的考驗，都是不切實際的空談。

很幸運的，我的工作正好不太需要主動行銷（基本行銷仍是必須的），需要的客戶會主動找上門，不需要的即使強力推銷也很難刺激消費，差別只剩下客戶會選擇誰來服務。

從事了適合自己的行業，避開個性上不擅於主動接觸人群的缺點，專業能力的優點就可以充分發揮出來，解答了客戶的所有疑問，並且提供更多沒有注意到甚至忽略掉的重要訊息，讓他們感受到專業知識的豐富和為他們服務的執行能力，也因此得到了客戶的肯定和口碑上的相互推薦，在事業領域也有了立足之地。

瞭解自己的個性、認識自己的優缺點，在適合自己個性的領域中，把優點充分發揮出來，就能夠肯定自己的能力，任何事都能自信面對。

pressured. As long as I'm willing, after a period of self-growth and practice, I'll gradually become more confident.

- Am I aware of the people, things, or situations I like and dislike? And can I face them calmly without reacting too emotionally (e.g., being overly excited about things I like, or dismissive of things I dislike)? Can I smile when something makes me happy, and laugh things off when they don't?

Also, do I genuinely like what others like? For instance, others might enjoy socializing and networking, but do I really enjoy it?

Do the things others dislike truly bother me? For example, others might not like the way I dress, but does it really affect them?

When it comes to others' opinions about me, unless my actions harm someone, which would warrant correction, personal preferences and opinions shouldn't matter. As long as I'm not bothering anyone, I should be free to be myself.

For example, a friend might say I rarely join social gatherings. If I'm not fond of socializing, and it doesn't affect my relationships or work efficiency, and my friends can understand and accept that, then is my dislike for socializing really a weakness or could it be a strength?

My job involves business promotion, and traditionally, sales require proactively reaching out to and visiting potential clients. However, I'm well aware that my weakness lies in not knowing how to start conversations with strangers or engage in social events. On the other hand, my strength is my expertise in analysis and problem-solving. I can address all of my clients' concerns and provide the most appropriate advice, and I possess a deep understanding of the products I sell.

Yet, without proactively selling, clients won't come to me, and without building a network, those strengths become useless. My analytical skills will remain theoretical without real-world application.

Luckily, my job doesn't require aggressive sales tactics (though basic marketing is still necessary). The clients who need the product will come to me, while those who don't, even with heavy promotion, are unlikely to

1. Understanding Your Strengths and Weaknesses | 23

make a purchase. The only difference is who the clients choose to work with.

By finding a job that suits my personality, avoiding the shortcomings of not being good at proactively approaching people, I can fully utilize my strengths. I can answer all of my clients' questions and provide additional, often overlooked, crucial information, allowing them to experience the depth of my expertise and my capability to serve them. As a result, I've earned their trust and word-of-mouth referrals, establishing myself in my career.

Understanding your personality and knowing your strengths and weaknesses allow you to excel in areas that suit you. When you fully unleash your strengths, you can confidently face anything.

2. 照顧自己健康

　　懂得照顧自己，才能真正懂得照顧別人，關懷別人之前，我會先做到照顧自己。

　　在生活（生理、身體）層面中，讓身體健康。我會問自己：身體健康嗎？健康標準是什麼？外表正常未必表示正常，什麼是具體的照顧呢？

- 清楚健康檢查的一些數據（例如：血液各項檢查、血糖、尿酸、肝膽腎功能、腫瘤標記、糞便潛血、MRI……），這除了代表掌握多年來的健康狀況，更可以瞭解自己的體質，畢竟每個人對於同一症狀的療程未必完全相同，以自己的健康數據做為參考、診斷及治療，醫病合作會是最好的。

- 會經常「忘記」用餐、「忘記」休息，甚至「忘記」按時服藥，然後以忙碌來當藉口嗎？對於自己的健康在乎嗎？愛自己，自然愛上健康。

- 照顧健康不是醫師的責任，醫師是專業在疾病的醫治，自己才是健康的照顧者。必須確實配合

　　醫師的服藥及療程的指示，更要正確提供自己身體治療過程的反應，讓醫師做下個療程的正確判斷。

　　我曾經調侃朋友：「醫師指示服藥一天吃三次，結果你三天吃一次，甚至說沒效就不吃，然後說這個醫師不好，那個醫師沒效，你不醫自己，誰能醫你？」，照顧健康，操之在己！

　　30來歲就加入了會員制的健康檢查機構，連續做了3年的檢

2. Taking Care of Your Health

To truly care for others, you must first know how to take care of yourself. Before showing concern for others, I make sure to care for myself first.

On the physical （physiological） level, I ensure my body stays healthy. I often ask myself: "Is my body healthy? What is the standard of health?" Just looking normal on the outside doesn't always mean you're healthy. So, what does it really mean to take care of yourself?

- Being aware of various health check-up data （e.g., blood tests, blood sugar, uric acid, liver and kidney function, tumor markers, fecal occult blood, MRI...） not only helps monitor your health over the years but also gives insight into your body. Since treatments can vary from person to person for the same symptoms, using your own health data for reference, diagnosis, and treatment can help foster better collaboration with doctors.

- Do you often "forget" to eat, "forget" to rest, or even "forget" to take your medicine on time, using being busy as an excuse? Do you care about your health? Love yourself, and naturally, you will start to love being healthy.

- Taking care of your health isn't solely the doctor's responsibility. Doctors specialize in treating diseases, but you are responsible for maintaining your health. You must follow the doctor's medication and treatment instructions and accurately communicate how your body responds during treatment so the doctor can make informed decisions for the next steps.

查之後，認為年輕而且檢查數據還不錯，健檢安排也就停頓下來。大約6年後，有一陣子一直覺得身體不是很舒服，於是又安排了檢查。

結果可想而知，醫師分析檢查結果，再比較之前的檢查數據後告誡我，再不注意，身體可能就會出問題，加上體重長期維持在82公斤上下，自己的確覺得很不舒服，於是開始認真的在各方面正確的照顧健康（運動、飲食熱量控制、食物種類選擇、生活作息調整），體重漸漸回到之前的62公斤，1年後再次檢查，結果連醫師都驚訝。

我不可能永遠完全健康，重要的是瞭解自己身體情況，即使在身體逐漸退化的時候，也能夠在最佳狀態下漸漸老化，讓生命健康的誕生，「健康」的結束，這是最美好的愛自己。

在心靈（心理、精神）層面中，讓情緒正向。我會讓情緒經常維持著平順的感覺。

- 對內心：常常發脾氣嗎？討厭或不喜歡的事情或人多嗎？常常動不動就緊張嗎？挑食嗎？總覺得自己是對的而不滿或委屈嗎？悲傷難過的時候多於快樂自在嗎？覺得沒有人瞭解我嗎？

- 對外在：人際關係不佳嗎？家人相處不好嗎？覺得工作壓力大嗎？覺得不公平的事情多嗎？生活覺得煩躁無趣嗎？

健康的身體，是人生的基礎。照顧自己的健康，從實際行動做起：

- 飲、食、三餐，懂得如何安排。即使可能因為交際、應酬，有一餐或幾餐難免大魚大肉，也知道如何在接下來的幾餐調整回來。例如：萬一這一餐吃了數千卡熱量的食物，那麼在往後幾餐就食用清淡、低卡食物平衡回來，自己清楚明白一天熱量攝取控制在1200卡~1800卡之間（熱量每日攝取值因人、因工作量而異）。

- 把運動融入每日生活裡，成為日常生活的習慣，能走不坐（車）、能爬不搭（電梯）、能站不躺（椅子、沙發），不知不覺每天都已經隨時在運動，例如：某些事情若非迫切需要，偶而以走路代替交通工具、走樓梯替代坐電梯；搭公車或捷運回家，何妨提前一站下車，再以稍微類似快

I once jokingly told a friend, "The doctor tells you to take medicine three times a day, but you take it once every three days and then complain that it's not working, or that the doctor isn't good. If you don't take care of yourself, who can help you?" Taking care of your health is in your hands!

In my early 30s, I joined a health screening membership program. After three years of consistent checkups, I stopped because I was young, and my health data looked good. About six years later, I started feeling unwell and arranged another checkup.

The results were as expected. After comparing the recent data with the previous ones, the doctor warned me that if I didn't start paying attention to my health, I could be in serious trouble. I had maintained a weight of around 82 kg for a long time, and I was feeling very uncomfortable. So, I began to take my health seriously, focusing on exercise, calorie control, food selection, and adjusting my lifestyle. Gradually, my weight returned to 62 kg, and after a year, the doctor was surprised by the results.

I understand that I can't be perfectly healthy forever. What's important is knowing my body's condition, so that even as I age, I can do so in the best possible state. A healthy life is a beautiful way to take care of yourself, from birth to "healthily" reaching the end.

On the emotional （psychological, spiritual） level, I strive to maintain positive emotions. I try to keep my mood steady and balanced.

- Internally: Do you frequently lose your temper? Are there many things or people you dislike? Do you often get anxious or tense? Are you picky with food? Do you always feel you're right and become dissatisfied or aggrieved when others disagree? Are you more often sad than happy? Do you feel misunderstood by others?
- Externally: Are your relationships with others strained? Do you have difficulty getting along with your family? Do you feel a lot of pressure at work? Do you frequently encounter things that seem unfair? Do you find life boring or frustrating?

A healthy body is the foundation of life. Taking care of your health starts with practical actions:

- Manage your meals. Even if you occasionally indulge due to social

步走的方式走回家；午、晚餐後坐著看電視、看報紙、打電玩，其實站著看或玩也可以，何妨順便站著動一動腳、甩甩手，未必要排出固定的時間去運動場、游泳池、健身房，畢竟去那些地方需要時間的安排，往返也需要時間。

例如：為了1小時的運動，還必須付出半小時甚至1小時的往返時間（如果走路去就另當別論），如果天氣太熱、太冷、颱風、下雨、工作偶爾忙碌等等因素，多數人是很難365天持之以恆的，因此，把運動成為日常生活習慣才會不知不覺的持久下去。當然，如果有人把去運動場合可以持續或成為常態，也是不錯的方法。

- 正確掌握自己的健康檢查數據，不會因為年輕而忽略健康檢查。每年的健檢資料，長期累積下來，可以成為自己往後醫療的重要參考，這裡提到的健檢並非一般勞健保所提供的免費檢查，畢竟那些檢查太表層、項目太少、某些健保免費檢查是三年一次，感覺時間相隔太久了，而是大型醫療院所或會員制健檢機構詳細的大項小項檢查。

- 健保、勞保、公保、農保之外，要有屬於適合自己的終身醫療保險。以自己的需求為考量，先列出需求項目，再找符合需求的醫療保單，這種終身保單，一份就夠了，而不是別人推銷什麼保單或有多少紅利就心動，畢竟終身醫療保險，應該著眼於照顧自己的終身醫療保障，而不是可以賺多少紅利，是保障自己活著的時候有最好的照顧，而不是過世後可以得到多少錢，因為保障的目的不同，保險的主要需求內容就不同，照顧健康，應以終身醫療保險能夠提供最多、最高的保障為優先考量。

曾經聽過很貼切的一句話：「40歲以前健康照顧你，40歲以後你照顧健康」，現在幾歲了呢？情緒影響心理、心理影響健康，從小、從現在開始照顧健康，就會更懂得照顧自己的身、心、靈。

engagements, you should know how to balance things out afterward. For instance, if you have a high-calorie meal, balance it with lighter, lower-calorie meals later, keeping your daily calorie intake between 1200-1800 calories （depending on individual needs and activity level）.

- Incorporate exercise into daily life so that it becomes a habit. Walk when you can instead of taking transportation, climb stairs instead of taking the elevator, and stand rather than sit when possible. Before you know it, you'll have exercised throughout the day without even noticing. For example, you could walk instead of using a vehicle for short trips, take the stairs instead of the elevator, or get off the bus or subway a stop early and walk briskly home. Instead of sitting after meals to watch TV or play video games, stand up and move around. You don't always need to go to a gym, swimming pool, or fitness center, as these places require time and effort. Integrating exercise into everyday life is easier to maintain.

- Keep track of your health data and don't neglect check-ups just because you're young. Your health check-up results, accumulated over time, become valuable reference points for future medical treatments. These checkups should go beyond basic health insurance offerings, which are often too superficial and infrequent.

- In addition to health and social insurance, it's important to have lifelong medical insurance that suits your needs. Choose an insurance plan based on your personal health requirements, not based on what others suggest or on potential bonuses. The focus should be on ensuring the best possible care while alive, not on financial benefits after death. The goal of medical insurance should be lifelong health coverage, not posthumous payouts.

I once heard a fitting quote: "Before 40, your health takes care of you; after 40, you take care of your health." How old are you now? Emotions influence mental well-being, and mental well-being affects physical health. By starting to take care of your health—both body and mind—from a young age or from now, you will better understand how to take care of yourself holistically.

3. 內心充滿自信

　　內心充滿自信，不需要任何刻意的行為，意念是堅定、明確，態度是樂觀、穩定，那股特質和魅力，自然會傳遞給周遭的人，是一種陽光、積極、熱忱、正向的舒服感覺。

　　自信與個性的內向或外向無關，是發自內心很自然所表現出來的一種行為和感覺，外向活潑比較有自信嗎？有時候只是自我深層意識空虛的掩飾；內向寡言比較沒有自信嗎？有時候是認清一切而沉穩的表現，或心理扭曲、壓抑的隱藏。

　　肯定自己的人，會出現以下的態度：

- 跳脫教條式的學習框限，不會墨守成規，思想靈活順應變化，回歸內在，從心做起。
- 用自我喜歡的方式，探尋最適合的生活。
- 用最能體會和感覺的方法來激勵自己。
- 做到自己與自己溝通的心靈層次。
- 如果希望透過外在的協助，也會找到可以幫助自己的人和最適合成長的方法。

　　外在環境複雜多變很難全面掌握、面面俱到，唯一可以確定的就是，無論外在環境如何變化，都很清楚知道自己要的是什麼，很清楚內在和外在的一切，由於對自己的信任，更可以用單純的思想和篤定的態度去面對，因而看似複雜的人、事、物就不再複雜，這就是自信的表現。

3. Confidence from Within

When you have confidence from within, there is no need for deliberate actions. Your mindset is firm and clear, and your attitude is optimistic and steady. This quality and charm naturally radiate to those around you, bringing a sense of warmth, positivity, enthusiasm, and comfort.

Confidence has nothing to do with whether you are introverted or extroverted. It is a natural expression of an inner state. Are outgoing and lively people more confident? Sometimes, this is just a mask for a deep sense of emptiness. Are quiet and reserved people less confident? Sometimes, it's a sign of inner clarity and calmness, or perhaps a concealed, suppressed psychological state.

A person who affirms themselves will exhibit the following traits:

- They step out of rigid learning frameworks, avoid being bound by conventions, and embrace flexible thinking to adapt to changes. They return to their inner self and follow their heart.

- They find the way of life that suits them best by following their own preferences.

- They motivate themselves in ways that they deeply understand and feel.

- They communicate with themselves on a spiritual level.

- If they seek external help, they will find the right people and methods to aid their personal growth.

舉一些身體力行的作法：

- 很清楚知道「我－是－誰」。這在前面的文章有提過一些想法。
- 喜歡現在的自己、滿足現在的生活、知足現在的一切、可以一個人自得其樂，把握活在每個「這一秒」的感覺，平心靜氣面對每個「下一秒」的來臨，知道自己就是自己的貴人。
- 擺脫對別人的職稱、頭銜、身份、地位、財富，盲目崇拜的迷思。
- 相信自己、正向思考、個性溫和、情緒平靜。
- 勇於表達自己的想法，以理性、客觀、同理心的思維和方式與人互動。

從小就滿臉雀斑，朋友曾經建議我去做現在很流行的雷射脈衝光去除雀斑。

我這麼回答：有雀斑的人多還是少？

朋友：有雀斑的人少。

我：所以有雀斑的人稀有。

朋友：是。

我：所以「物以稀為貴」。

朋友：對。

我：那何必把它弄掉！

朋友：？！？⋯⋯（傻眼，無言以對）

內心充滿自信，就會喜歡自己真實的內在和展現出來的外在，就像我喜歡我的雀斑一樣。

多年前和朋友去中美洲旅遊，看到當地的人，居然有一家8口擠在10幾坪的木造房子裡，沒水沒電沒瓦斯，以台灣的生活水平來衡量，設備算是非常簡陋的。

透過翻譯，我說：看起來生活有點不方便吧。（其實心裡是想，生活一定很艱難！）

他一派輕鬆的回答：不會啊。

The external environment is complex and ever-changing, making it difficult to control everything. But the one certainty is that, regardless of how the outside world shifts, they know exactly what they want. They have a clear understanding of both their inner and outer worlds. Because of their trust in themselves, they can face challenges with simplicity of thought and a firm attitude, making seemingly complex situations much easier to handle. This is the expression of confidence.

Here are some ways to embody confidence:

- Have a clear sense of "Who-I-am." I've touched on this in earlier writings.

- Love who you are now, be content with your current life, be grateful for everything you have, and find joy in being alone. Savor each moment, remain calm when facing the next, and know that you are your own greatest ally.

- Let go of blind admiration for others' titles, status, identity, or wealth.

- Trust yourself, think positively, maintain a gentle personality, and keep a calm emotional state.

- Be brave enough to express your thoughts and interact with others with rationality, objectivity, and empathy.

Growing up, I had a face full of freckles. Friends once suggested I try the popular laser treatments to remove them.

My response: "Are there more people with freckles or without?"

Friend: "Fewer people have freckles."

Me: "So people with freckles are rare."

Friend: "Yes."

Me: "So 'rarity makes things precious.'"

Friend: "Right."

Me: "Then why remove them?"

Friend: "?!?...." （Speechless）

我滿臉狐疑,心想:怎麼會呢?

　　他繼續說:要吃魚、蝦,我家旁邊的河裡抓就有;青菜、水果,自己種、山裡摘都很多;要吃雞還是豬肉,山上就抓得到,還有很多好吃的野味。河邊就可以洗澡、洗衣服,住家周圍木材隨手可得,吃的、住的、用的,要什麼有什麼,住這裡真的很棒。

　　一頓簡單而原始的當地風味午餐,證明了他所說的,各式難得一見的美味珍饈,令我難忘。

　　從他的口氣和眼神裡,我感受到他的滿足、喜悅和自信,如果是我,也會喜歡那種衣食無慮、生活無憂的方式,豪宅、富貴的標準是什麼?其實,就是喜歡自己的生活模式和發自內心的滿足。

When you are confident from within, you will love both your inner self and the way you appear externally, just like I love my freckles.

Years ago, I traveled with friends to Central America and saw a local family of eight squeezed into a small, basic wooden house with no water, electricity, or gas. Compared to the living standards in Taiwan, the conditions were very simple.

Through a translator, I said, "It looks like life might be a bit inconvenient here." (Honestly, I was thinking, life must be really tough!)

He responded casually, "Not at all."

I was skeptical, thinking, "How could that be?"

He continued, "If we want fish or shrimp, we can catch them in the river next to my house. Vegetables and fruits? We grow them ourselves or pick them from the mountains. If we want chicken or pork, we can hunt in the mountains. There's also plenty of delicious game to eat. We can bathe and wash clothes by the river. There's plenty of wood around the house for shelter and cooking. We have everything we need. Living here is great."

A simple, rustic lunch proved his point. The rare and exquisite dishes were unforgettable.

From his tone and gaze, I sensed his satisfaction, joy, and confidence. If I were in his shoes, I would also enjoy such a carefree, worry-free lifestyle. What is the real standard for luxury or wealth? Ultimately, it's about liking your way of life and feeling genuine satisfaction from within.

4. 規劃自己人生

　　愛自己、關心自己，也清楚人生的規劃和目標，在生活、工作各方面不依賴，不必他人操心。與其期待出現一位關心、照顧我的人，何妨讓自己就是那個人，不但沒壓力、沒負擔，更可以隨時按照自己的喜好來規劃人生，那是件多麼自在、自由的心情。

　　自己的人生自己規劃，做自己人生的主人和貴人。孩童階段，懵懵懂懂，一切都在摸索、學習。求學讀書階段，也談不上什麼明確的人生規劃，當然，如果這段期間已經有人可以從中灌輸人生規劃的觀念，甚至指導該怎麼做，那是非常幸福的一件事，雖然世事多變無法一概而論，然而觀念、原理、方法這類的知識越早知道越好，即使不懂或不明白，這樣的思想已經深植心中，一定會在日後產生影響。

　　人的一生充滿變數，面對生活、工作、家庭、收入、人際、健康等等層面，都不可能一成不變，因此，面對這些情況時，會去做一些規劃，我們聽過這句話：計劃趕不上變化！是的，也因為如此，計劃會隨著變化調整，然而，任何一種計劃，都有可能和其他計劃產生衝突，最後就不了了之或得到這個失去那個，難免留下缺憾，例如：工作計劃和生活、家庭、健康產生衝突；收入計劃和人際、健康產生衝突。

　　面對人生各種變化所做的規劃，總覺得千頭萬緒或相互衝突，得失之間難以平衡，仔細想想，能夠讓自己生活、工作的基本條件是什麼？健康！健康勝過的一切，這在「照顧自己健康」章節有提到一些想法。

4. Planning Your Life

Loving and caring for yourself includes having a clear life plan and goals. In every aspect of life and work, you can be independent and not rely on others to take care of you. Instead of waiting for someone to look after you, why not become that person for yourself? This way, there's no pressure or burden, and you can plan your life according to your preferences. What a free and easy feeling that is!

Plan your own life and be the master and benefactor of your own journey. As children, we are confused and learn through exploration. During the schooling years, it's rare to have a concrete life plan. Of course, if someone can instill the concept of life planning during this time and guide you on how to do it, that is a blessing. Although life is unpredictable and no plan fits all situations, the earlier you know about such concepts, principles, and methods, the better. Even if you don't fully understand them, these ideas will be ingrained in your mind and will influence you later on.

Life is full of uncertainties. In dealing with various aspects—such as living conditions, work, family, income, relationships, and health—things are unlikely to stay the same forever. Therefore, we often create plans to navigate these situations. You might have heard the saying, "Plans can't keep up with changes!" Indeed, plans need to be adjusted with changing circumstances. However, any plan can potentially conflict with others, leading to situations where something is gained but something else is lost, leaving regrets. For instance, work plans may conflict with personal life, family, or health, and income plans may clash with relationships or health.

其次，無論身處世界任何地方，在自給自足、以物易物或金錢財富的生活環境，「收入」（這裡所指的收入，物質或金錢都算），是無可避免用來維持生活、生命的必需來源。

財富的規劃，尤其希望在中晚年的生活可以無憂無慮，以此為目標，可以這麼思考進行：

- 無論現在是 20 幾歲、30 幾歲或 40 多歲，設定自己的退休年紀（退休，只是表示「多了更多自己的時間」，不代表完全退出職場），例如 55 歲。

- 假設生命是 100 歲，55 歲退休之後沒有任何收入、坐吃山空的最壞打算，那麼 45 年需要多少資金才能維持生活？

假設如之前「照顧自己健康」章節所提到，自己已經有終身醫療保險和房子，退休之後每個月需要新台幣 3 萬元的開銷（此為舉例，金額多少依個人生活能力及水平要求而定），那麼 1 年是 36 萬，45 年共需 1,620 萬現金（在此係指最穩定的定存或存款，還不包括可能有漲跌的股票、基金等等）。如果以 55 歲左右擁有 1,620 為目標，那麼，現在的年紀到 55 歲還有幾年？清楚知道每個月的生活支出之後，至少每個月必須為自己提存多少退休金？每年可以存多少下來？以此為努力目標，很明確的知道該怎麼完成這個計劃，就不會亂了方寸或半途而廢、前功盡棄。

- 其實，那 1,620 萬的現金，是假設往後 45 年坐吃山空時的最壞打算，然而即使 55 歲之後，如果繼續工作或改變成輕鬆的工作，每個月依然有收入，所以如果在 55 歲時能夠擁有 1,620，那還需要擔心什麼？或許某些人現在已經有符合退休需要的 1,620 了，如果真是這樣，那更要慢慢放慢腳步，該是好好愛自己的時候了。

20 歲在軍中服役時，一位老士官長的一句話，讓我至今依然印象深刻，他說：「XXX 的（三字經），俺年輕時有體力沒錢，俺現在有錢沒力了」。你，現在是在什麼階段呢？有「錢」有「力」，我們都喜歡！就看自己如何定義它、規劃它。

掌握健康與收入的人生規劃，也同時會讓其他方面得到平順。如果有了健康的身體，有了滿足於自己生活標準的財富，達到目標之後懂得放慢腳步，不再貪求，一切順其自然，會讓整個心情

When planning for life's many changes, it often feels like there are endless details or conflicting interests. The balance between gains and losses can be difficult to achieve. Think carefully: What is the most fundamental condition that allows you to live and work? Health! Health is everything, as mentioned in the "Taking Care of Your Health" section.

Next, no matter where you are in the world, whether living in a self-sufficient, bartering, or monetized economy, "income" (whether in terms of material goods or money) is an unavoidable necessity for maintaining life.

In planning for wealth, especially if you hope to live worry-free in your later years, you can approach it as follows:

- Whether you're in your 20s, 30s, or over 40, set a target retirement age (retirement here means "having more personal time," not necessarily withdrawing completely from the workforce). For example, aim to retire at 55.

- Let's assume you'll live to 100 years old. If you retire at 55 and plan for the worst-case scenario of having no income afterward, how much money would you need for the next 45 years to sustain your lifestyle?

Suppose, as mentioned in the "Taking Care of Your Health" section, that you already have lifelong medical insurance and own a house. If you estimate your monthly expenses after retirement to be around NT$30,000 (this amount is just an example and depends on your personal lifestyle and standard of living), you'll need NT$360,000 per year. Over 45 years, that adds up to NT$16.2 million (referring here to a stable amount in savings, not considering volatile investments like stocks or funds). If you set a goal of having NT$16.2 million by age 55, then you can calculate how many years you have until that age, how much you need to save monthly for retirement, and how much you can set aside each year. Once you have a clear goal, you'll know how to work towards it without getting lost or abandoning the plan halfway.

- In fact, that NT$16.2 million is based on the worst-case scenario of spending down your savings for the next 45 years. But even after 55, if you continue working or shift to a more relaxed job, you may still have income each month. So, if you can reach NT$16.2 million

4. Planning Your Life

感到放鬆、無壓力，當健康、收入無慮時（財富的滿足點在於自己，不與他人相比），沒有了不安全感，在心態上會有滿足的感覺，而這樣的心情，自然而然會讓生活、工作、家庭、人際等等其他方面感到順利，人生各方面的規劃所希望的是什麼？其實就是讓心境感到滿意罷了。

by age 55, what is there to worry about? Some people might already have that amount saved for retirement. If that's the case, it's time to slow down and take more time to love yourself.

When I was 20 and serving in the military, an old sergeant said something that stuck with me: "When I was young, I had strength but no money; now I have money but no strength." What stage are you in now? Having both "money" and "strength" is what we all desire. It depends on how you define and plan for them.

A life plan that balances health and income will also lead to smoother outcomes in other areas. If you have good health and wealth that satisfies your standard of living, and if you understand how to slow down and avoid being overly greedy once you've achieved your goals, everything will naturally follow. When health and income are secure (remember, financial satisfaction comes from within and should not be compared to others), a sense of security will settle in. You will feel content, and this state of mind will lead to smoother experiences in other aspects of life, such as work, family, and relationships. What do we ultimately want from life planning? It's simply to feel content in our hearts.

5. 擁有愉快心情

　　如果情緒長期比較偏向生氣、壓力、緊張、憂鬱、負面思緒，想要開心、愉快會是短暫而且困難的，往往只是表層的曇花一現而已，畢竟，內在情緒沒有真正得到宣洩和抒發，外在的喜悅會因為不是發自內在的自然流露，所以變得短暫，甚至只是壓抑而不自知的現象而已，這也是為什麼有些人會覺得常常開心並不容易的原因之一，讓自己情緒在不知不覺中轉變，在書裡提了很多觀點，期待靜心慢讀、字字體會，彼此分享。

　　「擁有」愉快心情和「保持」愉快心情，在心境上的感覺不同。例如：保持第一名和擁有第一名，「保持」會有股壓力，「擁有」是順其自然的獲得，有一句大家熟悉的話：不在乎天長地久（就是保持的意思），只在乎曾經擁有（就是擁有的觀點）。同樣期待愉快的想法，壓力而來的愉快和自然獲得的愉快，我們會喜歡情緒上順其自然的快樂，尤其是擁有了愉快心情之後，幾乎都在不知不覺中一直保持下去。

　　感恩、捨得、接納、笑、愛、慈悲、滿足、溫馨……，想想還有哪些字句可以形容愉快的心情，慢慢試著體會字意，相信一定會想到更多的美好字眼，心中擁有這些感覺，心情自然輕鬆、愉快。

　　感恩，是懷抱著對所有人、事、物的珍惜，內心自然流露出來的行為。擁有感恩的心，心境會變得柔軟、情緒會保持穩定、視野會擴大客觀，由外在事物所得到的心懷感恩，那是很開心的感覺（例如：精神、物質的支持），如果是由內在散發出來感恩的心情，那是種源源不絕、分秒存在的喜悅，那樣的感覺，讓我

5. Having a Happy Mood

If your emotions are often inclined toward anger, stress, tension, depression, or negative thoughts, it will be challenging and fleeting to experience true happiness. Such happiness is often superficial and short-lived because the inner emotions haven't been fully expressed or released. External joy that doesn't come from within tends to be brief, and sometimes we may not even realize we're suppressing our true feelings. This is one reason why some people find it hard to remain consistently happy. By gradually shifting your emotions, as discussed in various perspectives throughout this book, you can mindfully reflect on these ideas and share them with others.

The feeling of "having" a happy mood and "maintaining" a happy mood is quite different. For example, there's a difference between maintaining first place and having first place. "Maintaining" implies pressure, while "having" suggests naturally obtaining it. As a familiar saying goes, "It's not about lasting forever（which refers to maintaining）, but about cherishing the moment（which refers to having）." Similarly, when we expect to feel happy, happiness that comes from pressure versus happiness that comes naturally—most of us prefer the latter. Once you experience happiness, it often continues unconsciously.

Gratitude, generosity, acceptance, laughter, love, compassion, satisfaction, warmth… Take time to think about what other words can describe a happy mood. Slowly try to understand the meaning behind these words, and you'll likely come up with more beautiful expressions. When

們自然愉悅。

　　與人相處，無論是熟悉還是陌生、和善或是敵意，都可以用感恩的心去面對。當然，如果目前正處於受到某人的傷害，這個過程或許會持續一段時間，心情難免還在憤怒、難過或恐懼，怎麼可能心懷感恩？然而，會因為心境感恩於生活周遭其他的人事物，而讓當下這個不如意的心情得以變得感覺不那麼難以渡過，也就是對生活中的人事物擁有越多的感恩，就會擁有更滿足的愉快心情，就好像心中對 100 件人事物心懷感恩，那樣的感覺自然可以化解一件的不如意，自然而然擁有愉快的心情。

　　感恩的對象，不限於人而已，對事物一樣可以有著相同的態度，就是對現況的滿足感，未來遙不可知，對現況的不知足，就難有感恩的心，當然就難有愉快的心情。例如：工作、收入、交友、生活，即使不是自己目前覺得最滿意的，一樣可以用感恩的心去感謝現在存在的現況，這樣的心情，會讓自己朝積極、陽光的思維去面對一切，因為即使維持現況已經讓內在感到滿意，未來如果更好，自然更加感到感恩，感恩的心情就會一直長留心中。

　　感恩非盲目、非強迫，壓抑而來的感恩不是真正的感恩，讓自己的心境自然而然去接納和擁抱那份感覺，才會全然而真實的擁有它。

　　笑，不僅僅只是臉部表情的展現，內心的笑，更讓心情持續擁有愉快的感覺。對於人、事、物，無論好或壞的狀況，都可以用「笑」的心情去面對，尤其是碰到逆境時，內心的「笑」，可以讓心情在平復中冷靜思考及應對，所謂一笑置之，會覺得似乎不是那麼的困難，讓心情感到輕鬆許多。

　　內心的「笑」，會自然影響外在的表情而展現在臉部、聲音、肢體動作中，除了自己擁有愉快的心情，周遭的人也會感受到愉快的氛圍，這樣的感覺會形成一股氣息，而且隨時散發著那種魅力，做個愛「笑」的人，是多麼愉快的事。

　　心境的轉變，會讓一切變得愉快，擁有愉快的心情，會發現更多的美好！

your heart holds these feelings, your mood naturally becomes light and happy.

Gratitude comes from cherishing all people, things, and experiences. It's a behavior that naturally flows from a heart filled with appreciation. When you have a grateful heart, your mindset softens, your emotions stabilize, and your perspective broadens. Feeling gratitude for external things, such as spiritual or material support, brings joy. But if your gratitude comes from within, it's an endless and constant joy, present in every moment. This feeling brings natural happiness.

In interactions with others, whether they are familiar or strangers, kind or hostile, you can face them with gratitude. Of course, if you're currently hurt by someone, it might take some time to overcome feelings of anger, sadness, or fear, and you may wonder how it's possible to feel grateful. However, gratitude for other people, things, and experiences around you can help ease the difficult emotions, making them feel more bearable. The more you feel grateful for the people and things in life, the more content and happy you become. It's like feeling grateful for 100 things can help you naturally resolve dissatisfaction with one thing, allowing you to maintain a happy mood.

Gratitude is not limited to people; you can have the same attitude toward things and situations. It's about feeling satisfied with the present. The future is unknown, and if you are dissatisfied with the present, it will be hard to cultivate gratitude or happiness. For example, work, income, friendships, and life—these may not be at their best, but you can still be thankful for your current circumstances. This mindset helps you approach everything with a positive outlook, because even maintaining the status quo already brings inner contentment. If the future turns out even better, you'll naturally feel even more grateful, and gratitude will stay with you forever.

Gratitude should not be blind or forced. Gratitude that comes from suppression isn't true gratitude. Let your mind naturally accept and embrace this feeling, and only then will you truly possess it.

Laughter is not just an outward expression on the face, but a feeling within the heart that allows happiness to continue. No matter the situation—good or bad—you can face people, events, and circumstances with a "smile"

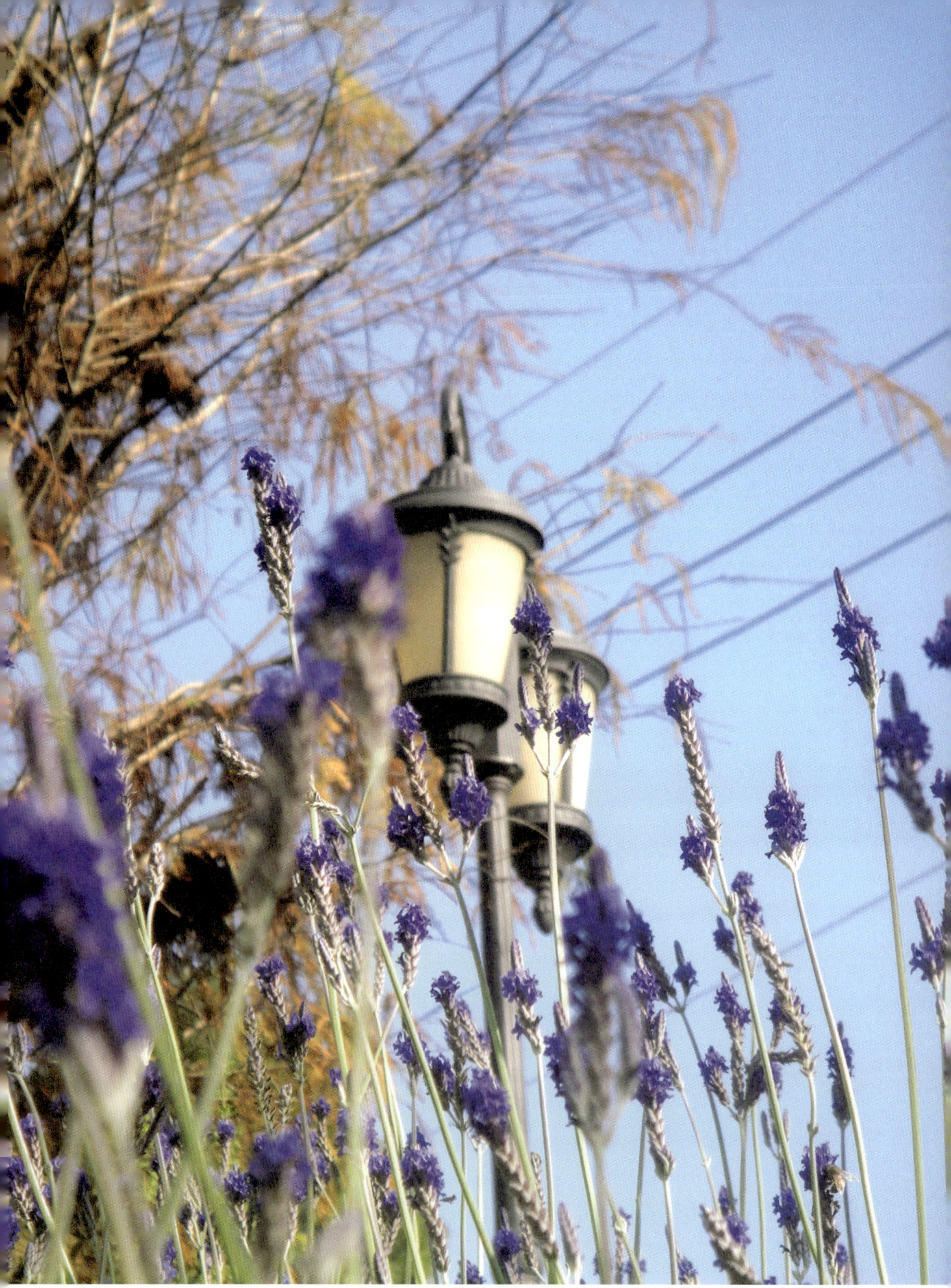

in your heart. Especially when facing adversity, internal laughter helps calm the mind, allowing for thoughtful responses. As the saying goes, "laugh it off," and it suddenly doesn't seem so difficult anymore. Your mood will feel much lighter.

The "smile" within will naturally influence your facial expressions, voice, and body language. Not only will you feel happy, but those around you will also sense the joyful atmosphere. This feeling forms a positive energy, constantly radiating charm. Being someone who loves to "smile" is such a joyful thing.

A shift in mindset makes everything more enjoyable. When you have a happy mood, you'll discover more beauty around you!

6. 與我共舞、享受單獨的喜悅

　　與我共舞，就是在各方面和自己「玩」，享受屬於自己的時間與空間，感受一種很特別「單獨」的喜悅！

　　如果長時間只有自己一人，通常會是什麼感覺？無聊、孤單、寂寞、害怕；還是，輕鬆、快樂、自在、滿足？有些人喜歡長時期的自我獨處，可以自得其樂；有些人經常需要陪伴，無法忍受孤單。

　　人，很難甚至無法離開人群自己一個人生活，需要和人們交流來滿足各種需求，然而，過程中也難免衍生互動中的種種問題。

　　我不能沒有朋友也不能離開人群，不過，至少可以用簡單的態度、觀念和行為，去面對外面的一切。首先，先讓內心踏實，肯定自我存在的價值，明明白白讓自己知道：我－不－孤獨。因為，永遠有我及「自己」兩人相隨。

　　我和「自己」，有非常深層的意境與心靈感受，那種體悟，就是可以做到：在人群裡，享受單獨的喜悅！

　　享受單獨的喜悅，不是孤僻、不是不與人互動，更不是宅不出戶，有了這個境界，內心是踏實、篤定、清淨、喜悅、滿足。享受單獨的感覺，可以先從小地方試著一點一滴慢慢培養，試著找到自己喜歡的獨處方式，然後去感受其中的快樂，當發現自己喜歡那樣的感覺時，就會懂得享受單獨的喜悅。

　　獨處時，我會體會這樣的感覺：

- 在熙來攘往的人群中，例如車站、捷運、機場、百貨公司、

6. Dance with Me, Enjoy the Joy of Solitude

"Dance with me" refers to playing with yourself in various ways, enjoying your own time and space, and experiencing the special joy of being "alone."

If you are alone for a long time, how would you usually feel? Bored, lonely, afraid; or relaxed, happy, free, and satisfied? Some people enjoy extended periods of solitude, finding joy in their own company, while others constantly seek companionship, unable to bear being alone.

Humans find it difficult, if not impossible, to live in complete isolation. We need interaction with others to meet various needs, but these interactions often bring their own set of challenges.

While I can't live without friends or disconnect from society, I can adopt a simple mindset, attitude, and behavior to face the outside world. First, I must make my heart steady and affirm my self-worth, clearly understanding that: I—am—not—lonely. After all, I always have myself as a companion.

There is a deep, profound connection between myself and "me," a spiritual realization that allows me to experience the joy of solitude even when surrounded by others!

Enjoying the joy of solitude doesn't mean being withdrawn, avoiding social interaction, or staying home all the time. When you reach this state of mind, your heart is steady, confident, calm, joyful, and satisfied. You can begin cultivating the feeling of enjoying solitude from small things, slowly

街道、景點，有時候會放慢腳步，找個地方坐下來，靜靜的看著人們的穿著打扮、臉部表情、走路動作、種種互動，細心的去感覺人們忙碌、緊張、輕鬆、快樂等等的行為，雖然只是坐著欣賞，其實也讓自己感受到而且融入了人們種種互動時的一種心靈交流。

- 家裡的陽台、公園、郊區、踏青、大自然（例如：海邊、山林、溪谷），置身這些環境時，會放慢腳步，體會一下當下所產生的感覺和心情：

  - 陽台的花長出嫩芽了！今天的花，有些謝了、有些開了！
  - 樹木的枝葉因風而搖擺，每次的擺動都不一樣！會好奇、會期待著每次不同擺動的樣貌！
  - 一些不知名的小草、小花，綻放著它們獨有的美麗！
  - 一片緩緩飄落中的葉片，有著一種輕盈、旋繞緩落的美！
  - 葉片上的滴滴朝露，原來早晨薄霧的清新空氣，就留在這裡！
  - 石頭千變萬化的紋路，吸引著好奇的心情，繼續尋找永遠不同的下一個！
  - 看著不知名的小蟲，想著牠的生命力、想著牠在做什麼！
  - 空氣中飄來自然淡香，抬頭看看、環顧四周，想知道是哪棵樹的芳香！
  - 專注望著藍天中不斷飄移變化的雲朵，期待著下一秒的雲朵會變出什麼樣的圖像！

細細品味那些景象，感覺它們的生命力和每次不同的樣貌，獨處的時光，是沒有孤單、孤獨的。

- 下雨了，車子的雨刷不斷的刷動著，雨刷每刷動一次，眼前一片清晰，雨大雨小，雨水往玻璃兩邊滑下的條紋都不一樣，好奇下次的紋路是什麼，會一直想看下去。
- 坐在車裡、坐在樹下，好像「看不到」風，而我依然可以感覺它如影隨形的存在著。風，讓身體覺得清涼、寒冷，當風與樹草的邂逅，樹與草因風而搖曳，透過內在的體會，我看到了風的存在。

discovering the happiness within, and once you find that you enjoy the feeling, you'll know how to embrace the joy of being alone.

When I'm alone, I experience the following sensations:

- Amidst busy crowds, like in a train station, metro, airport, department store, street, or tourist spot, I sometimes slow my pace, find a place to sit, and quietly observe people—their outfits, facial expressions, walking movements, and interactions. By attentively observing people's busyness, tension, relaxation, and happiness, I feel connected to them, as though there is an unspoken exchange of emotions.

- On my home balcony, in a park, countryside, or in nature （by the seaside, in the mountains, or near a stream）, I slow down and savor the feelings and emotions of the moment:
  - The flowers on the balcony have sprouted new buds! Some have withered, and others have bloomed!
  - The branches of the trees sway in the wind, and each movement is different! I feel curious and look forward to seeing how they move each time!
  - Some unknown little grasses and flowers are blooming with their unique beauty!
  - A leaf gently falling has a kind of light, swirling grace!
  - The dewdrops on the leaves are proof of the fresh morning mist, and they remain right here!
  - The intricate patterns of stones intrigue my curious heart, leading me to search for the next unique one!
  - Watching unknown little bugs makes me think about their life force and wonder what they're up to!
  - The air carries a faint natural fragrance, and I look around to find out which tree is spreading its scent!
  - I focus on the ever-changing clouds in the blue sky, excited to see what shape the clouds will take next!

- 獨處時，聽著下雨的水滴聲、浪濤拍打岩石或沙灘的聲音、溪水沖刷溪石的聲音、風與樹木樹葉交會的聲音，聽著這些大自然的自然音樂，感覺各種不同聲音與心靈的對話。

自己懂得和自己玩，會體會出一股在孤獨中不寂寞的感覺，是一種投入、充實、寧靜、自在的滿足，就好像擁有一種可以自己一個人就能自得其樂的嗜好一樣，例如：繪畫、獨旅、一人環島（汽車、機車、單車、徒步）、聆聽音樂、看書、園藝、大自然、靜心修行。

眼睛看、耳朵聽、內心想、用心靈去感受，有了這些滿足、喜悅的感覺，就能體會出單獨的喜悅，那是回歸內在後自然呈現出來的生趣。自己與內在心靈，永遠是最忠實的朋友，與「自己」相處，最自然、無負擔、無孤單。

By carefully savoring these scenes and sensing their vitality and diversity, I realize that solitude is far from lonely.

- It's raining, and the car's windshield wipers are constantly moving. Each swipe clears my view, and the raindrops create different patterns as they slide down. I'm curious about what pattern will come next, and I keep watching.

- Sitting in a car or under a tree, it seems like I can't "see" the wind, yet I can feel its constant presence. The wind brings coolness and coldness to my body, and as it interacts with the trees and grass, I sense its existence.

- When I'm alone, I listen to the sound of raindrops, waves crashing against rocks or the beach, streams flowing over stones, and the wind rustling through trees and leaves. Listening to this natural music, I feel as if I'm having a conversation with the different sounds.

When you learn how to play with yourself, you'll experience a sense of being content and fulfilled, never feeling lonely despite solitude. It's like having a hobby that brings joy even when you're alone, whether it's painting, solo traveling （by car, bike, or on foot）, listening to music, reading, gardening, enjoying nature, or meditating.

Looking with your eyes, listening with your ears, thinking with your mind, and feeling with your heart—all of these bring fulfillment and joy. When you embrace these feelings, you'll experience the joy of solitude, which naturally emerges from a connection with your inner self. Your inner self is always your most loyal companion, and spending time with "yourself" is the most natural, stress-free, and lonely-free experience.

7. 觸動心靈

　　什麼樣的感覺，能夠觸動情緒和心境？有時腦海會突然莫名其妙的閃過一些念頭，例如：離職、休息、旅行、工作、大自然景物、音樂旋律、各種情緒的反應，這是潛意識的自然反應，跟當下的情境、心情、工作，一點關係也沒有。

　　這些突如其來的想法，可能只是一瞬間的感覺而已，如果沒有留意，那個念頭很快就會溜走，甚至事後都回想不起來，跟夢境的感覺有點類似。

　　如果出現那種念頭，我會先用紙筆把它寫下來，等獨處或空閒時再拿出來看，慢慢感受代表的意思是什麼？要告訴我什麼？那個瞬間的念頭可能是內心要說的話，是潛意識想要表達的呼喚，那種感覺觸動了心靈的渴望和需求，是很貼切的自我對話機會。

　　每個人心中會觸動到的點和感動的事情都不盡相同，可能只是音樂當中的幾個旋律、文章當中的幾個字、電影中的一幕、朋友的一句話、眼睛看到的景物，心中就會產生悲傷、難過、哭泣或喜悅、溫暖、感動的種種情緒反應。

　　無論是什麼樣的反應，當那種感覺來的時候就靜靜的接納它，悲傷的感覺就讓它盡情宣洩，喜悅的感覺就靜靜的享受它，這是外在情境觸動了內心意識的反應，對正面或負面情緒都是很好的釋放。

　　曾經有這麼一次，排好了兩天的業務拜訪行程，清晨從台北開車到屏東，在屏東市區偶然瞥見「墾丁」的指標，心中產生一種奇怪的感覺，只是當時馬不停蹄的拜訪多位客戶也沒有在意。

7. Touching the Soul

What kind of feeling can stir up emotions and affect our mood? Sometimes, random thoughts flash through my mind unexpectedly—resigning, resting, traveling, work, nature, music, or emotional reactions. These are natural subconscious responses, completely unrelated to the current situation, mood, or task at hand.

These sudden thoughts might only last for a fleeting moment. If unnoticed, the thought slips away quickly, and later, it's hard to recall, much like the feeling of a dream.

When such thoughts arise, I write them down on paper and revisit them when I have time alone or when I'm free. I slowly reflect on what they mean. What are they trying to tell me? That fleeting thought could be my inner self speaking—an expression from the subconscious, touching on desires or needs, and providing a meaningful moment for self-dialogue.

What touches people's hearts and moves them varies for everyone. It could be just a few notes from a song, a few words in an article, a scene from a movie, a friend's comment, or something seen with the eyes. Such triggers can evoke a range of emotions—sadness, sorrow, tears, joy, warmth, or deep emotional response.

Whatever the reaction, when that feeling arrives, I simply embrace it. If it's sadness, I let it flow; if it's joy, I quietly savor it. These are responses triggered by external situations, and they offer a good release for both positive and negative emotions.

到了晚上8點多行程結束又再次看到「墾丁」的指標時，奇妙的感覺越來越強烈。

我把車停在路邊，閉上眼睛與自己心靈對話，然後張開眼睛，看看車窗外的人群和熙來攘往的車輛。

我再次發動引擎，直奔墾丁！到了南灣，在靠近海邊的民宿住了下來。

不需要五星級豪華飯店，我要的是海的感覺、海的聲音、海的呼吸和放鬆。原來，那是內在心靈告訴我，長期的疲憊需要休息了，機械式的行程和市區飯店已經麻痺了我的生活行為，墾丁的指標，其實就是觸動了我內心的需求。

第二天清晨，踩著海沙、呼吸著海的味道，向著大海伸展懶腰、欣賞旭日朝陽，帶著滿足又愉快的心情開始一天的工作。

心靈深處的潛意識要表達什麼，有可能就是自己想要的、想知道的、在乎的，如果可以抓住那種感覺，然後去探索、瞭解，試著用自我對話來找出答案，結果會越來越清楚，越來越認識真實的自己。

內心無論出現什麼樣的想法，不要否認它，我會試著去探索及瞭解這個想法真正的背後原因是什麼，因為，表層的壓抑也無法掩飾內在真實的自己，那是內在自己要告訴表層自己可貴的接觸。

經常與自己心靈對話、開啟內在心門，會越來越清楚自己、愛自己！

Once, I had planned a two-day business trip. I started driving early in the morning from Taipei to Pingtung, and while passing through the city, I noticed a sign pointing to "Kenting." A strange feeling arose in me, but I was too busy visiting clients to pay it much attention. By 8 PM, after my appointments, I saw the "Kenting" sign again, and the feeling grew even stronger.

I pulled over, closed my eyes, and had a conversation with my inner self. When I opened my eyes, I looked at the people and the bustling traffic outside the window.

Then, I restarted the car and headed straight to Kenting! I stayed at a simple guesthouse near South Bay, close to the sea.

I didn't need a five-star luxury hotel. All I wanted was the sensation of the sea, the sound of the waves, the breath of the ocean, and a moment of relaxation. It turned out that my inner soul was telling me that my long-term exhaustion needed a break. The mechanical routine and city hotels had numbed my life. That "Kenting" sign had triggered my inner need.

The next morning, I walked on the sandy beach, breathed in the ocean air, stretched toward the sea, and admired the sunrise. With a contented and joyful heart, I began my day's work.

What the subconscious wants to express may very well be what I desire, want to know, or care about. If I can catch that feeling, explore it, and understand it, and try to engage in self-dialogue to find answers, things become clearer. I will come to know my true self more and more.

Whatever thoughts arise within, I won't deny them. I will try to explore and understand the true reasons behind them because surface-level suppression cannot hide the authentic self. That inner self seeks to communicate something precious to the surface.

By frequently engaging in dialogue with my soul and opening the door to my inner self, I grow more and more aware of who I am and come to love myself even more.

8. 為自己、為所愛的人而活！

　　這個世界不缺我，一樣會一直持續下去，我的存在之於世間萬物而言是那麼的微不足道、沒什麼了不起。然而，我沒了，卻是什麼都沒了，我，就是那麼的獨特、唯一。明白自己的出現是很奇妙的唯一，「天下之大、唯我獨尊」，這句話的另一個詮釋就是：為自己而活！

　　人們會為了一個希望、目標、責任、財富，放棄其他的一切，甚至行屍走肉而活著，依附著這唯一的誘因來感覺自己的存在，讓自己有了一個生活下去的寄託。

　　我們會因為責任感的驅使而覺得自己非常重要，有一種「非我不可、別人不行」的想法。例如：門庭若市的診所只因為每個病人只找我看診；所有的廠商都找我只因為是我負責；這種課程只有我最瞭解非我來教不可；我們團隊不眠不休、日以繼夜研發是因為整個集團只相信我們……，因為上面那些感覺「唯我可以」的重要感，讓自己全心付出，也確實可能完整了每一件事，然而超出自己體能極限的辛苦甚至過勞，得到我們如此付出的人，恐怕全然不知、不以為意甚至覺得應該如此、理所當然。

　　我們為自己的工作全心付出是當然的，然而，真的那麼重要到非「我」不可嗎？仔細想想，其實人們需要的是「這個位置上的人」，而不是「這個位置上的我」，也就是沒了我，這個位置上還是永遠有人可以繼續下去，絕對不是非我不可。在為別人努力付出的同時，似乎忽略了為自己而活的醒思，兩者能夠平衡，才是成熟的自我。

　　因為懂得愛別人、照顧別人、為別人服務，更要懂得自己的

8. Live for Yourself, Live for Your Loved Ones !

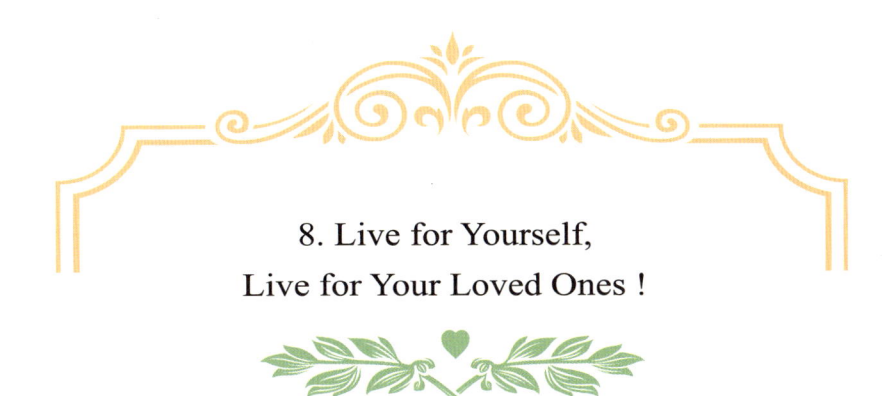

The world doesn't need me; it will continue as it always has. My existence seems so insignificant and unremarkable in the grand scheme of things. However, if I were gone, everything would be lost. I am unique and irreplaceable. Understanding that my presence is a remarkable singularity—"In a world so vast, I alone am supreme"—is another way of interpreting: Live for yourself!

People often sacrifice everything else for a hope, goal, responsibility, or wealth, sometimes living like zombies, clinging to this single source of purpose to feel their own existence. This provides them with a reason to continue living.

We may feel very important due to a sense of responsibility, thinking "I am indispensable, and no one else can do it." For example: A busy clinic where every patient insists on being seen by me; all vendors seek me out because I am responsible; a course only I understand and must teach; our team works tirelessly because the entire group only trusts us… Because of this feeling of being "irreplaceable," we give our all and may complete every task, yet those who benefit from our efforts might be completely unaware, indifferent, or even take it for granted.

While it's natural to dedicate oneself fully to work, is it truly so important that only "I" can do it? Upon closer reflection, people need "someone in this position," not "me specifically in this position." If I'm not there, someone else will continue from where I left off—it's not absolutely necessary for it to be me. In striving for others, we may overlook the

重要性、為自己而活的觀念。並非以自我為中心、目中無人、毫無顧忌的為所欲為，而是因為關心別人，希望他們因為我而過得更好、更順利，因此更加珍惜、愛護自己，懂得先為自己而活，才能為別人而活，如同愛自己才能真正懂得愛別人一樣，這是為自己而活的真正意義！

　　沒有什麼比自己的存在更可貴，即使擁有了傲人的生活、財富、事業，卻失去了自己的時間、自由、喜好甚至生命時光，當年齡、壽命接近尾聲時，才恍然大悟一生似乎沒有為自己而過時，身邊所擁有的名聲、榮耀、富裕等等的外在襯托，也無法挽回已經過往失去的自己，虛度真正無價、唯一一次必須好好把握的生命，是非常非常可惜，再也無法重來的。

　　無論現在幾歲，以上面所說的想法，來好好先為自己而活都來得及，尤其我們也希望身旁的家人、朋友都能因為我而過得更好，那麼「我」更應該要照顧好自己，當我已經充分能愛自己、活出自己，那種氣息與氛圍會擴散給身邊的人，也就能夠很自然的為自己的所愛的人而活！

importance of living for ourselves. Balancing both aspects—contributing to others and living for oneself—is the mark of a mature self.

Understanding how to love, care for, and serve others is important, but it is equally crucial to recognize our own worth and the concept of living for oneself. This doesn't mean being self-centered or inconsiderate, but rather, caring for oneself to better serve and love others. Just as one must love oneself to truly love others, living for oneself is about valuing one's own life and well-being first.

Nothing is more precious than one's own existence. Even if one has achieved impressive success, wealth, and status, losing personal time, freedom, preferences, and life's moments can lead to a profound regret when approaching life's end. Realizing too late that a life was not lived for oneself—while fame, glory, and wealth cannot recover the lost self—leaves a deep sense of missed opportunity, as this irreplaceable life cannot be relived.

No matter what age you are, it is always a good time to start living for yourself. Especially if you want your family and friends to benefit from your presence, you should take care of yourself first. When you fully love and live for yourself, that energy and atmosphere will naturally extend to those around you, allowing you to live not only for yourself but also for those you love.

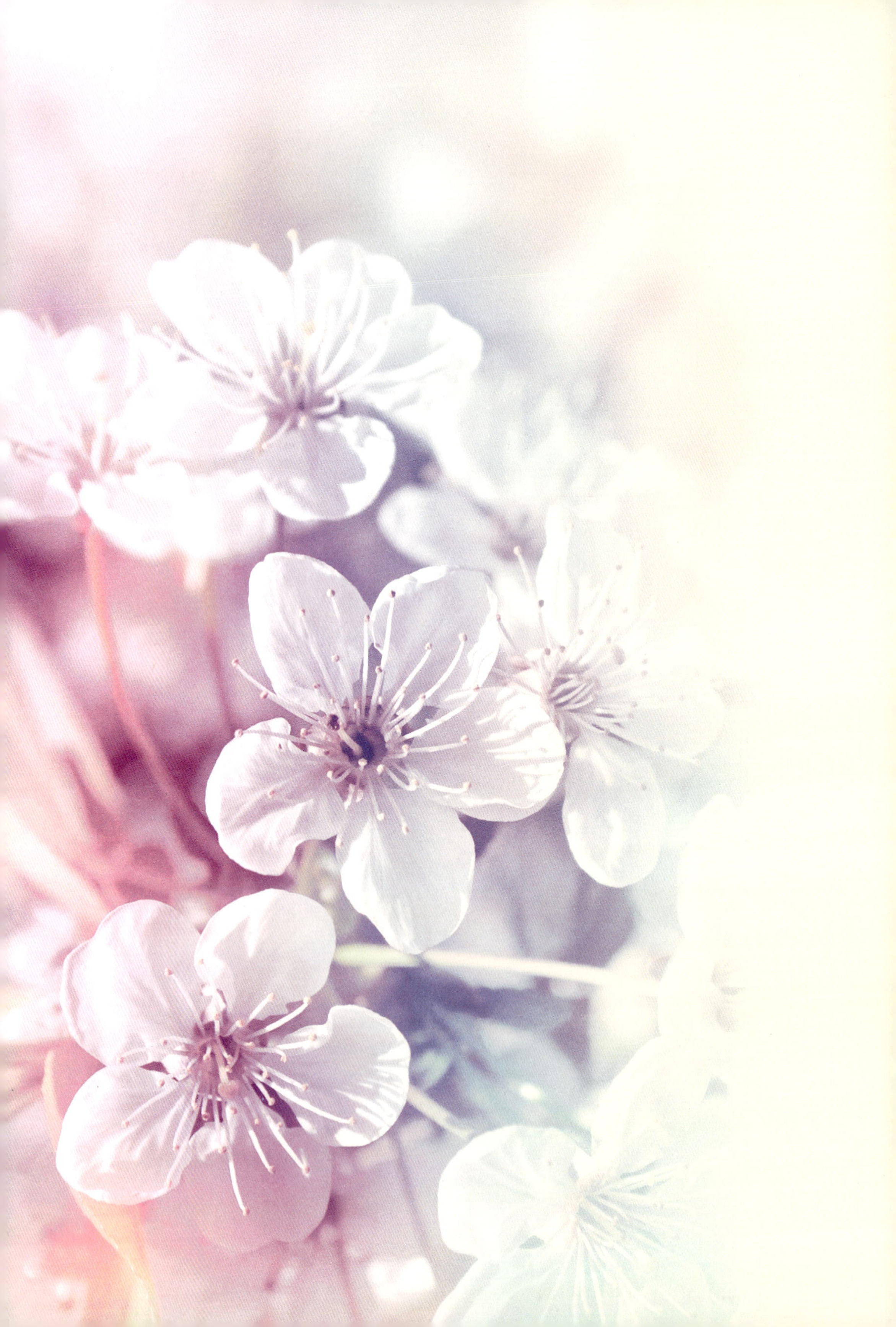

愛的傳達

The Transmission of Love

愛，有一股強大的正向能量，代表了關懷、接納，是一種很奇妙的心理反應，當我們將這個訊息給對方時，無論用什麼方式表達出來，只要讓對方感受到：你懂我，我懂你，也就接受到愛的訊息。

Love carries a powerful positive energy, representing care and acceptance. It is a fascinating psychological response. When we transmit this message to others, no matter how it is expressed, as long as the other person feels: "You understand me, and I understand you," they receive the message of love.

貳、愛的傳達

　　所謂「愛」，不僅僅只是愛情、親情、友情的「愛」，而是來自於身、心、靈的情感表達、互動及愉悅的心靈矜動，包含了對所有人、事、物的特殊情感，那種感覺，就是「愛」。

　　直接還是含蓄的表達，有形或無形的感應，重要的是勇於把愛「表達」出來。表達心中的愛，除了用說的之外，也可以用唱的、用寫的、用畫的、用表情、用肢體動作、擁抱、行動，甚至心靈感應等種種方式，可以想像的是，當發自內心傳達這個訊息給對方時，自己心裡也會是溫暖的，如果也得到了對方的回應，心情會是多麼的喜悅，我們都會喜歡那樣的感覺。

　　很熟悉的一句話：把愛「說」出來！說，是非常直接又立即的一種表達方式，無論是面對面或透過網路、電話，都會馬上接收到傳遞的訊息，尤其以當面說出來，對方的感受最直接。

　　說出心中的感覺，也是一種內在情緒的表達，把心裡的感覺說出來，無論是讚美、欣賞、輕聲細語、結結巴巴、氣憤急躁，在「說」的過程，已經同步傳遞了自己情緒的反應，有時候這樣的表達，是最直接讓對方感受到自己的方式。

　　懂得愛自己、做到愛自己，無形中會很自然的散發出一股愛的氣息，周遭的人，會感染到那種陽光、正向的氛圍。日常生活中，我們會有這樣的經驗，即使不是一直互動，某些人就是會讓我們感到輕鬆、愉悅，某些人卻是讓我們感到壓力、不舒服，這也證明，任何人，其實無時無刻都在表達「愛」的能量，差別在於是正向「愛」能量或負面「愛」能量而已，相信我們都希望自己能夠擁有正向「愛」的能量，因為，接收到別人積極、正向的互動，那是非常快樂的。

　　愛，有一股強大的正向能量，代表了關懷、接納，是一種很奇妙的心理反應，當我們散發這個訊息給對方時，無論用什麼方式表達出來，只要讓對方感受到：你懂我、我懂你，也就接收到愛的訊息。

Part Two: The Transmission of Love

"Love" is not just about romantic love, familial love, or friendship; it encompasses the emotional expression, interaction, and joyful resonance of the body, mind, and spirit. It includes a special feeling towards all people, things, and events. This feeling is what we call "love."

Whether expressed directly or indirectly, through tangible or intangible means, what's important is the courage to express love. Besides verbal expressions, love can be conveyed through singing, writing, drawing, facial expressions, body language, hugging, actions, or even telepathically. When we convey this message from the heart, it warms our own hearts as well, and receiving a response from the other person adds to our joy. We all appreciate that feeling.

A familiar phrase is: "Speak your love out loud!" Speaking is a very direct and immediate way of expression. Whether face-to-face or through digital means like phone or internet, the message is immediately received. Especially when spoken face-to-face, the other person experiences the feelings directly.

Expressing feelings is also an expression of internal emotions. Whether praising, admiring, whispering, stammering, or expressing anger, the act of speaking transmits one's emotional response. Sometimes, this is the most direct way for the other person to feel what you are conveying.

Understanding and practicing self-love naturally emits a sense of loving energy. The people around us can be influenced by this positive and uplifting atmosphere. In daily life, we may experience how certain people make us feel relaxed and joyful, while others create pressure or discomfort. This shows that everyone is constantly transmitting "love" energy, whether positive or negative. We all hope to have positive "love" energy, because receiving positive interactions from others is truly delightful.

Love carries a powerful positive energy, representing care and acceptance. It's a fascinating psychological response. When we transmit this message to others, no matter how we express it, as long as the other person feels: "You understand me, and I understand you," they receive the message of love.

9. 有質感的擁抱

　　如果不會讓對方產生唐突或侵犯的感覺，那麼，「擁抱」是很好的表達。即使語言不通甚至沒有

　　聲音，一次的擁抱勝過千言萬語，說了上百次的愛而沒有擁抱或肢體接觸，對方還是不會有深刻的感受。

　　離別前、久別重逢、悲傷、恐懼、快樂、感動、人際交往、緊張或情緒受到很大的波動時，一個深深的擁抱會讓對方感到溫暖、安定、放鬆。無論是有形或無形的擁抱，都會讓心裡感到安全、滿足。有形的擁抱，具體、深刻；無形的擁抱，則是另一種心靈的溫暖。有形的擁抱，傳達了很多愛的感覺，擁抱時「無聲勝有聲」的感受，對於情緒的安撫幫助最大，擁抱絕對有心理治療效果，尤其親子間如果經常擁抱，對孩子的人格發展絕對有正向的幫助，大人間的適度擁抱，會感到溫暖、安全、真實、原諒、接納等等的心理反應。

　　除了擁抱，肢體接觸也是很好的一種表達方式，像：拉拉手、手牽手、拍拍肩膀、摸摸頭、相互抓背、抓癢、按摩等等，都是肢體接觸很愉快的感覺。

　　有一次搭機遇到亂流，有好幾次飛機如雲霄飛車般上下劇烈搖晃，大大小小長達十幾分鐘，驚聲連連，可想而知是多麼可怕。

　　當飛機順利降落後，好多人不管認識還是陌生，彼此開心擁抱、落淚、握手、鼓掌歡呼甚至在飛機上就跳起舞來，把剛才所有緊張和恐懼的心情，透過那些肢體動作完全釋放出來，馬上得到了內心的溫暖和安定，無國界的肢體語言，的確是很好的一種

9. The Embrace of Quality

If it does not make the other person feel abrupt or violated, then a "hug" is a great expression of love. Even if there are no words or if language barriers exist, a hug can convey more than a thousand words. Repeatedly saying "I love you" without a hug or physical touch may not leave a deep impression on the other person.

Whether before parting, reuniting after a long time, during sadness, fear, joy, or emotional upheavals, a deep embrace can make the other person feel warmth, stability, and relaxation. Both tangible and intangible embraces bring a sense of safety and fulfillment. Tangible embraces are concrete and profound, while intangible embraces provide a different kind of spiritual warmth.

A tangible hug conveys a lot of love, and the feeling of "silence speaks louder than words" during a hug helps the most with emotional soothing. Hugs undoubtedly have a psychological therapeutic effect. Frequent hugging between parents and children can positively aid in the child's personality development. For adults, moderate hugging can evoke feelings of warmth, safety, authenticity, forgiveness, and acceptance.

In addition to hugs, physical contact is also a good way to express feelings, such as holding hands, hand-holding, patting on the shoulder, rubbing the head, patting the back, scratching, or giving a massage. These are all pleasant forms of physical contact.

Once, during a flight encountering turbulence, the plane shook

表達。

　　無形的擁抱，是用自己的心，去擁抱外在無形的一切，讓心情感到滿足與平靜。在情緒低沉或心情愉悅的時候，都可以用這種無形的擁抱來洗滌心靈、深化靈魂，並且體會其中的意義和哲理，我尤其喜歡大自然的擁抱，讓心情經常可以單純、寧靜、輕鬆。

　　擁抱大自然的一切，都可以用眼睛看、用耳朵聽，與身處的大自然心靈交會、彼此感應、相互擁抱。靜下心來面對大自然，用自己覺得最自在的姿態放鬆自己，經由眼、耳、皮膚、呼吸、心跳，體會融入大自然、彼此一體的感覺，把這股感覺引領到心靈深處。

　　之後，把擁抱大自然那種滿足及愉悅的心情，透過意念及感應傳達出去，去呼喚大自然，再把對大自然的情感全部收進心靈裡面，此時，漸漸感覺到一點風聲、水聲、空氣清香、蟲鳴鳥語，靜靜的感覺大自然相同的擁抱。

　　一年四季，特別喜歡秋的感覺，尤其是秋天所帶來的大自然景象。漫步松林、楓紅灑落、芒草舞動、陣陣秋風迎面吹拂，夏已遠離寒冬未至，空氣中瀰漫著一種欲冷還暖的氣息，因秋的感動，牽引出很多關於秋天的心情、音樂、歌曲、文章、詩句，因擁抱秋天而感動，內心因此感到安定、平和與喜悅。

　　無論有形或無形的擁抱，都會釋放出溫馨的能量，是彼此心靈互動很棒的一種雙向溝通。

violently up and down for several minutes, causing much fear. After the plane landed safely, many people, whether familiar or strangers, embraced, cried, shook hands, cheered, and even danced on the plane. They released all their tension and fear through these physical actions, immediately finding warmth and stability. The universal language of physical touch is indeed a wonderful form of expression.

An intangible hug involves embracing the unseen aspects of the outside world with one's heart, bringing satisfaction and peace. During emotional lows or highs, this kind of intangible hug can cleanse the soul and deepen the spirit. I especially enjoy the embrace of nature, which allows for simplicity, tranquility, and relaxation.

Embracing everything in nature can be done through sight and sound, connecting with the spirit of nature, sensing, and mutually embracing. By calming oneself and facing nature in the most comfortable posture, one can experience the feeling of blending with nature through the eyes, ears, skin, breath, and heartbeat, leading this feeling deep into the soul.

Afterwards, convey the satisfaction and joy of embracing nature through intention and perception, calling out to nature, and then incorporating all the emotions towards nature into the soul. At this moment, one gradually feels the sounds of the wind, water, fresh air, and the songs of insects and birds, quietly experiencing nature's embrace.

Among the four seasons, I particularly love the feeling of autumn, especially the natural scenery it brings. Walking through pine forests, watching red maple leaves fall, seeing the dancing reed grass, and feeling the autumn breeze, with summer having passed and winter yet to come, the air carries a scent of lingering warmth and impending cold. The emotional impact of autumn inspires much music, songs, articles, and poetry about autumn. Embracing autumn brings a sense of stability, peace, and joy to the heart.

Whether tangible or intangible, an embrace releases warm energy and is a wonderful form of two-way communication in the interaction of hearts.

10. 文字的憾動

　　文字的美，美在它的千變萬化，是一種很奇妙的表達方式，可以詮釋出無窮盡的思想、情感和抒發情緒。尤其文字的落筆，是經由感覺和思考之後，再一字一句呈現出來，讓想法能夠更充分及完整的表現。

　　無法當面說、不好意思直接說、擔心說的辭不達意或語無倫次，那麼用寫的，同樣可以把想法傳達給對方，尤其在無法碰面的時候，更可以把感覺寫下來。

　　拿起紙筆，腦海思索想要表達的話和文字，遣詞用字透過手中的筆，字字句句完成它，之後反覆閱讀，再做一些修飾或句子的重新組合，等到覺得最能表達意思時，再傳達給對方，這是多麼含蓄、多麼棒的一種表達。

　　我們都有這樣的經驗，桌上的一張紙條、一封信、一則簡訊、一通電子留言，字句間滿滿的讚許、無限的感謝、溫馨的問候、真誠的關懷、甜蜜的愛意，或許沒有見到對方，然而已經感受到對方所要表達的「愛」，會覺得開心、喜悅、甜蜜，即使不像說的那麼快速又直接，然而它卻可以反覆迴盪、久久留在眼中、心中。

　　文字，可以檢視個性、宣洩情緒和溫暖心靈。

　　寫出最有感覺的文字，不必在乎什麼字、什麼詞、什麼文筆，就是當下發自內心最確實的訊息而已，可能只是一個字、一直重複某個字、一句話、一篇文章，無論什麼方式，就是透過寫，把心裡所有的感覺源源不斷宣洩出來。

10. The Resonance of Words

The beauty of words lies in their infinite variety; they are a wonderfully unique form of expression, capable of conveying endless thoughts, emotions, and sentiments. Especially in writing, words are crafted after feeling and thinking, allowing ideas to be expressed more fully and completely.

When direct verbal communication is not possible, or when one feels embarrassed or worried about miscommunicating, writing becomes a powerful alternative. Writing allows us to convey our thoughts, even when face-to-face interaction is not feasible.

By picking up a pen and paper, one can carefully think through and express their thoughts and feelings. Choosing words and phrases, and crafting them into sentences, followed by careful review and revision, helps to convey the intended message with subtlety and precision. This is a profoundly effective way of communication.

We have all experienced how a note, letter, message, or email filled with praise, gratitude, warm greetings, genuine care, or sweet affection, can make us feel appreciated and loved, even without direct interaction. Though not as immediate as spoken words, written words resonate deeply, lingering in the mind and heart.

Words can reveal personality, express emotions, and warm the soul.

Writing heartfelt words doesn't require perfect grammar or elaborate language. It's about conveying the most genuine message from the heart at that moment, whether it's a single word, a repeated phrase, or a complete piece of

心情不好的時候，我會用寫字來釋放負面情緒，用文字來平復心情的變化。好心情的時候，寫下美好的想法，愉快的氛圍會留在心裡。這兩種心情所寫下來的感覺，同樣可以傳遞給有形的對方或無形的心靈感應，充分表達出愛的氣息。

　　當這樣的感覺傳遞出去時，別人也同樣會接收到我心情的變化，雖然文字沒有聲音，卻可以讓對方透過眼睛的看，把我要表達的心意留存在心中。

writing. Writing allows us to continuously release and express all the feelings within.

When feeling down, I use writing to release negative emotions and soothe my changing mood. During happier times, I write down positive thoughts, keeping that joyful atmosphere in my heart. Both kinds of writing—whether addressing tangible individuals or intangible spiritual connections—effectively convey the essence of love.

When these feelings are communicated through writing, others can also perceive the emotional changes I experience. Although text lacks sound, it allows recipients to see and hold onto the sentiments I wish to express.

11. 用行動的表示

　　現代科技發達，人們的互動有如遠在天邊、近在咫尺，不分晝夜、世界各地，都可以透過各種行動，把愛說出來，比起古人的飛鴿傳書、遙寄星辰，我們真的幸福多了。

　　有些行動會讓人覺得溫馨、愉悅，例如：

- 打開手機，看到訊息：「中午了，要記得吃午餐」、「感冒好多了嗎？早點休息。」
- 電子信箱、臉書、微博、Skype、Line……，看到朋友、家人溫馨的關懷文字。
- 公司加班，桌上放了一杯咖啡、一張問候便條。
- 拍拍肩膀、緊握著手、一個微笑、朋友、家人關心的問候，遇到困難時，得到照顧、幫忙和關懷。
- 屬於自己特別的日子，得到家人、朋友精神上或物質上的問候。

　　有了電腦和手機的發明，讓表達愛和關懷變得無遠弗屆，可以無時無刻隨時傳遞，有些的照顧未必要在身邊，用行動的方式表達出來，讓對方心情愉快、感覺溫馨的遙遠問候，也是很好的方法。

　　世界上有非常多的善心人士和慈善團體，在各個角落以實際行動去幫助需要的人，將愛的表達付諸實際行動，即使語言不通或無法言語，都會感到一股暖流湧上心頭，人間處處有溫暖，這就是用行動來展現愛的最好證明。

11. Expressing Through Actions

With the advancement of modern technology, interactions between people feel like they're both distant and near at the same time. Regardless of time or location, people can express their love through various means. Compared to the ancient methods of sending messages via carrier pigeons or entrusting wishes to the stars, we are indeed much more fortunate.

Some actions bring warmth and joy, such as:

- Opening a message on your phone that says, "It's noon; remember to have lunch," or "Is your cold better? Get some rest."

- Reading caring words from friends and family on email, Facebook, Weibo, Skype, or Line.

- Finding a cup of coffee and a note of greeting on your desk during overtime work.

- Feeling the support of a pat on the shoulder, a firm handshake, a smile, or the concern of friends and family when facing challenges.

- Receiving heartfelt wishes, whether in spirit or material form, on special personal days.

With the invention of computers and mobile phones, expressing love and care knows no boundaries; it can be shared at any time and place. Some forms of care don't require physical presence. A thoughtful, long-distance greeting expressed in actions can lift someone's spirits and bring warmth.

Around the world, many kind-hearted individuals and charitable

把自己的心意，透過行動表現出來，是最實際又直接的，會馬上讓對方感受到善意，那是無微不至的關懷和滿滿愛的感覺，我們都喜歡那種感覺。

organizations help those in need through concrete actions, proving that love can be expressed through deeds. Even if there are language barriers or an inability to speak, a warm feeling fills the heart, showing that there is warmth everywhere in the world—this is the best testament to love demonstrated through action.

Expressing our feelings through actions is the most practical and direct way to show kindness and care, allowing others to feel genuine goodwill instantly. It's a meticulous, caring love, a feeling we all cherish.

12. 心靈感應的傳遞

　　心靈感應是一種非常微妙、難以言喻、心久久不散的溫暖感覺。那種感覺只存在於兩個人之間，是身心靈交融到某種境界後，非常自然又微妙的呈現。

　　心靈感應，甚至會透過時空，無時無刻傳遞彼此的訊息，感受著無形卻似有形的存在。沒有時差、沒有刻意。不同的兩人，在不同時空或在相同的時間，做出相同的事，說出相同的話、做出相同的動作（例如：看到一景一物時，同步說出一字不漏、相同的一句話或同一時間裡，彼此在不同的空間裡同時寄發給對方的電子信件等等），而頻率之高、次數之多，難以計數，這是心靈感應的昇華。

　　這種感應也存在於人和動物之間，尤其是相當具有靈性的狗，太多太多人與狗心靈流動的感人故事，那種感覺當然也會存在於人與人之間，尤其思想、語言、心靈層次都可以雙向互通，更是難能可貴。

　　或許聽過這句話：你不用說我都知道。不需開口、不用文字，只是一個表情、眼神或動作，對方很直接就知道你要做什麼、想什麼、需要什麼，而且會彼此對等的擁有雙向的溫暖和感應，這樣的動作會令人倍感溫馨和快樂。

　　彼此用心靈感應來相互傳遞訊息，因為相互瞭解，個性、思想和觀念幾乎都不謀而合，一種磁場的特殊感應，就好像和另一個自己在互動，即使形體不在一起，依然很篤定的感覺到對方具體存在，那股無形而強大的力量，是永遠支持著彼此相互關懷與

12. Telepathic Communication

Telepathy is a subtle, indescribable, and lingeringly warm feeling. It exists only between two people, manifesting naturally and delicately when their minds, bodies, and spirits reach a certain level of harmony. Telepathy transcends time and space, allowing constant communication, where each senses the other's intangible yet seemingly real presence. There's no time difference, no forced intention. Two different people in different places, or even at the same time, might do the same thing, say the same words, or make the same gestures. For instance, upon seeing something, they might simultaneously utter the same phrase, or, at precisely the same moment, send each other an email from different locations. The frequency and repetition of such moments are countless, symbolizing the ultimate form of telepathic connection.

This phenomenon also exists between humans and animals, especially dogs, known for their remarkable sensitivity. Countless touching stories tell of the soulful bond between people and dogs, showing that this feeling can undoubtedly be shared between humans too. When thoughts, language, and spirit connect mutually, the experience is even more precious.

You may have heard the phrase, "I know without you saying it." Without words or texts—simply through an expression, a look, or a gesture—the other person instinctively understands your intentions, thoughts, or needs, creating a warm and joyful connection. This reciprocal telepathic exchange brings a comforting sense of belonging.

Through telepathy, two people transmit messages to one another,

成長的最大力量，或許形體無法分秒不離，然而心靈可以持續的感應，一樣會讓彼此感到溫暖的關懷。

　　心靈感應的傳達、互動和接收，是特定兩個人雙向的交流，在付出關懷的同時也立即得到對方的回應，是人生非常特別的際遇。懂得愛自己當然也會愛別人，因為，愛的是「自己」！

deeply understanding each other with an almost identical perspective, as if interacting with another version of themselves. Even if not physically present, they can feel each other's palpable existence, supported by a powerful, unseen force that fosters mutual care and growth. Though physical presence isn't constant, their minds continue to resonate, creating a warm bond of concern.

Telepathy's exchange, interaction, and reception form a unique, mutual connection between two people. As each shows care, the other responds instantly, forming a rare and special encounter in life. By learning to love oneself, one learns to love others, as the essence of that love is found within oneself.

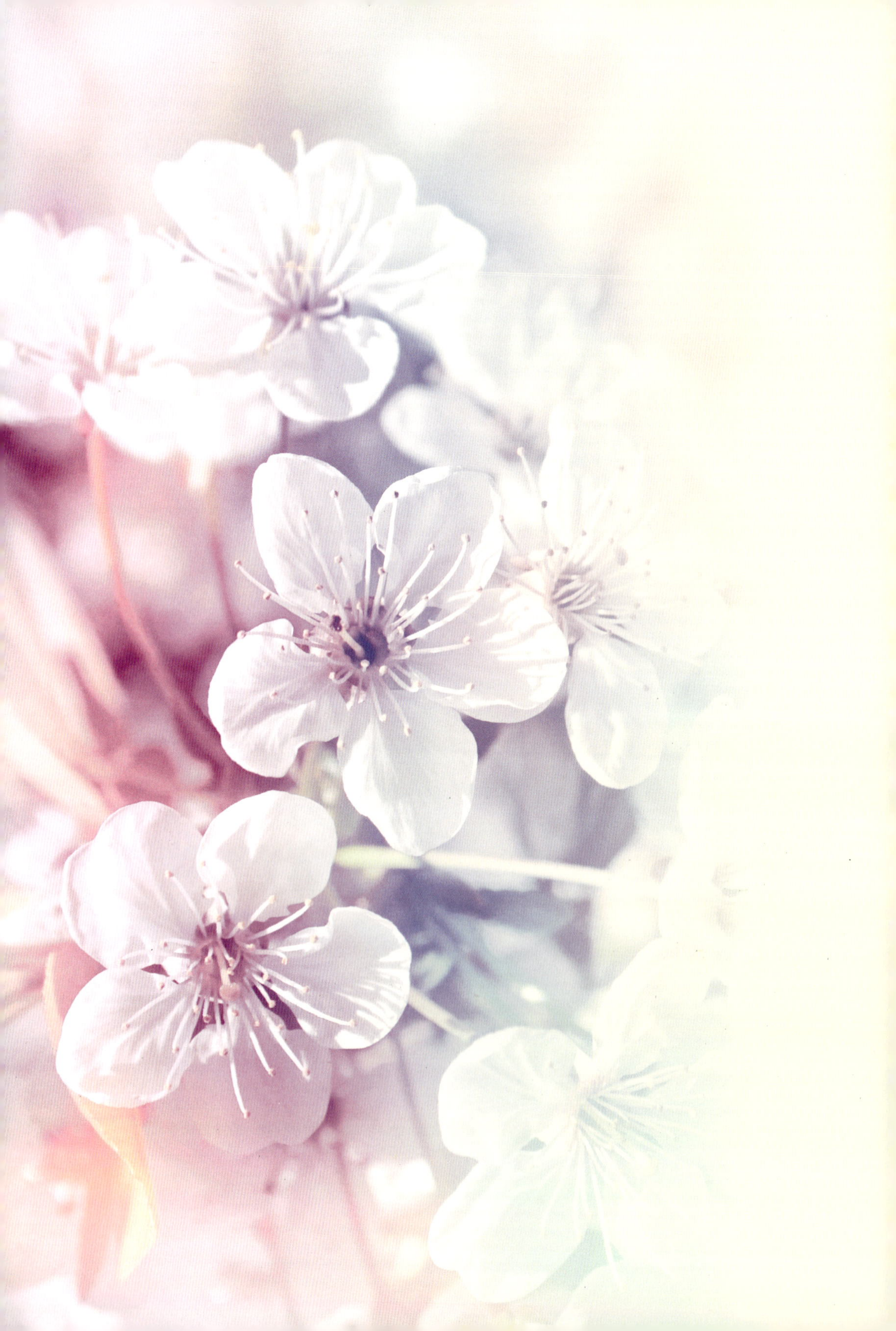

自我修煉與成長

Self-cultivation and Growth

什麼是土法煉鋼呢?就是不知道、沒接觸過任何成長方法,只是用著本身的思想和生活方式,以自己的方法來陪伴和改變。

What is is do-it-yourself"? It means using your own thoughts and lifestyle without exposure to growth methods, relying on your own way to accompany and change yourself.

參、自我修煉與成長

　　自我對話、自我探索、回歸內在、自我成長、生命修煉、心靈溝通，透過自我摸索或參加一些課程活動，都可以瞭解和改造自我原有的內在情緒，並轉換及提昇自我的性格素質，進而漸漸可以在不妨礙、影響別人的前題之下，做一個真正的自己。

　　以自我為中心的真正境界，不是自私自利、目中無人、我行我素、為所欲為，而是經由一些自我成長的方法來改變、認識及肯定自我的價值，非常清楚明白自己的一生真正要的是什麼，更懂得用簡單的態度、單純的想法，陽光、喜悅、滿足的心境去面對人世間所有的一切。

　　有哪些方法可以改變自己的觀念呢？如果覺得現階段心煩的事情多、意識到很想改變自己、情緒起伏大，不容易安撫自己的情緒，那麼，可以考慮參加一些方法正確而健康的課程、活動或一對一的引導，透過別人有系統、有步驟的輔導，是很好的一種成長方式，至少，可以比較有系統且立即把自己引導到正確的方向，之後，再選擇覺得合適的方法，慢慢來改變自己。

　　每個人的環境、背景、心理及情緒因素都不同，如果可以清楚知道要的是什麼，再向外尋求協助，效果會更好，而找到一位可以完全接納、完全同理心、真正經歷過一些傷痛的人來帶引，效果會事半功倍，因為，完全接納就能完全釋放。

　　除了向外尋找改變自己的方法，「土法煉鋼」，是我一路走來所想到和使用的方式，而改變是在不知不覺、悄悄變化中。

　　什麼是土法煉鋼呢？就是不知道、沒接觸過任何成長方法，只是用著本身的思想和生活方式，以自己的方法來陪伴和改變。沒有框架、教條約束、階段計劃、傳統束縛、目標設定、課程理論、任何壓力，最重要是會喜歡自己的方法而且成為生活習慣，自然而然的融入生活當中，在無形中慢慢的改變和成長，沒有什麼時候開始、什麼時候結束、邁向什麼階段的設限，這就是我對於土法煉鋼的思維和做法。

　　無論什麼樣的成長方法，只要適合自己，就是最棒的！

Part Three: Self-Cultivation and Growth

Self-dialogue, self-exploration, returning to one's inner self, personal growth, and spiritual communication can be understood and transformed through personal exploration or participating in courses and activities. This can improve and enhance one's character qualities and gradually become a true self without interfering with or affecting others.

The true realm of self-centeredness is not about being selfish, arrogant, or doing whatever one wants, but rather changing, understanding, and affirming one's own value through various personal growth methods. It involves being very clear about what one's life truly needs and facing everything in life with a simple, positive, and joyful attitude.

What methods can change one's perspective? If you are feeling overwhelmed by current troubles, want to change yourself, or have significant emotional fluctuations, consider participating in properly guided and healthy courses, activities, or one-on-one coaching. Structured and systematic guidance is a good way to grow and find the right direction.

Everyone's environment, background, psychological, and emotional factors are different. Knowing exactly what you want and then seeking help will yield better results. Finding someone who can fully accept and empathize with you, and who has experienced similar pain, can be even more effective because complete acceptance leads to complete release.

In addition to seeking methods from others, "do-it-yourself" is a method I have used throughout my journey. Change happens gradually and subtly.

What is "do-it-yourself"? It means using your own thoughts and lifestyle without exposure to growth methods, relying on your own way to accompany and change yourself. There are no frameworks, dogmas, constraints, stage plans, traditional limitations, goal settings, or pressures. The most important thing is to enjoy your own method and make it a habit, naturally integrating it into your life, leading to gradual change and growth without setting start or end points or stages. This is my approach and method for "do-it-yourself."

Regardless of the growth method, the best one is the one that suits you!

13. 我是三歲小孩

有時候我會說：我是三歲小孩。

朋友的反應有以下幾種：

- 你都幾歲了，還以為自己是小孩，真是幼稚。
- 你想法很天真，還真的有點像小孩。
- 非常有……。

　　面對經常接觸的事情，感覺幾乎都是由新鮮、好奇的興奮、喜悅，慢慢變為習以為常、理所當然、沒什麼特別，久而久之就司空見慣了，例如：陽台的一盆花、家裡的裝潢、買新車、出國、旅遊、美食、新工作、職位升遷、男女朋友、夫妻家人……。這未必是喜新厭舊的感覺，只是怎麼好像接觸久了，就越覺得沒什麼新奇或特別，有人心境因此感到不滿足或空虛，也有人因此覺得踏實、平靜。

　　回想還是小孩的時候，或看看現在的小朋友，似乎什麼事情都充滿好奇、好玩的心情，尤其年齡越小越覺得什麼都有趣，其實，我們也都曾經擁有那種感覺，只是為什麼經由時間的累積、年齡的增長，那份熱忱好像就消失了呢？是什麼樣的心境改變了想法？或許是被一些理所當然的觀念所框限了。

　　小孩的思想純淨、單純、直接、天馬行空、沒有約束，永遠保持著新奇、有趣、活力、創新，以大人的立場，或許覺得某些觀點有點不切實際，然而，大人因經驗而累積的觀念，好像也缺少了那種單純與直接，由於習以為常的想法，往往也箝制、忽略、壓抑了我們的心靈小孩。無論年齡大小，每個人的內心深處都依

13. I Am a Three-Year-Old Child

Sometimes I say, "I am a three-year-old child." My friends have different reactions to this:

- "How old are you now? Still thinking you're a child? How childish."
- "You have a very innocent way of thinking, a bit like a child."
- "Very much so..."

When we frequently encounter certain things, our feelings often shift from a sense of freshness, curiosity, excitement, and joy to something more ordinary, taken for granted, and unremarkable. Over time, these things become commonplace, like a flower pot on the balcony, home décor, a new car, travel, delicious food, a new job, a promotion, a romantic relationship, or family. This is not necessarily a case of always wanting something new, but rather that the more familiar we become with things, the less special they seem. Some people feel dissatisfied or empty because of this, while others find it grounding and peaceful.

Looking back at childhood or observing kids today, everything seems to be filled with curiosity and a sense of fun. The younger they are, the more they find everything interesting. We all once had that feeling, but why does that enthusiasm seem to fade with age and time? What changes our mindset? Perhaps it's the limitations imposed by the idea of things being taken for granted.

A child's thoughts are pure, simple, direct, and imaginative, without constraints, always filled with novelty, fun, energy, and innovation. From an

然存在著純稚、赤子之心,誰都無法否定它的存在,哪怕是 20 歲、60 歲還是 100 歲,永遠都是「三歲小孩」。

　　三歲小孩,是指心境如三歲孩童般,不會因為生命年齡的增長而失去心靈年齡的熱忱,心靈永遠保持著如孩童般的簡單、純淨、陽光,無論年齡增加了多少,心境不會因此而變得複雜。

　　[生命年齡],是人類創造時間觀念後所產生的年齡概念,而因為這樣的概念,對年齡累積的想法產生了影響,人們似乎就無法躲避生命年齡增加所產生的心理影響及生活行為。例如:我 30 多歲應該結婚生子了;我老花眼所以我老了;我到退休年齡我老了;我 70 歲我老了;我體力不如從前,好像開始變老了………。其實,即使無可避免這些年齡現象是存在的,然而在心情上,依然可以像三歲小孩般的快樂、自在。

　　[心靈年齡],年齡就定格在「三歲」小孩的境界,永遠保持孩童般的赤子之心,面對世間的一切,就像三歲小孩般的單純、樂觀與好奇。定格的心靈年齡加上生命年齡不斷增加所累積的成長經驗,會讓人生更顯得成熟與知足。

　　多年前,覺得眼睛偶而模模糊糊不是很舒服,忍不住去住家附近眼科診所檢查。

　　檢查完,醫師笑著說:你雖然看起來像 31、32 歲,不過,你絕對超過 40 歲了。

　　我:???(這跟眼睛不舒服有關嗎)

　　醫師:因為你老花眼啦,老花眼通常是 40 歲以後……,外表唬人,老花眼唬不了人的。

　　我:是喔。

　　醫師:當然啦。

　　我:管它的(指老花眼),那是它的事(指眼睛),它老它的,不干我的事啦。

　　醫師被我突如其來的這一句,當場傻眼,笑的無法開口說話。

　　我也笑著說:本來就是啊,眼睛 40 歲會老花,我還早的很咧。

　　凡事樂觀,永遠年輕,這就是「三歲」小孩。

adult's perspective, some of these ideas might seem impractical. However, adults, with their accumulated knowledge from experience, might lack that simplicity and directness. Our accustomed way of thinking often suppresses, ignores, or restrains the inner child within us. Regardless of age, everyone still has a pure, childlike heart deep down inside. No one can deny its existence, whether they're 20, 60, or 100 years old—they are always a "three-year-old child."

The term "three-year-old child" refers to a mindset like that of a three-year-old, not losing the passion of a youthful spirit despite the progression of age. It means keeping a child's simple, pure, and sunny attitude, no matter how many years pass, without letting life's complexity change that state of mind.

[Physical age] is a concept that arose after humans created the idea of time, and it has since influenced our thoughts about aging. People seem unable to escape the psychological and behavioral effects of increasing physical age. For example: "I'm in my 30s, so I should be getting married and having kids"; "I have presbyopia, so I must be getting old"; "I've reached retirement age, I'm old"; "I'm 70 years old, I am old"; or "I'm not as strong as before, I must be aging." Although these signs of aging are inevitable, our spirits can still remain as joyful and carefree as a three-year-old child.

[Mental age] is where one's mindset remains fixed at the level of a "three-year-old" child, always maintaining that childlike innocence. Facing the world with the simplicity, optimism, and curiosity of a three-year-old, this fixed mental age, combined with the life experience accumulated as physical age increases, can make life feel more mature and fulfilling.

Years ago, I noticed my eyes occasionally felt blurry and uncomfortable, so I couldn't resist visiting an eye clinic near my home. After the check-up, the doctor smiled and said, "You look like you're around 31 or 32 years old, but you're definitely over 40." I was puzzled: "What does that have to do with my eyes being uncomfortable?" The doctor replied, "Because you have presbyopia, which usually happens after 40... your appearance might deceive people, but presbyopia doesn't lie." I said, "Oh, is that so?" The doctor replied, "Of course." I responded, "Well, who cares? That's its business (referring to the eyes); let it age on its own. It has nothing to do with me." The doctor was taken aback by my sudden remark

有人會問：為什麼是三歲,不是五歲、……歲呢?直覺告訴我,「三歲」是心靈最純稚的階段。其實不必太拘泥於「幾歲」這個數字,重要是無論年齡幾歲,永遠可以保有孩童那份真摯的心靈。

and was at a loss for words, laughing uncontrollably. I laughed too, saying, "Exactly, my eyes might be 40 years old, but I'm still far from that age."

Staying optimistic and forever young—that's what it means to be a "three-year-old child." Some might ask, "Why three years old and not five or another age?" My intuition tells me that "three years old" is the purest stage of the soul. It's not necessary to be fixated on the number itself; what matters is that no matter how old you are, you can always retain the sincerity of a child's heart.

14. 我是溫室花朵？

很多朋友羨慕我的樂觀，認為從小就是備受呵護的溫室花朵，才能如此的陽光、自信。

從懵懵懂懂的幼兒時期開始，印象中，父母就不曾「安靜」過，那麼，成長過程就不如意嗎？好像也未必，因為喜歡跟自己玩，很能自得其樂的生活著。

小小年紀就會一個人：播聽黑膠唱片、欣賞音樂；拿著釣竿去公園、池塘釣魚；挖地洞烤地瓜、烤玉米、烤雞蛋；抓蜜蜂、蜻蜓、蝴蝶；灌蟋蟀、黏知了（蟬）、彈弓打麻雀；爬樹摘水果；養貓、養狗、養魚、養昆蟲、小動物；天馬行空寫文章、寫計劃；喜歡上學、不喜歡讀書……，腦袋整天就是繞著自己創造的各種遊戲玩耍。只要聽到、看到父母開始「不安靜」，我就「躲」起來，日子也就這麼過下去。

人生起起伏伏，大大小小的挫折可能隨時出現，順遂或逆境，就看用什麼心態面對。自己曾經遭遇了連續接踵而來的事件，應該稱得上是嚴重的打擊。

離開任職多年的公司後自行創業，草創初期胼手胝足、兢兢業業，然而，就在出國洽商期間，以前任職公司的主管，竟連同一位會首惡性倒閉數十人新台幣數千萬的會錢，我當然慘遭牽連，積蓄立即一無所有，公司業務面臨無法周轉、家庭生活費、小孩奶粉錢……，如何追討是一回事，眼前每天開銷如何過下去？我可以一日一餐都無妨，嗷嗷待哺的孩子怎麼辦？

我沒有求助任何人，傷心不到兩天（就是兩天，非比喻的形

14. Am I a Greenhouse Flower?

Many friends envy my optimism, believing that I must have been a carefully nurtured "hothouse flower" from a young age to be so sunny and confident. From my early childhood, I recall that my parents were never "quiet," but does that mean my upbringing was unhappy? Not necessarily, because I enjoyed playing by myself and was quite content living in my own little world.

At a young age, I could do things like play vinyl records and enjoy music, go fishing in the park or at ponds, dig holes to roast sweet potatoes, corn, and eggs, catch bees, dragonflies, and butterflies, play with crickets, cicadas, and sparrows using slingshots, climb trees to pick fruits, and raise cats, dogs, fish, insects, and other small animals. I loved writing stories, creating plans, and while I liked going to school, I didn't enjoy studying. My mind was always busy with games and activities that I invented. Whenever I sensed my parents getting "noisy," I would hide away and continue on with my life.

Life has its ups and downs, and setbacks can appear at any moment. Whether things go smoothly or not depends on your mindset. I have faced a series of challenges that could be considered major setbacks.

After leaving the company where I had worked for many years, I started my own business. In the early days, I worked diligently, but during a business trip abroad, my former manager and another person maliciously caused a financial collapse, taking millions of New Taiwan Dollars from dozens of people, and I was inevitably affected. My savings were wiped out instantly, the business struggled to stay afloat, and I had to worry about daily expenses, household needs, and my child's formula. How was I supposed to keep going? I could survive on one meal a

容詞），心想至少還有公司，加足馬力打拼應該可以暫時扭轉眼前情況，先穩住家庭生活比什麼都重要。然而身無分文的確寸步難行，因此，用走路代替騎機車、搭公車；擺攤位、發廣告單代替報紙打廣告，只是，有些最基本的支出還是難免，怎麼辦？

　　就在那時候一位客戶願意資助我，條件是公司過戶讓他成為負責人（當時我這行業執照的申請是凍結的）。不是錢或誰是負責人的問題，我的個性不喜歡合夥的經營方式，所以婉拒了。然而他一再保證一切都以我的理念為依歸，共同打拼又有資金，何苦一人獨撐？

　　我同意公司變更他為負責人，一切似乎有點起色，只是沒多久全走了樣，他對內、對外以老闆自居，生意手法讓人難以認同，最後，我只能選擇忍痛離開一手創立的公司。短短不到幾個月，幾乎所有的積蓄都被奪走，一無所有的傷痛還沒平息，僅剩唯一翻身希望的公司又被別人拿去，這豈非真的要斷了我所有的生路？

　　這兩件接踵而來的打擊，平常嗎？嚴重嗎？該怎麼應對？眼前全沒了，未來一片茫然，雙重打擊要如何面對？影響家人要如何降到最低？朋友聽了之後，反應包括：打官司、要回來、先跟父母或朋友借錢……，甚至有人說，這恐怕要社會事件了。

　　我選擇自我療傷和調整心情。面對困境及打擊，把最糟的可能情況仔細的全盤思考一下，想想能否承受，再思考如何處理，如果最壞情形還能承受，那還有什麼大不了，事實上很少結果真的最壞，如果萬一無法承受，再思考其他補救和解決的方法，讓傷害降至最低。

　　那段期間省吃儉用、等待機會，規劃未來重新申請公司的營運方案和文宣，一年多以後，終於等到執照重新開放申請，被拿走的公司後來反而因經營不善而消失了。

　　我始終相信，即使碰到嚴重打擊，必須讓自己能夠勇於承受現況，並且自我調適心情慢慢走過低潮，若爭吵或惡性循環，只有讓事情更複雜甚至惡化，整天意志消沉也解決不了問題，發生在自己身上的事自己解決，自己才是最佳的處理者。

　　我的確是溫室花朵。我對溫室花朵的另一種感覺是：經過各種不同歷練後，心境走向了單純、陽光、積極的一面，心靈益發安寧與無為，從此面對任何好或壞的情形時，都可以簡單面對、一視同仁。

day, but what about my hungry child?

I didn't ask anyone for help. After two days of feeling down (literally just two days, not a figure of speech), I thought, at least I still had my company. If I put in enough effort, I might be able to temporarily turn things around. Keeping the household stable was my top priority. But without a penny, it was hard to move forward, so I started walking instead of riding my scooter or taking the bus, and I promoted the business by handing out flyers instead of advertising in the newspaper. Still, some expenses were unavoidable. What could I do?

During that difficult time, a client offered to support me financially, on the condition that I transfer ownership of the company to him (since business licenses for this industry were temporarily frozen at the time). It wasn't about the money or who was in charge; I just didn't like the idea of a partnership. I declined politely. But he insisted, assuring me that everything would follow my vision, and with funding and shared efforts, why struggle alone?

I eventually agreed to make him the official owner of the company. Things seemed to improve slightly, but soon everything changed. He started acting as the boss, both internally and externally, with business methods that I couldn't agree with. In the end, I had no choice but to leave the company I had built from the ground up. In just a few short months, I lost almost all my savings, and the pain of losing my only hope of recovery was overwhelming. The company, which was supposed to be my last chance, was gone. Was my path completely cut off?

These back-to-back blows were tough to handle. How serious were they? How should I cope? I had nothing left in the present, and the future seemed uncertain. How could I minimize the impact on my family? Friends offered advice like filing a lawsuit, borrowing money from my parents or friends, or even making it a social issue.

I chose to heal myself and adjust my mindset. When facing challenges and setbacks, I think through the worst-case scenarios thoroughly and consider if I can bear them. If I can, then it's not that bad after all, because the worst seldom happens. If the situation is unbearable, then I look for other ways to mitigate and solve the problem to minimize the damage.

During that period, I lived frugally while planning for the future, reapplying for my company's license and creating new promotional strategies. After more than a year, I finally had the chance to reapply, and the company that was taken

14. 我是温室花朵？

from me eventually disappeared due to poor management.

I've always believed that even in the face of severe setbacks, you have to be able to bear the situation and gradually adjust your mindset to get through the tough times. Arguing or dwelling in negativity will only make things worse, and staying depressed won't solve any problems. The best way to deal with what happens in your life is to handle it yourself; you are your own best problem-solver.

I am indeed a "hothouse flower." But my view of being a hothouse flower is this: After going through various life experiences, my mindset has become simpler, more positive, and more proactive. My spirit has become more peaceful and content. Now, when I face good or bad situations, I can handle them with a simple, open-minded approach.

15. 音樂滋潤心靈

　　我很喜歡隨興聆聽各國音樂和各種音樂的曲風，欣賞屬於他們特有的樂曲、旋律和風格，心境上會有一種包容與接納的感動。

　　動態音樂可以釋放情緒，靜態音樂可以療癒心靈。音樂對於心靈的重要，就好像空氣對於身體的重要，好的音樂可以淨化心靈，什麼才是好音樂呢？好音樂，我會由自己的喜好和感覺來決定，無論什麼旋律或曲風，只要是自己喜歡的、有感覺的，就是好音樂！未必是聽說的或別人建議的，因為，別人喜歡或推薦的音樂，或許不符合自己的個性和喜好，可能就難以觸動心靈的感動。

　　因為，自己喜歡的音樂是來自於自身深切的感受，未必適用於別人，畢竟不喜歡或沒感覺的音樂，很難勾起心靈迴響，當然，如果能遇到懂得以音樂治療來帶領進入那些音樂情境裡的人，就另當別論。

　　隨時聽著喜歡的音樂，只要不妨礙別人（尤其是獨處時），此時的我不會在乎別人的觀覺或評價，因為，音樂裡有著某種特殊的情感、成長的記憶和種種的喜怒哀樂。音樂伴我成長，指的就是深植心靈深處永遠存在的音樂。

　　記得13歲那年，收音機傳來一首清音樂，不知何故，只要聽到那首音樂，整個心境感覺全部放空與寧靜，似乎一切全部停頓下來，覺得心不停的往內一直縮小，越縮越小又一直無止境的縮小，可以真實感到自己的存在，腦海浮現了生命存在的真實感。

　　閉上眼睛，眼前竟是一片光明，出現紫光、白光、藍光、金

15. Music Nourishes the Soul

I really enjoy casually listening to music from different countries and various musical styles, appreciating the unique melodies and characteristics they bring. It gives me a feeling of openness and acceptance. Dynamic music can release emotions, while calm music can heal the soul. Music is as important to the soul as air is to the body; good music can purify the mind. What is good music? I let my personal preferences and feelings decide. No matter the melody or style, as long as it resonates with me and I like it, that's good music. It doesn't have to be what's recommended or popular because other people's tastes might not align with mine, and their suggestions might not touch my soul.

After all, the music that moves me comes from my own deep feelings, which might not necessarily resonate with others. It's difficult for music that you don't enjoy or feel connected to evoke any kind of emotional response. Of course, if you can find someone who understands how to use music to guide you into those emotional states, that's a different story.

Whenever I listen to music I like, as long as I'm not bothering anyone else (especially when I'm alone), I don't care what others might think or say. To me, music carries a special kind of emotion, memories of growth, and all kinds of experiences of joy and sorrow. Music has accompanied me throughout my life—it's like a permanent presence rooted deep in my soul.

I remember when I was 13 years old, I heard a piece of instrumental music on the radio. For some reason, every time I listened to it, I felt a sense of emptiness and peace, as if everything had stopped. I felt my mind shrinking

黃色的光和閃爍不停的星星，好像漩渦不停的向內、向遠處一直旋轉進去，可以看到宇宙的星光燦爛及宇宙遙望無際深層又深層的景象，也清楚聽到心臟規律跳動的聲音，在音樂旋律的牽引過程中，身體偶而會出現汗毛豎立、起雞皮疙瘩的現象，那種感覺是溫暖和舒服的，這樣的感覺，隨著那首音樂一直反覆出現。

我很喜歡那樣的感覺，希望感覺一直存在著，只是，音樂只有3分多鐘，而且一直不知道那首音樂的曲名，無法找到那首音樂的錄音帶，怎麼辦？

我，將整首音樂旋律收錄到了腦海裡！之後，不斷從腦海裡反覆播放出來，有時甚至除了睡覺，就是整天迴盪耳際，在那段青少年的歲月裡，它無時無刻陪伴著我，撫慰與滋潤了我的心靈。

數十年後，我終於知道那首音樂的曲名，然而什麼曲名已經不重要了，重要的是它感動了我、伴我成長，直到現在依然是我的最愛。

現在正在寫著對這首音樂感覺的同時，音樂在腦海裡播放了起來，那些感覺又回來了！雞皮疙瘩出現了好幾次，已經過了數十年了，它對我的影響永遠與生命同時存在。

一首熟悉的音樂，代表了自己的一個故事、一個回憶、一個成長背景，最能勾起過往的回憶和感動心靈，把最有感覺的音樂記憶在腦海裡，獨處時，喚醒心靈深處那些感動的音樂，無時無刻欣賞、聆聽、哼唱，有種踏實的感覺，也牽引出所有的喜怒哀樂，情緒因此得到認同和撫平，心境因而平靜與滿足。

inward, smaller and smaller, infinitely smaller, and I could sense the reality of my own existence. In my mind, I saw a bright scene with flashes of purple, white, blue, and golden light, with twinkling stars that seemed to swirl inward like a vortex leading into the depths of the universe. I could hear the rhythmic beat of my own heart, and the melody made me feel a pleasant, warm sensation that sometimes even gave me goosebumps. That feeling came back every time I heard that piece of music.

I loved that feeling and wished it would last forever, but the music was only three minutes long, and I didn't know its name, so I couldn't find the recording. What could I do?

I memorized the entire melody in my mind! After that, I played it over and over in my head. Sometimes, apart from when I was sleeping, it was constantly echoing in my ears. During those years of adolescence, that music was always with me, comforting and nurturing my soul.

Decades later, I finally learned the name of that piece of music. But by then, the name didn't matter anymore. What mattered was how it moved me and stayed with me as I grew, and it remains my favorite to this day.

As I write these thoughts now, the music is playing in my mind, and those feelings have returned! I've felt goosebumps several times, even after all these years. Its impact on me continues to be as real as life itself.

A familiar piece of music represents a story, a memory, or a backdrop to your growth. It evokes past memories and deeply moves the soul. By keeping that music alive in your mind, you can relive those emotions and experiences whenever you're alone, enjoying, listening, or humming to yourself. It brings a sense of grounding, drawing out all your joys and sorrows, and it allows your emotions to be recognized and soothed, bringing peace and contentment to your heart.

16. 哭、蛻變與成長

　　哭和笑一樣的重要。大人、小孩都會哭。哭，可以表達內心的感覺，只是，隨著年齡的增長，這種方式被壓抑和控制了，表面上好像懂得自我控制，其實是把悲傷塞回自己的情緒倉庫，而且累積的越多，未來爆發的力量會越可怕，適度發洩悲傷的情緒，才會變得理智。

　　任何人都有情緒、都會發脾氣，差別在於什麼時候、什麼場合、什麼方式讓它適度的宣洩出來。情緒不是用「控制」來呈現表面的溫和，而是用適當的方式讓它得到出口、降低強度，所謂的控制情緒，不是塞回去、忍下來、吞回去，然後當做沒事，而是在適當的時機去抒解掉。

　　只有真正、勇敢的面對自我內心起伏的情緒，才會明白自己也有軟弱與無助的時候，才有可能以柔軟的心和同理心來自我療癒和成長，也才能懂得關懷、體貼別人和為別人著想。

　　哭，是表達和發洩情感很好的方法。尤其一個人的時候，如果知道如何處理或由懂得釋放情緒的人來引領，那麼，盡情、無負擔、放心的哭出來，是很快的情緒釋放方法，哭過之後，能使人心情舒暢。

　　如果清楚明白為什麼傷心、難過，那麼自我療癒或借助外在協助（例如：閱讀、靜心、課程、活動）都很有幫助。如果不是很清楚，可能就需要一位有深層同理心的人來協助層層回溯根源和探索隱藏內在的原因，也可以讓情緒和壓力得到釋放，使自己得以明白哭泣、難過的真正背後因素是什麼，得到真正的蛻變和

16. Crying, Transformation and Growth

Crying is as important as laughing. Both adults and children cry. Crying can express inner feelings, but as we age, this way of expression becomes suppressed and controlled. On the surface, it seems like we've learned self-control, but in reality, we are just stuffing sadness back into our emotional storage. The more it accumulates, the more explosive the future outburst can be. Properly venting sadness can lead to rationality.

Everyone has emotions and gets angry. The difference is when, in what situation, and how these emotions are properly expressed. Emotions are not about showing surface calmness through "control," but rather about finding appropriate ways to express them and reduce their intensity. So-called emotional control is not about stuffing emotions away, enduring them, or swallowing them, but about releasing them at the right moment.

Only by truly and courageously facing our fluctuating emotions will we understand that we also have moments of weakness and helplessness. This understanding allows us to heal and grow with a soft heart and empathy, and to care for and consider others.

Crying is a good way to express and release emotions. Especially when alone, if you know how to handle it or if someone who understands emotional release guides you, crying freely and without burden can be a quick method of emotional release. After crying, people often feel relieved.

If you understand why you are sad or upset, self-healing or external help (such as reading, meditation, courses, activities) can be very helpful. If you're not clear, you might need someone with deep empathy to assist

成長。

　　透過哭，會讓心情得到暫時的平復，也能清除負面情緒垃圾，即使是難以撫平的遺憾也比較容易釋懷，如果一直壓抑著負面的思維沒有做適度的抒解，可能就會產生越來越嚴重的負面想法，整個心境也就會往負面的方向發展。

　　心中持續著悲傷、難過、委屈、思念、心酸的感覺，眼眶會漸漸泛紅、泛淚、眼淚奪眶而出，此時，拿起毛巾或衛生紙拭拭淚、擤擤鼻涕，讓淚水盡情宣洩出來，感覺放鬆或疲累、沉默不語或全身癱軟無力都沒關係，之後再好好睡一覺，當一覺醒來感覺會好很多。

　　每個人或多或少都有自己不自知的負面情緒，它隱藏在情緒倉庫裡，這些不自知的負面情緒在自然而然的哭泣過程中，很自然的放聲大哭甚至是嬰兒哭聲，之後會開始重新檢視自己，哭過以後，會漸漸變得自信、理性、放下。

　　一位朋友因為家裡的寵物突然過世，居然持續的哭泣了7天之久，怎麼會因為寵物的過世而這麼的傷心難過？連他自己也覺得奇怪。

　　後來在閒聊的過程中，終於明白情緒崩潰的真正背後原因：對感情的執著無法放下。突然和寵物的分離，牽引出小時候被家人暫時拋棄的無助和恐懼。表面上是寵物過世的哭泣傷心，實際上是幼年時期親情分離的悲傷。那7天的情緒釋放，幫助他明白了原因，也漸漸釋懷。

　　每個人都有情緒，如果有正向的思維，就可以把情緒和生氣做切割。就像以下的兩種情況：

第一類：事件出現、情緒瞬間出現。

　　激動、發脾氣、打、罵、傷害自己，無論哪一項，都是一種發洩動作。如果自己很難控制或希望獲得深層抒發、治療，那麼找專業的人協助是不錯的方法，也可以去上一些內在成長或情緒清理的課程，先幫助自己的情緒找到出口，當然一定要找適合自己的專業人員。

第二類：出現不滿情緒時，先想一下怎麼了？再想一下該怎麼處理最恰當。

in tracing the root causes and exploring the hidden internal reasons. This can help release emotions and stress, allowing you to understand the true reasons behind your tears and sadness, leading to genuine transformation and growth.

Through crying, emotions are temporarily calmed, and negative emotional clutter is cleared. Even deeply troubling regrets become easier to let go of. If negative thoughts are continuously suppressed without appropriate release, they may lead to increasingly severe negative thoughts, causing one's mindset to develop in a negative direction.

When sadness, distress, grievances, longing, or heartache persist, and tears well up, it's okay to use a towel or tissue to wipe away tears and blow your nose. Let the tears flow freely, and if you feel relaxed or exhausted, or if you're silent and limp, that's okay. Afterward, have a good sleep. You will likely feel much better upon waking up.

Everyone has some unconscious negative emotions, hidden in their emotional storage. During the natural process of crying, these emotions are released, and crying, even like an infant's cry, will eventually lead to self-reflection. After crying, people gradually become more confident, rational, and able to let go.

A friend cried continuously for seven days due to the sudden death of a family pet. Why such deep sadness over a pet's death? Even he found it strange.

Later, in a casual conversation, he finally understood the true reason behind his emotional breakdown: his attachment to emotions was hard to let go. The sudden separation from the pet triggered the helplessness and fear of being temporarily abandoned by family during childhood. The seven days of emotional release helped him understand the cause and gradually come to terms with it.

Everyone has emotions, and if we have positive thinking, we can separate emotions from anger. Consider the following two situations:

First Type: An event occurs, and emotions arise instantly. Expressing anger, venting, hitting, scolding, or harming oneself—any of these are forms of release. If you find it hard to control yourself or seek deep emotional

如果是針對「人」，想一下怎麼處理可以讓自己和對方都接受；如果是對事或物，怎麼處理會最恰當；如果是複雜的事情，分析最壞和最好的情況是什麼，想出最圓滿的解決方法。

　　第二類的過程，少了發洩情緒的動作，這就是情緒和生氣的切割，是屬於情緒還可以控制，理性較高的類型。

　　大人會因為面子問題而放不開，尤其一句：男人有淚不輕彈，不知壓抑了多少男人情緒發洩的機會，女性有著比較柔軟的性情，容易用哭泣來宣洩情感，這也是女性平均壽命多於男性的一項重要心理因素。

　　誰沒情緒？只要在覺得安全自在的場所，例如：自己的房間或汽車裡，都是隱密又放心的地方，準備衛生紙和垃圾桶，盡情的把情緒垃圾倒出來吧！

　　如果朋友在哭泣，不用說話，不要勸告，只要靜靜陪著他，感受他的難過就好，只要沒有傷害自己或他人的動作，就讓他一直宣洩悲傷，時間多久都無所謂。任何人只要情緒獲得充分的釋放，心情就會好很多，也會漸漸比較清楚自己要的、期待的是什麼。

release and healing, consulting a professional can be a good method. You can also take internal growth or emotional clearing courses to help find an outlet for your emotions. It's essential to choose a suitable professional.

Second Type: When dissatisfaction arises, first consider what's happening. Then think about the most appropriate way to handle it. If it's about a person, think about how to handle it in a way that both parties can accept. If it's about an event or object, how can it be handled most appropriately? If it's a complex issue, analyze the worst and best scenarios and find the most satisfactory solution.

The second type involves less emotional venting and represents a situation where emotions can still be controlled and reasoning is higher.

Adults often struggle to let go due to issues of pride, especially with the saying: "Men don't shed tears easily." This represses many emotional release opportunities for men. Women, with their generally softer nature, are more prone to expressing emotions through crying. This is an important psychological factor contributing to the longer average lifespan of women.

Who doesn't have emotions? As long as you are in a safe and comfortable place, such as your room or car, with tissues and a trash can ready, let out the emotional clutter freely.

If a friend is crying, don't speak, advise, or criticize. Just quietly accompany them and feel their sadness. As long as there's no self-harm or harm to others, let them continue to release their sadness for as long as needed. Anyone who fully releases their emotions will feel much better and will gradually become clearer about what they want and expect.

17. 聆聽、回應、同理心

　　感覺被接納、被認同、被瞭解，是非常愉快的。期待別人懂我之前，我會先瞭解自己、檢討自己，知道我要的是什麼，先聆聽、回應、認同自己，再用那樣的心情去理解和回應別人的想法，這和愛自己而後懂得愛別人的想法一樣，會讓對方感受到得到彼此的認同。

　　聆聽別人之前，要先懂得如何聆聽自己。能夠清楚聆聽自我內在的想法，確實瞭解想法的真正原因而且回應自己，這樣的感覺，就是「自我同理心」。有了這樣的修為，會很自然的感染給別人，這會是最自然、最貼切的同理心，最能感受對方的心情，也會讓對方真實的感受到被瞭解的溫暖。

　　被「聆聽」，每個人都喜歡那種感覺，懂得聆聽的人，自己的心情會很開心，被聆聽者也會感到愉快和被瞭解。

　　聆聽時，全神貫注的聽對方所說的每一字、每一句和看著對方的肢體動作（例如：眼神、表情、姿勢、語調、情緒起伏），這樣可以清楚明白對方真正要表達的是什麼，在適當的時候把所聽到的說出來，例如：簡單的一些「嗯」「喔」「是」、「你的意思是……是嗎？」、「你覺得……很生氣，是嗎？」或是「我明白你為什麼傷心……」、「能在再多講一些關於……」，這樣的聆聽與回應，會讓對方感受到被瞭解、尊重和接納。

　　聆聽時，不批評、不責備、不評斷、不先入為主、情緒不隨對方起伏、不打斷不駁斥，尤其要有感同身受的心，讓對方知道我明白他的感受和想法。其實，「感同身受」和「贊成想法」是

17. Listening, Responding, and Empathy

Feeling accepted, recognized, and understood is very pleasant. Before expecting others to understand me, I first need to understand and reflect on myself. Knowing what I want, listening to, responding to, and recognizing myself first, and then understanding and responding to others' thoughts with the same mindset, is akin to loving oneself before loving others. This approach makes others feel mutually recognized.

Before listening to others, one must first know how to listen to oneself. Being able to clearly listen to and understand one's own inner thoughts and respond to oneself is what is called "self-empathy." With such cultivation, it naturally extends to others, resulting in the most genuine and fitting empathy. This makes others truly feel understood and supported.

Everyone enjoys being "listened to." Those who are good at listening will feel happy themselves, and those being listened to will feel pleased and understood.

When listening, focus fully on each word and sentence spoken by the other person, and observe their body language (such as eye contact, facial expressions, posture, tone, and emotional fluctuations). This helps to clearly understand what the other person is trying to convey. At appropriate times, express what you've heard, such as with simple responses like "Mm," "Oh," "Yes," "Is this what you mean?" "You seem very angry about this," or "I understand why you are sad…". Asking them to elaborate, such as "Can you tell me more about…," shows that you are listening, respecting, and accepting them.

可以切割的，也就是：可以認同對方的感受，然而不贊同對方的想法。

例如：孩子和同學口角，回家告訴父母想打那個同學，父母可以聆聽孩子的生氣，感同身受他的憤怒，然而不贊成打人。只要聆聽，讓孩子說完心裡的話，發洩所有不滿和憤怒後，讓孩子明白父母的感同身受，等孩子情緒緩和了，自然可以平心靜氣的討論恰當的想法和作法。無論是正面或負面情緒，同理心就是聆聽、接納、回應，對事情的認同或支持或對錯，是沒有關連的。

同理心要用實際行動來表達，而非只是口號、說說而已，同理心和同情心不同，同理心會讓自己變得更自信、積極、務實、包容、接納、感恩、寬容，無論是自己獲得認同或認同別人，那樣的感覺，是溫暖而陽光的。

While listening, avoid criticizing, blaming, judging, or interrupting. Especially, avoid being swayed by their emotions or dismissing their feelings. Instead, truly feel their emotions and thoughts. In fact, "empathizing" and "agreeing with their ideas" can be separated. You can empathize with their feelings while not necessarily agreeing with their ideas.

For example, if a child argues with a classmate and wants to hit them, the parents can empathize with the child's anger but should not support hitting. By listening to the child's frustrations and letting them express their feelings, the parents can show understanding. Once the child's emotions calm down, a discussion on appropriate actions can follow. Whether the emotions are positive or negative, empathy involves listening, accepting, and responding, and does not necessarily correlate with agreeing or disagreeing with their actions.

Empathy should be expressed through actions, not just words or slogans. Empathy differs from sympathy; it makes one more confident, positive, pragmatic, tolerant, accepting, grateful, and forgiving. Whether receiving or giving recognition, this feeling is warm and sunny.

18. 鼓勵別人、說服自己？

　　我們都曾經受過別人的鼓勵，也有過這樣的經驗：為什麼我這麼努力的鼓勵他，就是講不聽、不肯做？而自己是否曾經想過，如果別人用同樣方式鼓勵我時，會是什麼感覺？聽得進去嗎？道理有用嗎？還是根本覺得：對方不瞭解我（甚至覺得是壓力）。

　　鼓勵真的有幫助嗎？當有人在我心情低落或遇到挫折時，說了一大堆道理和方法，或許真的有道理，然而，我真的心情有變好了嗎？被鼓勵了嗎？覺得建議有用嗎？或者心情還是一樣，甚至覺得不被瞭解，沒有真的幫助到我，或認為對方的建議根本不是我要的。

　　幾乎所有的規勸或鼓勵，都是先否定他的感覺、想法、做法，然後再告訴他現在提供的方法才是最好的，希望把自己成功的方法複製到別人身上，相信按照我建議的方法去做是正確的，其實被否定的感覺誰都會不舒服，有些的鼓勵，只是在說服自己、肯定自己而已。

　　如果無法瞭解別人在想什麼、原因是什麼、需要的是什麼，那麼，所有鼓勵都只是在對牛彈琴，因為，那些話是來自於自己的經驗，自己的方法未必適合別人，尤其是自己的經驗未必等同於別人的遭遇和環境。

　　如果感覺不被瞭解，任何的鼓勵和好意反而給對方壓力。鼓勵別人，要從內心著手。傾聽他怎麼說，讓他把內在的想法和疑惑說出來，回應他真實的想法，讓他覺得被瞭解和支持，才願意把心中話說出來，並且在不斷說出困難的過程，會覺得問題似乎

18. Encouraging Others, Persuading Oneself?

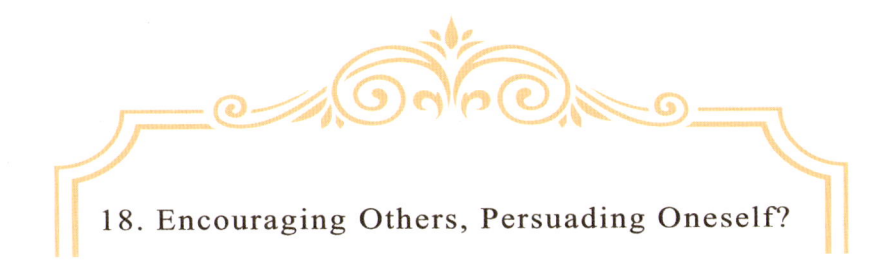

We've all received encouragement from others and have experienced this: Why is it that no matter how hard I encourage someone, they just don't listen or act? Have you ever thought about how you would feel if someone encouraged you in the same way? Would you be receptive? Are the reasons useful? Or would you feel that the person doesn't understand you （even feeling pressured）?

Does encouragement really help? When someone gives a lot of advice and methods while you're feeling low or facing setbacks, even if the advice is reasonable, does it actually improve your mood? Do you feel encouraged? Do you find the suggestions useful, or do you still feel the same, perhaps feeling misunderstood or that the advice isn't relevant?

Most advice or encouragement involves denying the other person's feelings, thoughts, or methods and then offering one's own successful methods as the best way. The intention is to replicate one's own success, believing it is correct. In reality, being denied often feels uncomfortable. Some encouragement is merely about convincing oneself rather than truly helping the other person.

If you cannot understand what the other person is thinking, their reasons, or their needs, then all encouragement is like playing to a deaf audience because those words come from your own experience. Your methods may not suit them, especially if your experiences are not equivalent to theirs.

If you feel misunderstood, any encouragement or goodwill might add to the pressure. Encouragement should come from within. Listen to their

沒那麼的困難，甚至找到了適合他的方法，而不是否定他、標榜自己。

　　鼓勵別人之前，要先聆聽他的心聲，感覺被認同、被瞭解，在沒有壓力和防衛的情緒之下，讓他充分說出內在的聲音和想法，再由他依照本身的環境所造成的想法中，幫助他找到適合而且可行的方法，這樣的鼓勵，會讓他覺得就是他要的。

　　一位朋友的孩子，數學一直不及格，成績經常只有十到二十幾分，補習、找家教、做更多的練習考卷、訂定獎勵標準，結果都沒有起色，後來，他終於說：「我討厭背數學公式，我問老師公式是怎麼產生的？老師說：就是這樣、這樣所以變成這樣。叫我不要一直問，背起來就對了，背得滾瓜爛熟就會熟能生巧，然後不斷的做很多練習題，數學成績自然就會很高分。可是，我討厭背，我要知道公式為什麼是這樣的結果，而不是那樣的結果」。

　　結果，家長終於找到一位願意耐心告訴他為什麼的數學家教，半年後參加全校同年級的數學競試比賽，從半年前的全校最後第一名，成為這次全校前面第一名，半年內連得兩個「第一名」，連老師和家長都驚訝不已。

　　鼓勵其實很簡單，就是：你的想法我知道。這樣的鼓勵，最貼切，也最有效果，而不是用說服自己的方法，去鼓勵別人，因為，那是說服而不是鼓勵。聆聽、接納、回應、同理心，無論是鼓勵別人或整理自己的情緒，都是最貼切的鼓舞。

words, let them express their inner thoughts and doubts, and respond to their real thoughts. This makes them feel understood and supported. Through this process of expressing difficulties, they may find that their problems are not so daunting and may discover suitable solutions, rather than feeling negated or that you are showcasing yourself.

Before encouraging others, listen to their feelings and ensure they feel recognized and understood. With no pressure or defensiveness, allow them to fully express their inner voice and thoughts. Then, help them find feasible solutions within their own context. This kind of encouragement feels right and effective.

A friend's child had consistently failed math, with scores often ranging from just ten to twenty points. Despite trying tutoring, hiring private tutors, doing more practice exams, and setting up reward systems, there was no improvement. Later, the child finally said: "I hate memorizing math formulas. I asked the teacher how the formulas are derived, but the teacher just said: 'It's like this, so it becomes this way. Don't keep asking, just memorize it, and with enough practice, your math scores will naturally improve.' But I hate memorizing. I want to understand why the formula results in this outcome and not that one."

Eventually, the parents found a math tutor who patiently explained the reasons behind the formulas. Six months later, the child participated in a math competition for the entire grade and went from being the lowest-scoring student to being the top scorer, impressing both teachers and parents.

Encouragement is actually quite simple: "I understand your thoughts." This type of encouragement is the most fitting and effective, rather than using one's own methods to persuade others, which is more about convincing than truly encouraging. Listening, accepting, responding, and showing empathy are the best ways to motivate others or manage one's own emotions.

19. 生命處處是溫暖

　　一覺醒來，開始面對一天的生活，我會去體會生活周遭的每一件事，感受身邊一些極細微的片刻，讓心情擁有陽光、積極、溫暖的感覺。

- 想像躺在床上，除了眼睛能動，身體其他部位都無反應（不能說話、四肢全部沒反應），感覺如何？期待什麼？多麼希望誰能幫我？

　　試著體會這樣的情境：被蚊蟲叮咬，想告訴照顧者，無奈不能說話，眼睛只能看著蚊蟲在身上爬動，心情如何？床鋪太冷、太熱、肚子餓、口渴、想上廁所、心情煩躁、生氣，這些平常看來實在簡單不過的事，怎麼處理？此時多麼希望身旁是一位細心呵護的照顧者，而不是一位公事公辦的照顧者。

　　那種不方便會持續一陣子，甚至永遠無法全部復原，脾氣會好嗎？心情會愉快嗎？我們可以感同身受和接納那種心情嗎？是不是正好有這樣的人需要我的關懷呢？未必一定是當事人，才能深刻感受那種不方便，一樣可以用心體會來真心照顧需要的人。

- 騎機車或開車等紅綠燈，一位行動不便的人，動作遲緩的穿越斑馬線，走到一半時紅燈亮了，當事人是什麼感覺？周遭的駕駛又是什麼反應？

　　行動不便單獨過馬路，已經感到壓力和緊張，即使用盡全身力氣和速度，無奈就是龜速，走到一半眼看就要變紅燈，心情更是無比緊張，此時如果有人按喇叭，甚至機車、汽車就從身前、身後行駛而過，有什麼感覺？如果有人幫忙，扶著過馬路或機車、

19. Everywhere in Life is Warmth

Upon waking up, as I begin to face the day, I try to experience every little thing around me and feel the subtle moments. I let my mood be filled with sunshine, positivity, and warmth.

- Imagine lying in bed, with only your eyes able to move and the rest of your body unresponsive (unable to speak, all limbs unresponsive). How would that feel? What would you hope for? How much would you wish for someone to help you?

Try to imagine this situation: being bitten by insects, wanting to tell the caregiver, but unable to speak, only able to watch the insects crawl on your body. How would you feel? If the bed is too cold, too hot, you're hungry, thirsty, need to go to the bathroom, feeling frustrated or angry—how would these seemingly simple things be handled? At this moment, how much would you wish for a caring caregiver instead of a bureaucratic one?

Such inconveniences might last for a while or even forever without complete recovery. Would your temper improve? Would you be happy? Can we empathize with and accept that feeling? Is there someone who needs my care just like this? It doesn't have to be the person experiencing it; anyone who needs care can be genuinely supported with empathy.

- While waiting at a traffic light on a motorcycle or in a car, what would a person with mobility issues feel when moving slowly across the crosswalk and the light turns red halfway? What is the reaction of the drivers around them?

汽車靜靜等待過完馬路才行駛，感覺又如何？

- 如果我是瞎子，走在路上的感覺如何？

看見瞎子走在路上，如果把自己的眼睛遮起來，眼前一片黑暗方向感全沒了，東西南北方位、路況高低起伏、牆壁在哪裡、現在安不安全、拿到的是什麼物品或食物，全都看不見、不知道。

全部的情況都因為眼睛看不見而全然不知，當下是什麼感覺？恐懼、害怕、無助、需要協助？試著用布把眼睛遮起來，體會看不見的感覺，會加深自己的同理心。

- 吃飯時如果沒有手，只有嘴和腳，如何設法一個人吃飯？

平常拿筷子、刀叉，實在簡單不過了，缺了雙手時要如何用餐呢？試著把雙手置於背後，要如何拿起筷子、刀叉？嘴巴要吃食物，只剩腳可以幫忙，那麼腳指如何拿筷子、刀叉？雙腳互相協助或身體彎向腳指，用嘴或臉去幫忙？

體會那種感覺，過程一定會碰到一些動作上的挫折，看似簡單的一餐，有些人竟如此辛苦，感受那些人的毅力，也給自己知足、珍惜的領悟。

- 一隻小蟲（例如：螞蟻、蚊子、蒼蠅、蟑螂、毛毛蟲）出現在面前，通常是什麼反應？如何處理？

跟地主買了一大片的農場，把草除了、樹砍了，整地、翻修，開始計劃想做的事，因為農場是我買的，真的是這樣嗎？

有些人碰到小蟲，不管是被叮咬或只是看到而已，幾乎就是出手把小蟲消滅掉，為什麼要這麼做？回答是：覺得討厭、噁心、被嚇到，所以要消滅。這只是以人類的立場所做出來的行為。

我會想，當小蟲看到人類時是什麼感覺：被巨大怪物驚嚇到，想趕快逃走或者認為這是我（小蟲）回家的路。只因為人類體型比它大，只因為人類一己的感覺，就順手結束了小蟲的生命，這對人類來說似乎沒什麼大不了，如果我是小蟲呢？

人類因為高智慧而操縱了地球所有資源，更應當與其他生命一起分享，而非控制甚至據為己有，要用心感受其他生命共同存在的可貴，因為，真實而純淨的心靈，是存在了對所有生命的尊重和包容的同理心。

Crossing the street with mobility issues is already stressful and tense. Even with all their might and speed, they move slowly. If the light is about to turn red and someone honks the horn or a motorcycle or car passes by, how would that feel? If someone helps, holding them across the street or waiting until they have safely crossed, how would that feel?

- If I were blind, what would walking down the street be like?

Seeing a blind person walking down the street, if you cover your eyes, everything is pitch black. There is no sense of direction, no understanding of the terrain, walls, safety, or what items or food you are holding.

What would it feel like to be completely unaware due to blindness? Fear, anxiety, helplessness, need for assistance? Try covering your eyes with a cloth to experience the feeling of blindness; it will deepen your empathy.

- If you had no hands while eating, and could only use your mouth and feet, how would you manage to eat alone?

Usually, using chopsticks or cutlery is very simple, but without hands, how would you eat? Try placing your hands behind your back. How would you pick up chopsticks or cutlery? How would you use your feet to help? Would your toes or body bend to assist, or would you use your mouth or face?

Experience the feeling of this process; it will involve some physical frustration. What seems like a simple meal can be very challenging for some. Feel their perseverance and gain an understanding of gratitude and appreciation.

- When a small insect (like an ant, mosquito, fly, cockroach, or caterpillar) appears in front of you, what is your usual reaction? How do you handle it?

If you bought a large farm and cleared the grass, cut down trees, prepared the land, and planned your activities, is it really yours because you bought it?

Some people, upon encountering small insects, whether bitten or just seen, often kill them out of dislike, disgust, or fear. Why do this? The answer is: because they find them annoying, gross, or frightening. This is a behavior from a human perspective.

19. Everywhere in Life is Warmth

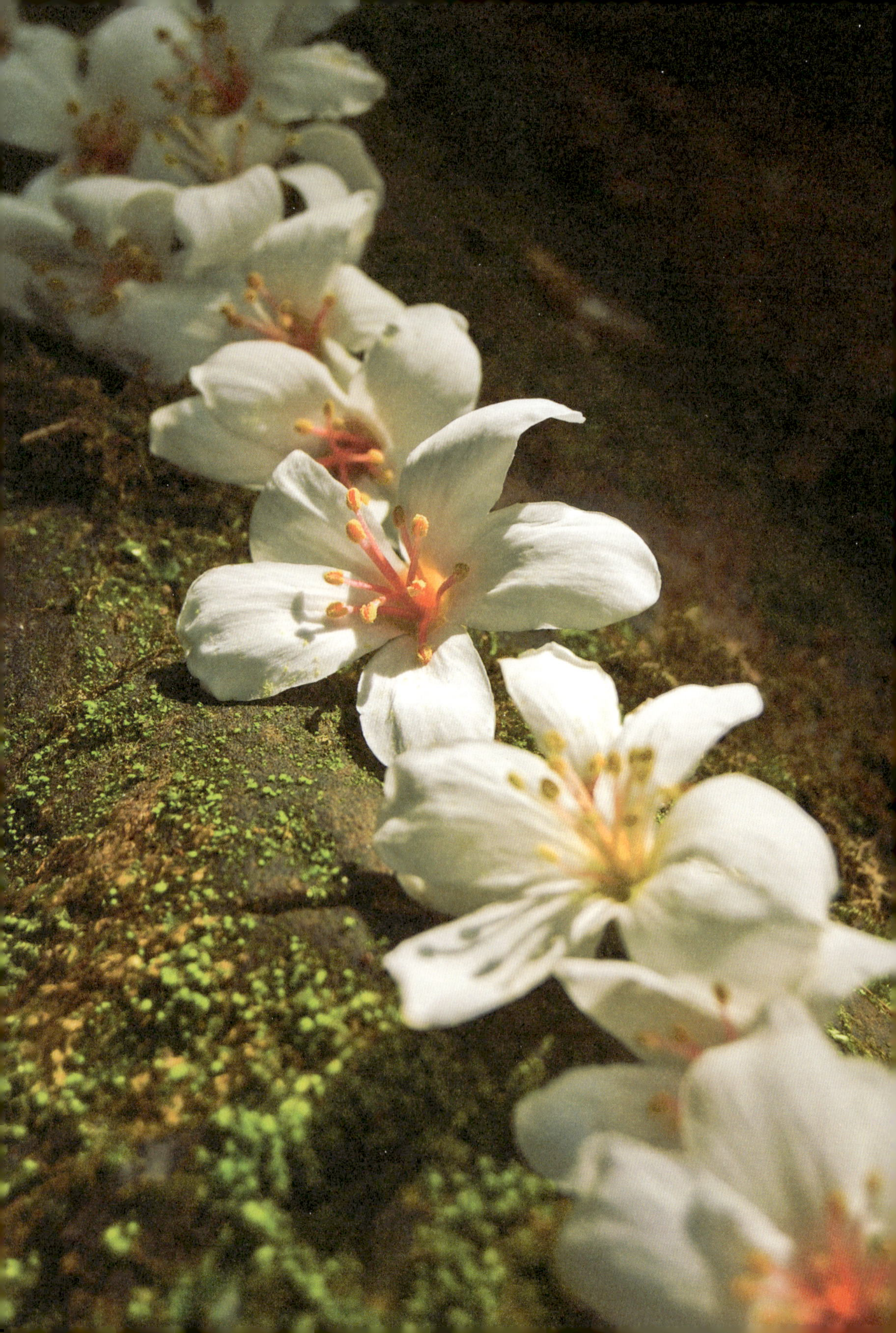

I wonder what the small insect feels when it sees a human: is it terrified by a giant monster, wanting to escape quickly, or does it think it is on its way home? Just because humans are bigger, and due to one's personal feelings, the insect's life is ended. It seems trivial to humans, but what if you were the insect?

Humans, with their high intelligence, manipulate all of Earth's resources and should share them with other lives rather than controlling or claiming them. We should appreciate the preciousness of all life together, as a genuine and pure soul exists in the respect and empathy for all life.

20. 觀念和習慣

　　在出生及生活環境的影響之下，很自然把聽到、看到、學到的，成為心中的觀念和習慣，尤其是幼年期所灌輸的觀念和習慣，從此會深信不疑、奉為圭臬，因為整個環境都是如此，很自然就會認為這是理所當然、應該這樣沒錯。

　　人不會做「自己認為不對、不好」的事。沒有人會故意做不好的事，而是以自己的思想去做認為對的事，只是，是對或錯，恰不恰當，適不適合，在別人的觀點和想法，可能會有所不同。

　　每個人都在自己的生活環境下發展出一套思想模式，因為適合當下的環境，所以認為是好的，和別人想法不同時，總希望把自己認為最好的告訴對方，甚至說服對方改變想法。其實，同樣一件事情，不同環境或許會出現不同觀念或做法，其實有可能都很好，只是觀念、環境、背景、方法、呈現的方式不同而已。

　　和朋友到馬爾地夫海釣，大家興高采烈的把漁獲交給餐廳主廚做魚湯料理，在台灣，鮮活的海魚煮薑絲清湯最清甜美味，如果再加幾滴米酒味道更棒，一夥人在餐廳期待美味上桌。

　　當魚湯端上桌時，大家傻眼了！整鍋料理由紅蘿蔔、洋蔥、馬鈴薯、辣椒和一些當地配料做成，就是遍尋不著最基本而且可以去腥味的薑，主廚卻非常熱心的介紹這道當地美味的魚湯料理，幾位朋友只能面有難色的勉強品嚐幾口略帶腥味的魚湯。

　　因為觀念和習慣的牽絆，即使只是同樣的一條魚，我們感覺的美味料理或許其他地區未必是美味，仔細想想，這就是人們多采多姿的料理觀念，都做出了符合自己覺得最棒的美味，其實，

20. Concepts and Habits

Under the influence of birth and living environments, it's natural to adopt the concepts and habits heard, seen, and learned into one's mindset, especially those instilled during childhood. These become deeply ingrained beliefs and norms, as the environment shapes the perception of what is right and acceptable.

People don't do things they believe are wrong or bad. No one intentionally does bad things; rather, they act according to their own beliefs of what is right. However, what is considered right or wrong, appropriate or unsuitable, may vary from person to person.

Everyone develops a thought pattern suited to their environment, believing it to be good. When differing from others' thoughts, there is often a desire to convey one's own beliefs as the best, even persuading others to change their views. In reality, the same matter might be approached differently in various environments, and each approach could be equally good, differing only in concept, environment, background, method, or presentation.

For example, when friends went fishing in the Maldives and eagerly handed their catch to the restaurant chef for fish soup, they expected the fresh fish to be prepared with ginger for a sweet and delicious taste, as is common in Taiwan. Instead, the soup came with carrots, onions, potatoes, chili peppers, and local ingredients, without the expected ginger. The chef enthusiastically introduced the local fish soup, and the friends had to reluctantly taste the slightly fishy soup.

放下過去的習慣和感覺，接納世界各地的料理模式，都是好吃的。

我品嚐那份魚湯發現，雖然沒有我們習慣的薑，然而洋蔥和辣椒其實有異曲同工之妙，加上紅蘿蔔的一點甜度和當地的配料，恰到好處的料理搭配，反而讓一點點腥味呈現出另一種不錯的海味。我喜歡品嚐異國風味料理，什麼都好吃。

在台灣，不同信仰的朋友告訴我相同的答案：信仰能淨化人心。同時也傳達了觀念和做法，的確感到尊重與感動。到了東南亞、美洲、歐洲、大洋洲的一些國家，不同的人說出了相同的想法，我確信那些思想對他們都是好的。

當這些朋友碰面聊到這個觀念上的差異時，也確信只要勸人為善，都是最好的，沒有因信仰不同而不同。某個區域的思想觀念在當地一定具有影響力，然而未必適合其他區域，也未必表示思想觀念有好壞、高低之分。

我們不能用自己的思想、觀念，去反駁、否定或改造別人的思想觀念，而是應該用心體會不同思想觀念產生的原因和內涵，用感同身受的心來體會其中的意境。

地球上任何一個角落所產生出來的每一種想法，都有它存在的道理，接納來自任何人、任何地方的思想觀念，會讓心境更加寬廣、思想更趨客觀、純熟，因為，否定如同關閉心門，接納就是敞開心窗。

Due to the constraints of concepts and habits, even with the same fish, what is perceived as delicious may vary. Reflecting on this, people's diverse culinary concepts lead to dishes they consider the best. Letting go of past habits and embracing diverse culinary styles can reveal that all can be tasty.

Tasting the fish soup, I found that although it lacked the familiar ginger, the onions and chilies provided a similar effect, complemented by the sweetness of carrots and local ingredients, creating a well-balanced dish. I enjoyed the foreign flavor and found it delicious.

In Taiwan, friends of different beliefs shared the same answer: faith purifies the heart. They also conveyed their concepts and practices, which I felt respect and appreciation for. In Southeast Asia, the Americas, Europe, and Oceania, people expressed similar thoughts, which I believe are good for them.

When these friends discussed the differences in concepts, they agreed that encouraging goodness is always the best, regardless of differing beliefs. Regional ideologies may be influential locally but might not suit other areas and do not necessarily imply superiority or inferiority.

We should not use our own beliefs and concepts to refute, deny, or reshape others' beliefs but should deeply understand the reasons and meanings behind different thoughts and beliefs with empathy.

Every idea from any corner of the Earth has its reason for existence. Accepting thoughts and concepts from anyone and anywhere can broaden our minds, making our perspectives more objective and refined. Denial is like closing the door to our hearts, while acceptance is like opening the windows.

21. 擁抱心靈淨土

　　我們內心一直存在著心靈淨土，就看自己是不是能夠感覺到它的存在，願不願意打開它，用什麼樣的方式和它互動。那是一種單純、無為、放空、自在、靜心、輕鬆、愉悅、柔軟的感覺，可能每天專注生活、工作、忙碌而忽略了它的存在，因此有時候心情會莫名的感到空虛、孤獨、情緒低落、負面思維。

　　心靈淨土就在深層潛意識裡，想像著心靈花園的各種感覺：藍天、湖泊、群峰、草原、星辰、碧海、白沙、晨曦、夕陽、亮光、悲傷、委屈、難過、孤單、恐懼、憤怒，這些都是心靈互動的感應。

　　擁抱心靈淨土，情境由大而中而小，漸漸往深層境界深入又深入，細細再細細的一直探索下去，用當下的直覺與自己對話，最能深刻體會那種神遊的感覺，無論是喜或悲，心情會因此而溫馨、安定、踏實。

　　表層自己與內在自己單獨相處，是敞開心靈最好的時機，在最自在和放鬆的環境中，閉目、靜心、放空，之後仔細體會那種感覺：

- 推開「心靈花園」的門，眼前呈現了：花團錦簇的景象；空氣裡瀰漫著陣陣的芬芳氣息；一整片彩虹般的花海；一朵嫣紅玫瑰；一株清香百合；一片桃紅花瓣；一片翠綠光潔的葉子。用喜歡的感覺慢慢開啟、慢慢塑造出屬於自己的花園。

　　進入這片花園，從一景（大），打開內心的門窗；到一物（中），看到了吸引目光的花朵；最後是特定的點（小），就像

21. Embracing the Spiritual Sanctuary

Our inner self always has a spiritual sanctuary; it depends on whether we can feel its existence and are willing to open it and interact with it in what way. It is a pure, effortless, empty, free, calm, relaxed, joyful, and soft feeling. Often, we might be so focused on life, work, or busyness that we overlook its presence, leading to feelings of emptiness, loneliness, low mood, and negative thinking.

The spiritual sanctuary lies deep in the subconscious. Imagine the feelings of a spiritual garden: blue skies, lakes, peaks, grasslands, stars, blue seas, white sands, dawn, sunset, light, sadness, grievance, sorrow, loneliness, fear, anger—these are the interactions with the spirit.

Embracing the spiritual sanctuary involves moving from large to medium to small, gradually delving deeper. Engage with your intuition and dialogue with yourself to deeply experience this sense of spiritual wandering, whether it is joy or sorrow. It will make your mood warm, stable, and grounded.

Being alone with the outer self and inner self is the best time to open the heart. In the most relaxed and comfortable environment, close your eyes, calm your mind, and empty yourself. Then carefully experience the feeling:

- Push open the door to the "spiritual garden" and see: a vibrant scene of flowers; the air filled with fragrant scents; a whole sea of rainbow-colored flowers; a red rose; a fragrant lily; a peach-colored petal; a glossy green leaf. Slowly open and shape your own garden

細細品味花瓣特別的顏色。更多的感覺和感動油然而生，慢慢進入心靈深處。

　　因為心情愉快、放鬆，可以不斷的深入自我靈魂，感覺是那麼的自在、無負擔、任我遨遊，原來，心情連結心靈是可以一片明亮的。

- 難過：悲傷的事情（大），牽引出悲傷的感覺（中），最後帶出悲傷的情緒（小），情境由大而中而小，當悲傷被牽引出來時，難過的感覺就會浮現出來，情緒不斷從這個缺口宣洩出來，哭、叫、打、轉、沉默，心靈會幫助釋放情緒，讓情緒得到安慰，撫平悲傷。

　　難過、哭泣、憤怒、委屈，這些傷痛別人不一定瞭解，朋友的規勸未必讓情緒得到撫慰，種種的不如意和傷痛，可以在心靈淨土裡，讓寧靜無聲的心靈，靜靜來療癒它、修復它。

　　擁抱心靈淨土，是一種靜態、沉澱的感覺，生活、工作、獨處，很多細微的感動無時無刻圍繞身邊，只要用一點心思就會發現它的存在。與自己的心靈互動和擁抱，它會溫暖每天起伏的情緒，心情會感到一片寧靜，就像一大片綠色草原、一望無際的藍天白沙、無垠的寰宇星空，置身「心靈大自然」的氛圍裡，倍感靜心與舒暢。

　　心情低落時，回到心靈淨土，可以得到安慰和療傷。

　　心情愉悅時，徜徉心靈淨土，多麼的奔放、陽光和喜悅。

with the feelings you like.

Entering this garden, from a large scene (macro), open the windows of your heart; to a specific item (medium), see the attractive flowers; finally to a particular detail (micro), like appreciating the unique color of petals. More feelings and emotions will naturally arise, gradually penetrating deep into the spirit.

Because of the joy and relaxation, you can continually delve into your soul, feeling so free, unburdened, and explorative. It turns out that connecting with the spirit can be bright and uplifting.

- Sadness: A sad event (macro) draws out the feeling of sadness (medium), ultimately leading to the emotional state of sadness (micro). When sadness is drawn out, the feeling of sorrow emerges, and emotions continuously flow through this gap—crying, shouting, hitting, turning, being silent—the spirit helps release emotions, providing comfort and soothing sadness.

Sadness, crying, anger, and grievance—these pains might not be understood by others, and friends' advice may not always soothe the emotions. Various disappointments and hurts can be healed and repaired in the spiritual sanctuary, where a quiet and serene mind gently tends to them.

Embracing the spiritual sanctuary brings a sense of stillness and calm. In daily life, work, and solitude, many subtle touches of emotion surround us; with a little attention, we can become aware of their presence. Interacting with and embracing one's own spirit brings warmth to the daily fluctuations of mood. The feeling of serenity can be like a vast green meadow, an endless blue sky with white sand, or a boundless starry universe. Being immersed in this "spiritual nature" ambiance provides deep tranquility and comfort.

When feeling down, returning to the spiritual sanctuary offers solace and healing.

When feeling joyful, wandering in the spiritual sanctuary feels so liberating, sunny, and full of delight.

22. 擬人化的情感抒發

　　擬人化的情感抒發，是一種的心靈感受和精神寄託，雖然表面物象不存在，實際上卻是紮紮實實的烙印在內心世界，是自我情感與內心連結，牽引出的踏實感覺。

　　「她」，是心靈交流的代名詞。我用「她、妳」，來代表所有看到的事和物（不包括人）、聽到的聲音、想到的事件和身體與心靈碰觸的感覺，不是男女感情的「她」，也沒有特定對象或目標，而是一種內在情感含蓄的轉換，把外在所接觸到的情境和感覺，回歸到自己的內心，再牽引出潛意識裡的「她」，體會和抒發「她」給我當下所觸動的感覺。

　　「她」，代表了內心所有的心靈意境，難過的時候找「她」訴說心事，宣洩悲傷；愉快的時候找「她」分享喜悅，共同歡樂。「她」，永遠是最忠實、最溫暖、最保密的心靈傾聽對象，擬人化的「她」會完全的聆聽、接納、回應、同理心，也就是自己和「自己」的心境相互輝映。

　　小時候去溪頭旅遊，看見一位女士打坐在孟宗竹林裡的一塊石頭上，經過她身旁時，我好奇的問：阿姨，妳幹嘛坐在石頭上啊？

　　她說：我在和自己聊天。

　　我呆呆看著她，然後趕快跑掉，心想是不是碰到神經病了。經過了二十多年，有機會再次造訪溪頭時，好奇的想知道什麼是「和自己聊天」。薄霧的清晨在山林間漫步時，我終於明白那位「神經病」阿姨幹嘛「和自己聊天」了。

22. Personification of Emotional Expression

Personifying emotions is a way to convey and anchor spiritual sensations, creating a meaningful connection between self-emotion and inner experiences. Although these personifications don't physically exist, they leave a profound imprint on our inner world, offering a tangible sense of connection.

"She" represents this inner dialogue. I use "she" and "her" to symbolize everything observed （excluding people）, sounds heard, thoughts processed, and the sensations experienced through body and soul. This "she" is not tied to romantic connotations or a specific individual but serves as a metaphor for transforming and internalizing external experiences. It helps channel and express the emotions that arise from these experiences.

"She" embodies the full spectrum of inner spiritual landscapes. When feeling sad, one can turn to "her" to express and alleviate sorrow. In moments of joy, "she" is there to share and celebrate happiness. "She" is always the most devoted, warm, and confidential listener—completely absorbing, accepting, and responding to emotions, thereby reflecting and amplifying the inner state.

I recall visiting Xitou as a child and seeing a woman meditating on a rock in a bamboo grove. Curious, I asked, "Auntie, why are you sitting on the rock?" She answered, "I'm having a conversation with myself."

I was puzzled and ran away, thinking I had encountered someone unusual. Over twenty years later, when I revisited Xitou, I was intrigued to understand what "talking to oneself" meant. During a misty morning walk

因為有了擬人化的「她」，如同心裡住了一個「人」，不再覺得孤單，心會變得柔軟豐富，情緒、情感會趨於寧靜和滿足，心靈因此得到平靜與滋潤。

　　即使單身，心中也可以擁有一個「她（他）」，有別於逃避現實而在心中虛擬的異性假象，更不是劃地自限、自我框架、與世隔絕的自我陶醉，而是無時無刻可以滋潤心靈及包容萬物的「她」。

　　因為風，我寫下了這個感覺：
風
依然聽到妳的聲音
依舊看見妳的輕飄
永遠記得妳的溫柔

無時無刻
朝朝暮暮
歲歲月月年年
圍繞獨處的我

春　讓我溫暖
夏　讓我奔放
秋　讓我感動
冬　讓我依偎

風
多麼希望伸手擁妳入懷
深深擁抱著妳
而妳
竟也無時無刻在我身邊

in the forest, I finally understood why that "strange" woman was engaged in such self-dialogue.

With the personified "her," it feels as though there is a companion within the heart, making solitude less daunting. This inner presence softens the heart, enriching emotions and creating a sense of peace and contentment, providing emotional stability and nourishment.

Even when single, one can maintain a "her" (or "him") within—distinct from avoiding reality by fabricating a fictional romantic figure or isolating oneself within personal constraints. Instead, it offers continuous spiritual nourishment and an inclusive, empathetic perspective towards everything.

Because of the Wind, I Wrote Down This Feeling:

Even when single, one can maintain a "her" (or "him") within—distinct from avoiding reality by fabricating a fictional romantic figure or isolating oneself within personal constraints. Instead, it offers continuous spiritual nourishment and an inclusive, empathetic perspective towards everything.

Because of the wind, I wrote down this feeling:

The Wind

I still hear your voice,

I still see your lightness floating,

I will always remember your gentleness.

At all times,

Morning and evening,

Year after year,

Surrounding me in solitude.

Spring makes me warm,

包圍著我陪伴著我

風
是我
還是妳
擁抱了我圍繞了我

喜歡妳的春夏秋冬
喜歡妳的圍繞相隨

擁有妳
愛戀妳
跟著妳

Summer makes me free,

Autumn makes me emotional,

Winter makes me snuggle.

The Wind

How I wish to reach out and hold you close,

To embrace you deeply.

And you,

Are always by my side,

Surrounding me, accompanying me.

The Wind

Is it me,

Or is it you,

Who embraced and surrounded me?

I love your spring, summer, autumn, and winter,

I love how you always surround and follow me.

To have you,

To love you,

To follow you.

23. 掌握先機

多年前和一位朋友聊天，聊到他創業初期的一些事情，提到了在某次公會召開的同業例行會議時，由於他是新成立的公司和剛加入不久的會員，原本抱持著拜會資深同業和學習的心情，沒想到會議開始沒多久，卻被其中幾位資深同業輪番言語圍剿。

同業抱怨他惡性競爭、削價搶客戶，說：「為什麼很多客戶才剛剛在詢價，DM、資料剛寄出，才不過2~3天而已，就被你簽走？」

這位朋友首先強調絕無削價競爭，簽約價格是公會建議的彈性範圍，他願意提供蓋掉客戶個人資料後的合約給同業看價格。

之後，他請教了同業幾個問題：

- 週六、週日、國定例假日、過年、除夕夜，請問各位在做什麼？

同業說：休息、渡假、準備過年。

朋友說：我在電話追蹤客戶，只要客戶同意，無論北中南東西部，馬上親自登門拜訪客戶。

- 颱風天、刮大風下大雨、寒流，請問各位在做什麼？

同業說：在家休颱風假、待在辦公室或家裡。

朋友說：只要客戶同意，無論地點哪裡，我開車拜訪客戶。

- 半夜、清晨1點、3點時，請問各位在做什麼？

同業說：睡覺。

23. Seizing the Opportunity

Years ago, I had a conversation with a friend about the early days of his entrepreneurial journey. He mentioned an experience during a routine guild meeting where, being a newly established company and a recently joined member, he was prepared to learn from more experienced peers. However, to his surprise, shortly after the meeting began, several senior colleagues started to verbally attack him.

They accused him of engaging in predatory competition, undercutting prices, and stealing clients. One person said, "Why is it that clients are just inquiring, and within 2–3 days after receiving our promotional materials, you've already signed them?"

My friend clarified that he wasn't engaging in price-cutting. He pointed out that the contracts he signed were within the flexible range recommended by the guild. He even offered to show the contracts（with personal information redacted）to prove the prices were legitimate.

He then asked his peers a few questions:

"What are you doing on weekends, national holidays, New Year's Eve?" They answered: "Resting, vacationing, getting ready for the New Year." He responded: "I'm following up with clients on the phone. If a client agrees, I personally visit them, no matter where they are."

"What do you do on typhoon days, when it's raining heavily, or when there's a cold front?" They replied: "Taking a storm day off, staying in the office or at home." He said: "If a client agrees, I drive to meet them

朋友說：我在高速公路上南來北往，無論幾點，只要客戶何時有空，時間我全部配合。

　　之後的相處，同業不再言詞攻擊，保持了良性的競爭和互動。

　　他又提到，曾經有一通國際電話從東南亞打來，詢問了相關事情後，表明了高度意願，然而客戶說他在東南亞，等有空安排時間到台灣，再委託辦理相關業務。這位朋友請教了客戶東南亞的電話和地址，告訴客戶說：我明天去拜訪你，幾點抵達東南亞，稍後買到機票會告訴你。客戶覺得難以置信、半信半疑，說：怎麼可能？

　　第二天，當地時間下午1點左右，他打電話給客戶時，客戶告訴他在入境大廳有人會舉牌，那是他的司機。見面後開心寒暄，客戶二話不說立即交付所有文件和費用，然後招待他品嚐當地海鮮大餐，第二天早晨去打高爾夫球，之後送他到機場搭下午飛機回台灣。

　　朋友說出了他的服務理念：客戶的需求要立即幫忙解決，不能耽誤了他們的計劃和商機，可以走路、捷運、開車、高鐵、渡輪、飛機，地球之內，都是我的服務範圍。

　　在瞬息萬變的商機中，以聆聽、回應、同理心的態度去理解客戶的需求，感同身受他的想法和做法，從中討論出最符合他需求的規劃，如果可以的話，是產品儘量量身訂作來配合客戶，而非客戶處處配合產品（某些產品一成不變，某些產品可以彈性調整），以客戶立場和角度來考量，這樣的心態和理念，會得到認同，客戶自然而然會因為確實符合需要而全然放心委託，不是只靠話術或說服能力來說服客戶配合。

　　掌握先機，不讓客戶感到壓力、沒有壓迫感，是一種自然關懷、熱忱、積極的態度，有了這樣的態度，自然會源源不絕的想出很多的方法、做出很多的事情，而這樣的行動力，會讓客戶自然而然感受到一股服務的熱忱，相信客戶都是會多方比較的，除了專業知識讓客戶信服之外，展現出與眾不同的行動力，會是爭取到服務機會的另一個重要因素。這也難怪我這位朋友為什麼有機會可以「跑」在同業之先了。

regardless of the weather."

"What are you doing at 1 a.m., 3 a.m.?" They answered: "Sleeping." He said: "I'm driving up and down the highway, meeting clients whenever they have time."

After that, his peers stopped attacking him verbally, and they maintained healthy competition and interaction.

He also shared a story about receiving an international call from Southeast Asia. After discussing business, the client, who was interested, said they would visit Taiwan when they had time. My friend asked for the client's contact information and told them, "I'll visit you tomorrow. I'll let you know what time I'll arrive after I book my flight." The client, skeptical, said, "Is that even possible?"

The next day, around 1 p.m. local time, my friend called the client, who had arranged for someone to meet him at the airport. After meeting, the client immediately handed over all documents and payments. They later enjoyed a seafood feast, played golf the next morning, and he flew back to Taiwan that afternoon.

My friend's philosophy is simple: clients' needs must be met immediately. Their plans and opportunities shouldn't be delayed. Whether by foot, metro, car, high-speed rail, ferry, or plane, anywhere on Earth is within his service range.

In the fast-changing world of business, listening, responding, and empathizing with the client's needs allows for discussions that lead to customized solutions. If possible, products should be tailored to the client, not the other way around. This mindset builds trust, leading clients to entrust their business with peace of mind. It's not just about using persuasive tactics but genuinely addressing client needs.

Seizing the opportunity without pressuring clients involves a natural, caring, and enthusiastic attitude. With this mindset, countless ideas and actions will naturally emerge, and clients will feel the warmth of the service. Clients often compare multiple options, but alongside professional knowledge, showing unmatched action is key to securing opportunities. It's no wonder my friend was able to "run ahead" of his peers.

24. 易受感動的心

人難免情緒起伏，也有某些的堅持和喜好厭惡，只是，無論外表再怎麼看似冷漠、惡劣，還是平和、順從，其實每個人的內心深處，都有柔軟易受感動的心，或許因為壓力的影響而受到壓抑難以牽引出來，女性比較容易受到感動，男性其實也有鐵漢柔情的一面。

易受感動的心，在深層潛意識裡一直存在著，那是純淨的本性，只是因為外表的壓抑而被隱藏、埋沒。那種感覺隨時都有，尤其在自我獨處或觸動到自己很有感覺的一個點時，就很容易浮現出來，每個人會感動的點不盡相同，知道自己會因為什麼人事物而感動，也會感受到別人因何事的感動而被感動，試著暫時放下包袱，讓感動的心在眼裡、心裡流動馳騁，就像洗滌掉心靈的包袱，那樣的感覺會讓我們發現，原來，生活處處充滿了美好的感動。

記得小學五年級還懵懵懂懂的時候，只因為手上有張免費電影招待券，興奮的想看期待已久的「看」電影，看看電影是長什麼樣子，根本不管內容是什麼。

電影是 "Love Story"，我當然不管什麼影片，能「看」電影就很高興了。

電影開始，第一幕是男主角獨自一人坐在雪中的運動場旁，之後開始電影情節，電影結束前的最後一幕，男主角又孤伶伶的坐在雪中的運動場邊，看到這一幕時，只是小學五年級的我，不知道為什麼竟然一陣鼻酸、眼眶泛紅、流下眼淚。

當時一直不清楚怎麼了？因為情節根本看不懂，然而那一幕幕「愛的故事」的意境和心靈感應，或許已經深深刻刻烙印在我稚嫩

24. An Easily Moved Heart

People inevitably experience emotional ups and downs, with certain preferences, dislikes, and principles. Regardless of how indifferent, harsh, calm, or compliant someone may seem on the outside, everyone has a soft, easily touched heart deep within. It may be suppressed by stress and difficult to draw out, but while women may express their emotions more easily, men also have their tender side.

The sensitive heart always resides in the depths of our subconscious, representing our pure nature, which is often hidden or buried by external suppression. This feeling is always present, and especially when we're alone or when something deeply resonates with us, it easily surfaces. Each person is touched by different things, and knowing what moves us allows us to feel empathy for what touches others. By letting go of our burdens, we allow these feelings to flow freely in our hearts and minds, like a cleansing of the soul, revealing that life is filled with moments of beauty and emotion.

I remember being in the fifth grade, still quite naive, when I got a free movie ticket. I was so excited to watch a movie I'd been anticipating, without even caring about the plot. The film was "Love Story," and for me, just watching a movie was a big deal.

The film began with the male lead sitting alone by a snow-covered sports field, and the story unfolded from there. At the end of the film, he was once again sitting there in solitude. At that moment, even though I was just a fifth-grader, I felt a sudden wave of emotion, with my nose tingling and tears welling up in my eyes. I didn't understand why I felt that way because

的心靈深處，牽引了我那原始又真誠易受感動的心。

　　感動的心是細微心境的呈現，是一種純真、直接的情緒反應，也代表了發自內心的認同，有時候眼睛看、耳朵聽到、心情想到某一景象時，一股奇妙的感覺瞬間冒出來，例如：一種大自然景緻、某人的一些舉動、一首音樂、某種回憶，都會產生觸景傷情或喜極而泣，相信任何人都有過這種感覺，那是潛意識真情的流露，流淚未必就是悲傷的負面情緒，也可以是感動、溫馨、滿足、安全的情感流露。

　　如果壓抑了自己的情緒，也會壓抑掉柔軟感動的心，少了感動的心情，會讓我們錯失溫暖的感覺，那是非常可惜的。感動的感覺，是美美的感覺，擁抱感動的心，真好！

I didn't grasp the plot at all. Yet, the imagery and the unspoken connection of that "love story" seemed to have deeply imprinted on my young mind, awakening my sincere and tender heart.

A heart that can be moved is a reflection of a delicate state of mind, a pure and direct emotional response, and a true expression of inner resonance. Sometimes, when we see, hear, or think of a certain scene, a magical feeling emerges instantly. It could be a natural landscape, someone's actions, a piece of music, or a memory that triggers tears of sorrow or joy. We all have these moments, where the expression of true emotion surfaces from the subconscious. Tears are not always a sign of sadness; they can also be an outpouring of joy, warmth, fulfillment, or a sense of safety.

If we suppress our emotions, we also suppress that tender, responsive heart. Without this feeling of being moved, we miss out on the warmth of life, which is a great pity. The sense of being touched is a beautiful feeling; embracing that emotion is truly wonderful!

25. 善解人意

　　有人瞭解我的喜怒哀樂、聽得懂我在說什麼、知道我要做什麼、以我喜歡的行為方式互動，那種感覺是非常舒服的。如果自己也懂得用這種方式跟別人互動，當看到別人開心、滿足、瞭解我的用心時，也會感受到同樣喜悅的氣氛。

　　善解人意是同理心的一種呈現，也就是懂得愛自己而後可以真誠的去愛別人的表現，是發自內心自然流露的態度及行為，和巴結、討好或有目的的付出不一樣，無法模仿或刻意學習，畢竟，如果不是發自內心的真誠，那麼，虛假或刻意表現出來的行為，都是難以持續很久的，也會讓人感到虛偽和空洞不實，因為，感受不到真心，就沒有真正的感動。

　　對自己的感覺而言，善解人意有一些特質：一切簡單、愛自己、接納自己、順其自然、體諒他人，這些很自然呈現出來的行為和特質，會讓別人感受到你散發出來的氣息。

　　對別人的感受來說，善解人意是感覺被接納、被瞭解，就像自己的喜怒哀樂，有人可以馬上瞭解和回應一樣，內心當然會有喜悅、舒服的感覺。

　　善解人意他人之前，先善解人意自己，我們都喜歡得到這樣的互動，因此，先懂得用這些方式對待自己，當自己深切體會到那些情感給自己帶來是什麼樣的感覺之後，自然能夠用那些相同的態度去對待別人，而且是很隨性的舉動，是那麼的自然又真誠，甚至只是自己習慣性的一些動作，就已經讓對方深刻感受到我們的善解人意。

　　善解人意絕非只是一方付出，一方接受，而是一種很愉悅的心靈提昇和雙向互動。

25. Understanding and Empathy

When someone understands my emotions, knows what I'm saying, recognizes what I want to do, and interacts with me in a way I like, it feels incredibly comforting. If I can also interact with others in this manner, seeing them happy, fulfilled, and aware of my thoughtfulness brings the same sense of joy.

Understanding and empathy are forms of emotional intelligence. They reflect self-love that allows us to genuinely love others. This attitude and behavior come naturally from the heart, unlike flattery, appeasement, or giving with ulterior motives. It can't be mimicked or intentionally learned. After all, if it's not genuine, then actions that are false or calculated won't last long, and they will come across as insincere and hollow. Without genuine emotion, there's no real connection.

From my own feelings, empathy has several traits: simplicity, self-love, acceptance, going with the flow, and understanding others. These naturally exhibited behaviors and qualities allow others to sense the energy you emit.

To others, empathy feels like being accepted and understood. It's as if someone can immediately understand and respond to your emotions, bringing joy and comfort to the heart.

Before showing empathy to others, we should first be empathetic toward ourselves. We all appreciate this kind of interaction, so by treating ourselves this way first and deeply feeling those emotions, we can naturally extend the same attitude toward others. It becomes a spontaneous, sincere action. Even small habitual gestures can convey empathy profoundly to others.

Empathy isn't just one person giving and another receiving; it's a joyful mutual upliftment and interaction.

26. 成功有效能的態度

　　成功的基本道理、觀念、技巧，其實是互通的。一位懂得照顧自己的人，在生活上通常都能夠獨立面對及解決各種瑣事，而在處理這些瑣事的過程當中，也自然學會如何面對其他事情的能力，這樣的能力運用在其他方面當然是互通的。

　　成功者之所以會想出各種的解決方法，最主要關鍵在於清楚問題的癥結點在哪裡、自己的需要是什麼、完全肯定自己和有效率的管理自己，而且內心踏實、篤定，可以用清晰的思維、簡單的態度去面對多變的事情，即使需要尋求協助，也清楚什麼人幫得上忙，不會盲、茫、忙，甚至錯失良機。

　　舉幾個印證的例子：

- 可以在30分鐘內完成5道菜的人，同樣的經驗、方法和技巧，也絕對有能力在30分鐘內出貨30件（所需時間和料理幾道菜、出貨件數多寡，依難易度而不同），因為會懂得如何運用完成5道菜的效率，去想出最短時間完成30件的辦法。

　　料理和出貨，同樣的一個觀念：最短的時間完成最多的事情。這當中的效率規劃，包括：物品的前後擺放位置、工作流程和順序的排列、動線的安排、時間的分配及運用、步驟的簡化（例如：5個動作是否可以簡化成4或3個動作）等等，把這些觀念和做法運用在居家生活管理、工作、讀書、業務推展、理財投資各方面，當然也會有效率。

26. Attitudes for Success and Effectiveness

The basic principles, concepts, and techniques of success are often universal. A person who knows how to take care of themselves can usually handle and resolve various life details independently. Through managing these tasks, they naturally develop the ability to handle other situations, and these skills are transferable to other areas.

The key reason successful people can come up with different solutions is that they clearly understand the root of the problem, what they need, and can fully affirm themselves while managing their time effectively. They remain grounded and confident, capable of using clear thinking and a simple approach to deal with complex situations. Even when they seek assistance, they know exactly who can help, avoiding blind or chaotic decisions that could result in missed opportunities.

Some examples to illustrate this:

- A person who can cook five dishes in 30 minutes can use the same experience, method, and skill to ship 30 items in 30 minutes (the time required varies depending on the difficulty of the task). This is because they understand how to use the efficiency of preparing five dishes to figure out the quickest way to complete 30 items.

Cooking and shipping share a common principle: accomplishing the most within the shortest time. This efficiency planning involves arranging items, organizing workflow, managing time, and simplifying steps (such as reducing five actions to four or three). These concepts can be applied to home management, work, studying, business development, financial

- 懂得管理自己的時間，例如：與朋友約早上 9 點見面。在 9 點前到達、不遲到的原則下，事先規劃開車（假設是開車）的時間大約需要多久，路上可能塞車的時間，再規劃出自己最慢幾點必須出門。

那麼，確認最慢幾點必須出門是大方向之後，就能規劃出早上必須幾點起床、盥洗、吃早餐、整理服裝儀容等等事情的安排，也就清清楚楚，不會倉促甚至遲到。這樣的態度運用在工作、理財、業務短中長期目標、人際關係、職涯規劃、讀書計劃、生涯規劃等等，活用這樣的方法和態度，絕對是相通的。

自己不自覺所呈現出來的態度反應，往往也決定了心態的正向或負面，在邁向成功之前，先肯定自己、愛自己，讓自己的態度樂觀、正向。世事看起來好像千變萬化，其實並不複雜，生活懂得變通、靈活運用資源的人，就有能力用相同的技巧去面對外在所有的變化及困難，因為，已經成功的運用相同的方式和技巧，解決了生活上、工作上的難題了，尤其是遇到重大難題時，也會清楚從哪裡可以得到援助。

investments, etc., leading to increased productivity.

- Managing your time, for example, if you agree to meet a friend at 9 a.m., you plan how long it will take to drive （assuming you're driving）, account for possible traffic, and set a deadline for when you need to leave. Once you determine the latest time you must leave, you can plan what time to wake up, get ready, and handle other morning tasks. By doing this, you avoid rushing or being late. This approach can be applied to work, finance, business planning, relationship management, career development, study plans, and life goals. Applying such methods and attitudes is highly effective.

Your attitude, often reflected subconsciously, determines whether your mindset is positive or negative. Before achieving success, first affirm yourself, love yourself, and cultivate an optimistic and positive attitude. While life may seem ever-changing, it isn't as complicated as it appears. People who know how to adapt and use resources flexibly can apply the same techniques to tackle external changes and challenges. After all, they've already successfully used these strategies to solve personal and professional challenges. When encountering major difficulties, they will also clearly know where to find help.

27. 家

　　看著動物頻道，一隻高空俯衝的老鷹，地上幾隻驚慌逃竄的土撥鼠，就在千鈞一髮，土撥鼠鑽進了地洞，安全逃過一劫。這一幕，讓我更深刻的感覺：有「家」真好！

　　家，是最熟悉的環境，提供了安全、溫暖、療傷的場所，是忙碌、疲憊後，身心都可依靠的歸屬感，沒有負擔、沒有壓力、沒有時間、完全隱私、輕鬆自在、毫無顧忌，褪去面對朋友、工作、應酬時刻意包裝的外表，呈現真實、放鬆的自我。

　　沒有家，一切變得飄泊、虛幻。累了、倦了，漂泊的遊子渴望回家，倦鳥懂得歸巢，就算在外餐風露宿、居無定所，然而內心深處永遠有著對「家」的思念。

　　無論是單身還是和家人同住，情緒低潮時，在家裡睡覺、發呆、寫字、打電話跟朋友發牢騷、盡情的掉淚、思考或者什麼事都不做，讓情緒完全放空，在最放心的家裡讓心情得到修復。

　　我喜歡在家渡假的感覺，沒有任何負擔，心情完全放鬆，賴在床上什麼都不想、打開音響、欣賞陽台花草、沖杯咖啡、做點料理、看書、上網、泡澡，家裡什麼都有，什麼都不用往外跑。

　　心情對了，待在家裡就很愉快，心情不對，其實去哪裡還是不開心，家，是舒服的地方。

　　有人喜歡回家，因為有很多美好的感覺；有人不想回家，其中的原因也很多，好或不好的感覺只能分享，很難讓別人複製或學習，因為，每個人的問題點不盡相同，自己的經驗未必適合別人。

27. Home

Watching the Animal Channel, I saw a scene where an eagle dives from the sky, and several groundhogs flee in panic. At the last moment, a groundhog dives into its burrow, narrowly escaping danger. This moment made me deeply appreciate how wonderful it is to have a "home."

Home is the most familiar environment, offering a safe, warm, and healing space. It provides a sense of belonging where you can rest both body and mind without burdens, pressure, or time constraints, enjoying complete privacy and freedom. You can shed the masks worn in front of friends, at work, or socializing, and just be your true, relaxed self.

Without a home, everything feels fleeting and unreal. When weary, wandering souls long to return home, just like birds naturally return to their nests. Even if they've been through hardships and homelessness, deep down, the longing for "home" remains.

Whether single or living with family, during emotional lows, you can sleep, daydream, write, vent to friends on the phone, cry, or simply do nothing, letting your emotions completely unwind in the safety of home, allowing your mood to heal.

I enjoy the feeling of vacationing at home, with no obligations and a completely relaxed mood. Lying in bed with no thoughts, playing music, admiring balcony plants, making coffee, cooking, reading, browsing the web, or taking a bath—everything is there at home, and there's no need to go out.

如果有人不喜歡回家，而別人卻把喜歡回家的種種美好感覺告訴他、鼓勵他，那可能不是他所要的，也許自己那些美好的感覺正好是他心痛的點，那樣只會更增加他的難過而已。

　　就讓他把不喜歡的感覺盡情的說出來，一起感受那種不愉快，不要打斷他的話，不要批評、糾正或加入自己的意見，只要靜靜的當個聆聽者就好。

　　這樣除了可以瞭解別人不喜歡回家的原因，也會讓自己更珍惜當下所擁有的溫暖，尤其是朋友不滿的情緒得到我們的聆聽、認同和適度的發洩後，他，終究會「回家」休息。

　　誰都無法否定「家」的歸屬感。落地生根，從出生那一刻開始，「家」就是一輩子的精神寄託，落葉歸根，更證明誰都會想「家」，在最安心的地方出生及終老。

　　家，給了人們安定和放鬆的美好感覺，有了喜歡回家的心情，外出工作會充滿熱忱、動力和效率，總希望以最短的時間完成工作，因為，可以快點回家，那是內心溫暖而甜蜜的期待，家的感覺真好！

When your mood is right, staying at home is delightful. When it's not, even going out won't make you happy. Home is a comfortable place.

Some people love returning home because of the warmth they feel. Others avoid going home, and the reasons vary. Good or bad, these feelings are personal and difficult to replicate for others, as everyone's problems are different, and personal experiences may not apply to others.

If someone dislikes going home and others try to share the joy of returning home with them, it might not be what they need. In fact, your pleasant experiences might deepen their pain, only making them feel worse.

Let them express their feelings fully. Share in their discomfort without interrupting, criticizing, or offering solutions—just listen. This not only helps you understand why they avoid home, but also deepens your appreciation for the warmth you have. Once your friend has vented and felt heard, they, too, will eventually "return home" to rest.

No one can deny the feeling of belonging that home provides. From the moment we're born, home becomes a lifelong spiritual anchor. "Falling leaves return to their roots" is proof that, in the end, we all long for home—a place where we are born and grow old.

Home gives people a sense of stability and relaxation. With a love for home, we approach work with passion, motivation, and efficiency, always wanting to finish quickly so we can return home to that warm and sweet anticipation. Home feels wonderful!

28. 貴人

　　多年前和一位朋友 A 君聊天，聊起 A 君在海外申請成立公司的過程。

　　申請執照等結果，A 君必須主動詢問進度才知道情況，補件、補資料的來回過程就耗掉四個多月，然而執照一直沒有消息（正常進度通常一個月），最後，竟然告訴 A 君無法核准。

　　公司設立的條件都符合規定，雖然以條例規定多次向幾個政府部門據理力爭，用盡了所有可以想到的方法爭取，無奈還是沒有結果。

　　已經六個多月了 A 君心灰意冷，仍然不想輕易放棄，A 君想起十多年前認識的一位朋友 B 君在當地曾經經商多年，只是已經將近十年沒連絡，好不容易翻箱倒櫃找到了電話，不知電話還通不通，反正試著做最後一搏，沒想到電話通了，經過一番寒暄，開始大吐苦水。

　　B 君說：你怎麼不早說，沒事，我這幾天忙完給你打幾通電話，你等我消息。A 君心想怎麼可能？過了一個星期，B 君沒有回電話，A 君心想自己已經盡了所有自助人助的努力，想就此放棄算了。就在他告訴家人只能放棄的同時，電話響了，是 B 君打來的。

　　B 君說：老張啊，你的執照下來了，你可以找時間去拿……。這簡直是驚天動地的大消息！完全是 180°的大反轉，從跌停板鎖死瞬間直衝漲停板的心情轉折！

　　A 君除了萬分感謝還是萬分感謝，從不問 B 君是如何做到的。A 君說：當時如果真的放棄了，選擇第二、第三方案轉往其他國

28. Benefactors

Years ago, while chatting with a friend, A, about his process of applying to establish a company overseas, he shared that despite meeting all the regulatory requirements and repeatedly arguing with various government departments using the regulations as a basis, he received no results. The process took more than four months, with back-and-forth documentation and requests, although the normal processing time is usually one month. In the end, he was told that his application couldn't be approved.

It had been over six months, and A was disheartened but unwilling to give up easily. He remembered a friend, B, whom he had known over ten years ago. Although they hadn't been in touch for nearly ten years, A managed to find B's phone number and decided to give it a try, even though he wasn't sure if the number was still in use. To his surprise, the call went through. After a bit of catching up, A poured out his grievances.

B responded, "Why didn't you say something earlier? No problem, I'll make a few calls for you after I finish up in the next few days. Wait for my news." A thought it was unlikely anything would come of it, but after a week and with no call from B, A decided to give up and inform his family that he would have to abandon his plans.

Just as he was about to give up, B called. "A, your license has been approved. You can pick it up at your convenience." This was a groundbreaking turn of events, a dramatic reversal from despair to triumph!

A was immensely grateful and never asked B how he managed it. A reflected that if he had truly given up and pursued other options or countries,

家，還是有路可走，只是計劃完全亂掉，要重新開始，B君的幫忙，真的太好、太重要了。看似淡淡的交往，卻是生命中的貴人！

　　我們聽過這類的話：做自己的貴人、自己就是自己的貴人。

　　遇到要求什麼就給什麼的人，沒有經過自己費盡心思努力而在無助下才得到的幫助，只能算是給予，是照顧而不是貴人，畢竟，靠牆牆倒、靠人人跑、靠自己最好。

　　自己就是貴人，自助而後人助，遇到任何困難或逆境，只要抱持著絕對不放棄的積極態度，任何事，都能夠找到解決的方式，無論結果如何，都是最好的安排，畢竟是努力的全部投入，過程中也最清楚知道需求和應對策略，如果在這個時候需要幫助，也會找到最恰當的人，經由本身最大努力和最需要的人的幫忙，任何結果都會清楚、明瞭，也會願意接受。

　　與其希望貴人出現，何妨先做好自己，具備了充足的能力和條件，當能力越充分時，別人助己一臂之力的成功機會越大，因為在各方面的能力都能夠幫助自己，萬一遇到剩下的一個點無法克服時，除了本身會想到其他的配套措施之外，貴人適時出現的機會會大大提高，而且，自己就是貴人當中的一位。

　　完全相信自己，是對自己的肯定，先建立自己的信心，就能運用智慧和身邊的資源處理所有的事情，貴人就在你身邊？是的，那位貴人，就是如影隨形的自己！

it would have completely derailed his plans and required starting over. B's help was crucial and invaluable, demonstrating that what seemed like a casual acquaintance was actually a benefactor in his life.

We often hear phrases like "be your own benefactor" or "you are your own benefactor."

A person who meets requests without effort, without having been through the trials and tribulations of securing help on their own, is not truly a benefactor but simply a caregiver. After all, relying solely on others or external help is not ideal; relying on oneself is the best approach.

Being your own benefactor means first helping yourself, then seeking help from others. When facing difficulties or adversity, maintaining an attitude of never giving up can lead to finding solutions. Regardless of the outcome, it's the best arrangement because it involves all your effort. Understanding your needs and response strategies during this process means you'll be able to find the right help when necessary, and any result will be clear and acceptable.

Instead of hoping for a benefactor to appear, why not first work on yourself? By being well-prepared and capable, the chances of others assisting you effectively increase. When you are fully equipped, the likelihood of receiving timely help from a benefactor also rises, and you become one of those benefactors yourself.

Believing in yourself is an affirmation of your abilities. By establishing confidence, you can use your wisdom and resources to handle all matters. The benefactor you seek is indeed yourself, always by your side!

29. 忍耐？不在意！

我們都知道「忍一步，海闊天空；退一步，怡然自得」，只是，真的就此心情平靜無事嗎？忍耐，似乎是化解情緒紛擾的方法，然而，我們不難發現，當同樣問題再次或持續發生之後，可能就會出現這麼一句：「忍無可忍」、「火大了」、「孰可忍，孰不可忍」、「每次都這樣」、「忍不下去了」……，似乎並沒有因為之前的忍耐，就此化解對這件事情的不滿，為什麼會這樣呢？

有人會說忍耐功力不足、修養不夠。仔細想想，如果是壓抑下來的情緒，一定會有反彈的一天，而且未必是同一件事的牽引而爆發，也有可能是其他事情的不滿帶出壓抑、忍耐已久的情緒，這也就是為什麼有人這麼說：「我才問你一下，幹嘛突然發這麼大的脾氣，今天是不是吃了炸藥啊？」。

忍耐的對應就是不忍耐！我們都明白一個觀念：忍耐，是有限度的。所以忍到最後，不滿還是爆發出來，其實是因為情緒並沒有得到出口和抒解。因此，忍，有時候是壓抑、退讓、逃避甚至妥協的心境，未必是自己真正的想法，忍耐的確可以化解某些不好的立即現況或場面，只是情緒的波動恐怕未必隨之煙消雲散，事後的自我探討，對自己的情緒真相和成長很有幫助也很重要。

通常我會這麼和自己對話：

- 剛才為什麼覺得不舒服而發脾氣或想發脾氣？（是什麼原因生氣）

- 為什麼要忍下來？（當時是什麼情境下而如此）

- 為什麼事情過了，我還是很不舒服？（哪個原因讓我沒過

29. Endurance? Not a Concern!

We all know the saying, "Endure a moment, and the sea will be wide and the sky vast; take a step back, and you'll find inner peace." But does patience truly lead to a state of calm and tranquility? Patience seems to be a way to resolve emotional turmoil, yet it's common to hear phrases like "I've had enough," "I'm so angry," "This is unacceptable," or "I can't take it anymore" when the same issue recurs or continues. It appears that previous patience does not always resolve dissatisfaction with the situation. Why does this happen?

Some people might say it's due to a lack of patience or insufficient self-cultivation. But if we think carefully, suppressed emotions will inevitably rebound someday, and they might not necessarily erupt over the same issue. Dissatisfaction with other matters could also trigger the pent-up emotions that have long been held back. This is why we sometimes hear someone say, "I just asked you a question, why did you blow up like that? Did you eat dynamite today?"

The counterpart of patience is impatience! We all understand the concept that patience has its limits. So when dissatisfaction eventually erupts, it's because the emotions did not have a proper outlet. Sometimes, patience is a state of suppression, retreat, avoidance, or even compromise, and it may not reflect our true thoughts. While patience can indeed diffuse an unpleasant situation in the moment, the emotional fluctuations might not disappear so easily. Post-event self-reflection is important for understanding the truth of our emotions and fostering personal growth.

I usually engage in a conversation with myself like this:

關）

- 這麼一忍，我的心情就真的沒事了嗎？（真的無所謂了嗎）
- 是不是真的已經不在意、無所謂？（確認自己的情緒反應是什麼）

　　忍耐不能是退讓、壓抑的心態，即使真的必須有所妥協或接受結果，事後也要清楚明白起初不愉快的心情，自己已經可以真正的不在意、無所謂，完全沒有忍耐或不忍耐的問題，這才不會把情緒壓抑下來或潛伏在潛意識裡持續發酵而不自知。

　　不在意和無所謂，不是掛在嘴上，而是要與自我的內在對話，不斷反覆的問自己：「無所謂了嗎？真的無所謂了嗎？」，這樣，會愈加清楚明白是忍耐、壓抑，還是真的不在意了，這對自己的情緒有很大的正向幫助。如果發現忍耐只是壓抑、不滿或不舒服的感覺還在，那麼事後就要設法找出原因，用自己知道的方法往自我內在去探索問題，或尋求專業協助，徹底釋放掉忍耐的壓抑和不滿（要注意不要找只會說大道理、指責、教訓、批判，而無真正輔導功效的人士，那會導致二度傷害）。

　　任何人都有情緒和脾氣，生氣是很正常的，只是瞬間爆發的脾氣可能就忘了後果，事後反而增加更多問題和困擾，因此，當下的忍耐是很好的修為，而事後如果可以去探索原因，然後感覺內心是真正的釋懷、不在意、無所謂，那會是自我心境平靜、愉悅的提昇，「凡事無所謂」，這種深層的感覺真的很輕鬆自在！

　　忍耐，是愛別人；釋懷，是愛自己。懂得愛自己（釋懷），自然可以愛別人（忍耐）。所以，釋懷當然就沒有忍耐的情緒，也就可以真實的愛別人。

- Why did I feel uncomfortable and get angry or want to get angry just now? (What was the cause of my anger?)

- Why did I choose to hold it in? (What was the context at that moment?)

- Why do I still feel uneasy even after it's over? (What caused me to remain unsettled?)

- Does my mood truly calm down after holding back? (Am I genuinely okay with it now?)

- Have I truly let it go and become indifferent? (Confirm what my emotional reaction is.)

Patience shouldn't involve a mindset of suppression or retreat. Even if you have to compromise or accept the result, it's important to clearly understand the initial discomfort. You need to reach a point where you truly no longer care or feel indifferent, with no lingering issues of patience or impatience. This way, you won't suppress your emotions or let them ferment in your subconscious.

Not caring and indifference aren't just words you say; they require an inner dialogue with yourself, repeatedly asking, "Am I really okay with it? Have I truly let it go?" This helps to clarify whether you're suppressing your feelings or genuinely at peace. If you discover that patience has only led to suppression and that dissatisfaction or discomfort remains, it's essential to find the root cause and address it. You can use methods you know to explore the problem within yourself or seek professional help to release that suppressed dissatisfaction (avoiding those who only preach or criticize without offering genuine support, as that could cause more harm).

Everyone has emotions and tempers; getting angry is normal. However, a sudden outburst of anger may lead to unintended consequences and more problems afterward. In such cases, patience is a valuable virtue. But if you later explore the root causes and genuinely feel at ease with yourself, it will significantly elevate your sense of inner peace and joy. Achieving a state of "indifference to all" brings a lightness and freedom to the soul.

Patience is about loving others; letting go is about loving yourself. When you learn to love yourself (by letting go), you can naturally extend that love to others (through patience). Letting go means there's no longer a need for patience, and you can genuinely love others.

30. 時差

　　台灣時間凌晨，整理資料、電話連絡事情……還在工作，家人曾經說：「都這麼晚了還在做事，睡飽明天再做」，我說：「他們現在是早上，開始上班工作了」。原來，我和國外朋友居住的地方是有時差的，台灣白天他們晚上早就下班了，台灣晚上他們白天正在上班，如果是台灣白天連絡？難怪「經常」連絡不上了！

　　我們居住地方（例如：台灣）的 24 小時運行時間，未必和地球其他地方一樣，對地球來說，永遠可以有 24 小時的白天、24 小時的黑夜，台灣的晚上未必是其他地方的晚上，我們理所當然的晚上睡覺，其他地方的人，可能才剛天亮準備工作。

　　這樣的體會和延伸，對於事情的認知和判斷，不能以自己的環境、思想、標準或習以為常、理所當然的生活模式，去看待其他事情，也就是不以自己侷限的角度斷定全世界，而是以世界的寬廣角度來成長自己，這是面對靜態的時差，可以領悟到的一種思維。

　　動態的時差，就是親身去體驗，搭乘長途飛行的國際班機最直接。很多人一想到飛行時數十幾個小時的時間，旅途的疲累加上出發地和目的地時差的關係，抵達目的地後，不論是白天或是夜晚，幾乎都還是昏昏欲睡、昏昏沉沉，很難直接接上當地的生活、工作步調。

　　時差調整，我會以飛機起飛的時間、飛行的時間和抵達時間來做全盤的考慮，重要是配合目的地的時間來調整在飛機上的作息。假設晚上 9 點起飛，飛行 18 小時，抵達時間是當地早上 9 點，

30. Time Difference

At midnight in Taiwan, I was still working—organizing data and making phone calls. My family once said, "It's so late, why are you still working? Get some sleep and do it tomorrow." I replied, "It's morning where they are, and they're just starting their workday."

It turns out that my foreign friends live in a place with a time difference from Taiwan. During the day in Taiwan, it's night where they are, and they've already left work. When it's night in Taiwan, it's daytime where they are, and they're just starting their day. No wonder it's often hard to reach them during Taiwan's daytime!

The 24-hour cycle where we live （for example, Taiwan） doesn't necessarily align with other parts of the world. For the Earth, there can always be 24 hours of daylight or 24 hours of darkness somewhere. Nighttime in Taiwan doesn't mean it's night everywhere else. While we sleep at night, others might just be waking up to start their day.

This understanding extends to how we perceive and judge things. We can't use our own environment, thoughts, standards, or routine life patterns to evaluate other situations. In other words, we shouldn't judge the entire world from our limited perspective but should broaden our minds to see things from a global standpoint. This realization is something we can learn from facing the static nature of time differences.

Experiencing dynamic time differences is something that one can fully understand by traveling long distances on international flights. Many people think about the exhausting journey that takes several hours, along with the

個人晚上睡眠習慣是 8 小時的話，那麼登機後千萬別馬上呼呼大睡，頂多小憩當午休，飛機飛行約 7~8 小時後才是晚覺時間，一口氣睡足自己的晚覺，到了當地剛好早上，開始一天的行程也不會有時差的疲累感。

　　瞭解靜態時差的存在，可以讓我們明白 24 小時隨時隨地都有人們正在白天工作，我們的休息不代表大家都在休息，這樣的概念，會讓我們在規劃計畫、工作進度、人際溝通中，懂得如何分秒必爭、把握機會、掌握先機的重要，這是自我積極態度、內在熱忱和活力的展現。

　　克服動態時差的問題，無論飛行多久、時差多少，抵達當地都可以神采奕奕，就像在原來居住的地方一樣的作息，不會因為時差的不適應而影響旅遊品質和心情，甚至耽誤商務行程和商機。面對自己的問題去解決它，這就是歷練自己思考解決問題的方法，不會讓它一再發生、持續困擾、甚至不知如何面對和處理，這樣的積極態度，是讓自己在面對任何困擾時，都可以想出最適當的方法。

　　有機會出國長途飛行的話，試試看解決時差的方法吧！

time difference between departure and arrival locations. This can make one feel drowsy and sluggish upon arrival, struggling to adjust to the local rhythm of life and work.

To adjust to jet lag, I usually consider the time the flight departs, the duration of the flight, and the time of arrival. It's crucial to align your onboard routine with the destination's local time. For example, if a flight departs at 9 PM, lasts for 18 hours, and lands at 9 AM local time, and if you're used to sleeping for 8 hours at night, it's best not to fall asleep immediately upon boarding. Treat the first few hours as a nap, like a midday rest, and then, after 7-8 hours of flight, consider it your bedtime. This way, you wake up refreshed just in time for the morning at your destination without feeling the effects of jet lag.

Understanding the existence of static time differences helps us recognize that somewhere, people are always working during those 24 hours. Just because we're resting doesn't mean everyone else is. This mindset enables us to make the most of our time, seize opportunities, and stay ahead when planning, working, or communicating. It's a sign of proactive thinking, inner enthusiasm, and vitality.

Overcoming the problem of dynamic time differences means that no matter how long the flight is or how significant the time difference, you can always arrive at your destination feeling energetic and maintain your usual routine. This way, the jet lag won't negatively impact your travel experience or mood, and it won't interfere with business trips or opportunities. Confronting the problem directly and solving it is a way to train yourself in problem-solving methods, ensuring that challenges do not persist or worsen due to uncertainty on how to handle them. This proactive approach helps you face any issue with the best possible solution.

If you ever have the chance to take a long-haul flight, give these jet lag solutions a try!

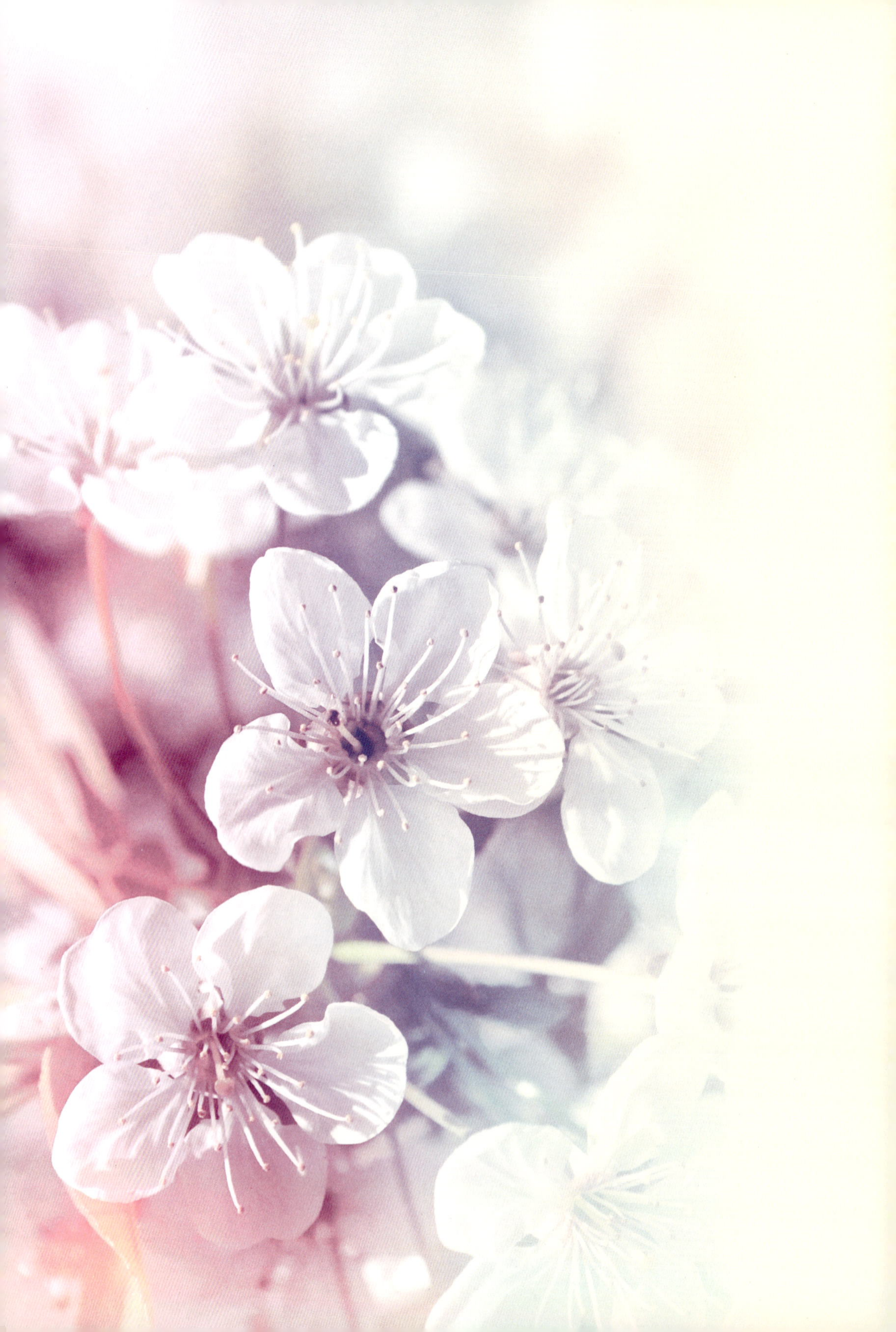

反向思考，無限寬廣

Reverse Thinking, Infinite Broadness

用擺脫傳統、毫無拘束、逆向探索、跳躍思考、天馬行空的想法去探索事情，完全不設限的思考模式，會因此瞭解更多的想法和事實。

With unconventional, unrestricted thinking, reverse exploration, and imaginative ideas, explore things without limits. This unrestricted way of thinking allows you to understand more ideas and facts.

肆、反向思考、無限寬廣

　　很多事情發生的原因和結果並非固定不變，很難用一定的規則或模式去面對、解決或論定。

　　一件事情呈現的是結果，而它背後的原因可能很多，或是相同的原因，結果未必一樣，例如：兩位銷售員得到服務單位業績第一名（結果），他們努力的方法未必相同（原因）；學習他們如何得到第一（原因），然而未必會得到第一（結果）。因此，除了學習別人的經驗，更要反向思考：為什麼別人會成功的原因和結果，清楚明白後，再試著找出適合自己的方法，突破思想觀念的自我設限，思緒會源源不絕，視野因此寬廣。

　　世界上有很多很多的事情，並不一定在自己所認知的範圍內想得到，因為自己生活環境產生的觀念、生活經驗，會習慣性的產生一些理所當然的邏輯、行為模式和思想的框限，而這樣的習慣也往往限制了觀念成長、視野領域與自我突破。

　　心中的一把尺是原則，然而接納和同理心，則會讓思考角度更廣闊，感受更多層面。想想自己為什麼會這樣的思考，再想想別人為什麼會是那樣的觀念，用開放的思維去面對人、事、物，不預設任何立場，也沒有先入為主的觀念，試著用各種層面的思考角度，去探索、思索、體會所有的事情，會因此發掘到更深層的意義和經驗，用這樣的模式去理解他人的想法，也是一種同理心的呈現。

　　接受與認同，是可以做切割的，也就是可以接受所有不同的觀念，卻不一定要認同那些所有的思維。敞開心門接受不同的觀念，放開心中根深蒂固的思想和成見去探究不同領域的想法。用擺脫傳統、毫無約束、逆向探索、跳躍思考、天馬行空的想法去探索事情，完全不設限的思考模式會因此瞭解更多的想法和事實，讓思想變得清晰及圓融，事情不再感覺那麼複雜，也不會陷入自我設限的泥淖，人與人之間的相處，就能夠做到你懂我、我懂你的同理心。

　　反向思考，人生無限寬廣！

Part Four: Reverse Thinking, Infinite Broadness

Many causes and effects of events are not fixed or predictable, making it challenging to address, solve, or determine them with strict rules or patterns.

An event presents a result, but the underlying causes can be numerous, and the same cause may not always lead to the same result. For example, two salespeople may both achieve first place in their service unit's performance (result), but their methods may differ (causes); learning how they achieved their top position (causes) does not necessarily mean you will achieve the same result (result). Therefore, besides learning from others' experiences, it's essential to engage in reverse thinking: understand why others succeeded, and then identify methods suitable for yourself. By breaking through self-imposed mental limitations, your thoughts will flow continuously, and your perspective will broaden.

The world contains many things that may not be within our current understanding, as our perspectives and experiences are shaped by our environment, leading to habitual logic, behavior patterns, and thought constraints. These habits often limit the growth of our perspectives, vision, and personal breakthroughs.

The principles in your mind are like a ruler, but acceptance and empathy will expand your thinking and allow you to experience various dimensions. Reflect on why you think in a certain way, then consider why others hold different views. Approach people, events, and things with an open mind, without preset positions or preconceived notions. Try exploring, contemplating, and experiencing everything from various perspectives to uncover deeper meanings and experiences. This approach also reflects empathy towards understanding others' thoughts.

Acceptance and recognition can be separated, meaning you can accept all different viewpoints without necessarily agreeing with all of them. Open your mind to different ideas, release deeply ingrained thoughts and biases, and explore various fields with unconventional, unrestricted, reverse thinking, and imaginative ideas. This unbounded thinking will help you understand more ideas and facts, making your thoughts clearer and more integrated. Things will no longer seem so complicated, and you won't be trapped by self-imposed limitations. Interactions with others will exhibit mutual understanding and empathy.

Reverse thinking makes life infinitely broad!

31. 我老了？

朋友說：「我老了！」

我回答：「人生70才開始，你老了？還早得很吶！」

為什麼這樣回答？因為，人生「70」才開始，所以，我們都還沒「出生」，老了？那當然還早得很。

如果還沒有70歲，要為開始的人生做準備，還沒出生怎麼會老？

如果70歲了呢？那表示人生開始了！所以才「1歲」而已，也就是70歲＝1歲，140歲才等於71歲。1歲才剛開始準備迎接美好的人生，哪裡會老？樂觀、知性又感性的想法，會讓心情永遠年輕，生活充滿朝氣。

對於年齡的心態和想法，我的心靈年齡永遠沒有年紀！

我的另一種回答是：「20歲的老人一堆，80歲的小孩也一堆！你還年輕得很！」

因為老不老，跟外表及年齡無關，跟內在心態有關。有些人外表看起來似乎年輕，然而思想僵硬、生活散漫、工作消極、負面情緒一堆、人生毫無規劃和目標，這類型的人，應該才是「老了」。

有些人無論什麼年齡，即使外表看起來似乎有點年紀，然而樂觀、開朗、積極、正向、思想靈活，這類型的人，就是真正的「年輕人」。

在捷克的一間酒吧裡，一位白髮蒼蒼的女士和一群人開心飲

31. Am I Old?

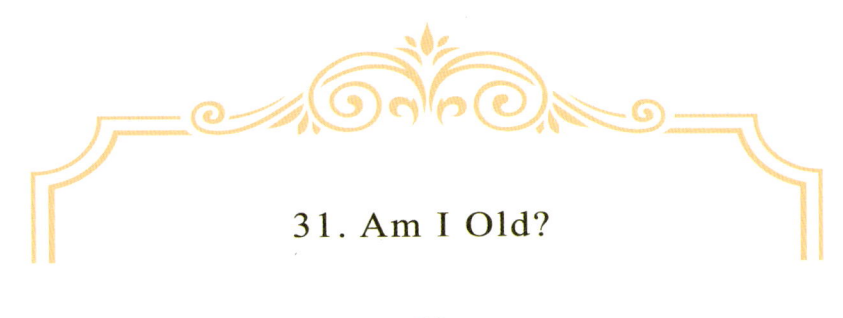

A friend said, "I'm old!" I replied, "Life starts at 70, so you're still very young!"

Why respond this way? Because life "starts" at 70, we haven't even "been born" yet. If you are not yet 70, how could you be old?

If you are 70, then life has just begun! At 70, you are only 1 year old, meaning 70 years = 1 year, and 140 years equals 71 years. At just 1 year old, you are beginning to prepare for a wonderful life, so how could you be old? Optimistic, intellectual, and emotional thinking will keep your mood young and your life vibrant.

Regarding age, my inner age is always ageless!

Another response I might give is: "There are many elderly people at 20 and many young people at 80! You're still very young!"

Being old or young is not related to appearance or age but to inner mindset. Some people may appear young but have rigid thinking, a disorganized lifestyle, passive work habits, and negative emotions. These people could be considered "old."

Conversely, some people, regardless of their age, may appear older but are optimistic, cheerful, proactive, positive, and flexible in their thinking. These people are the true "young" ones.

In a Czech bar, an elderly lady with white hair was joyfully drinking with a group of people at a family gathering spanning four generations. She was 88

酒作樂，原來是祖孫四代的聚餐，這位女士88歲。

她的滿頭白髮散發著光芒，臉上有皺紋依然滿臉笑容，臉色紅潤有光澤，朋友很好奇的問她是如何保養身體，怎麼還那麼年輕、快樂、有活力？

只見她靦腆的用手遮住嘴巴一直笑，沒想到她40幾歲的孫子搶著回答：「美滿的性生活！」她笑而不答，笑得更開心了。

人類創造了時間的觀念，所以時間會一秒一秒累積，因此有了年紀和壽命的想法，於是認為生命

時間累積的少就表示年輕，累積的多就認為是老，而這樣的觀念深植腦海後，心態和想法就不知不覺產生了變化，然而，這只是人類自我設限的枷鎖而已，地球上的其他生命不知道年齡是什麼，反而沒有煩惱，沒有年齡的觀念，一樣可以過得自在，若沒有了生命，年齡數字也就毫無意義。

年齡的枷鎖會讓我們很自然的認定：什麼年齡就該有什麼樣的行為。例如：6歲了，該開始讀書上學了；30歲了，該結婚了；40歲了，步入中年了；60歲了，該退休了；70歲了，我老了；100歲了，活夠了；……。其實這樣的想法，會讓自己掉入年齡行為級距的枷鎖，反而箝制了自己可以接觸各種人生層面的視野和機會，那是很可惜的。

一句：我老了。代表了多少心態的反轉。內心的想法會從行為表現出來，因此無形中，潛意識也會漸漸失去生命積極的動力，這樣的念頭會在不自覺的牽引下，自然而然把自己往「老」的方向前進。

跳脫年齡的觀念，根本忘掉年齡的框架，快樂做自己！

years old.

Her white hair radiated light, her wrinkled face was still full of smiles, and her complexion was rosy and vibrant. Curious friends asked how she maintained her health and remained so young, happy, and energetic.

She shyly covered her mouth and continued to smile, while her 40-something grandson quickly answered, "A fulfilling sex life!" She laughed even more, enjoying the moment.

Humans created the concept of time, so time accumulates second by second, leading to thoughts of age and lifespan. Thus, we think that less time accumulated means being younger and more time means being older. This idea, deeply embedded in our minds, causes subtle changes in our mindset. However, this is merely a self-imposed constraint. Other life forms on Earth don't know what age is and live freely without concern for age. Without life, age numbers become meaningless.

The shackles of age make us naturally assume certain behaviors based on age. For example: at 6, one should start school; at 30, one should be married; at 40, one enters middle age; at 60, one should retire; at 70, one is old; at 100, one has lived enough; etc. Such thinking can confine you to age-specific behavior patterns, limiting your exposure to various life opportunities and perspectives. It's a shame.

Saying "I'm old" signifies a shift in mindset. Internal thoughts manifest in behaviors, and subconsciously, this attitude may erode one's motivation for life, naturally guiding oneself toward "old" directions.

Break free from age concepts and forget age constraints. Be happily yourself!

32. 一代不如一代？

聽過這樣的話嗎？

「一代不如一代！」

「上一代落伍了，下一代吃不了苦，還是我們這一代最強！」

當我們這一代這麼告訴孩子時，讓我想起小時候，父母也對我說過同樣的話，相信祖父母在我父母小時候，一定也說過相似的話，也許我孩子長大成家之後，也會對他們的孩子說出這些類似的話。

一代一代往上推，再一代一代向下延續，好像每一代都會說著相同的話，結果呢？人類不是越來越進步、越來越進化、越來越棒嗎？

為什麼這一代會覺得自己才是最好的？原來，自己覺得承襲了上一代的優點，加上自己的努力和改造，當然覺得是目前最好的。這一代的優點當然希望下一代能夠延續下去，卻偏偏覺得下一代的觀念、態度、做法似乎不一樣，甚至不按照這一代的模式和觀念做事，所以就覺得下一代不長進、退步了。

事實上，我們比上一代優秀，而為什麼會被覺得不好？探究原因，上一代會因為他們那一代的觀念已經根深柢固，而且可以成功的模式也深信不疑，因此認為我們這一代的思想模式、行為習慣和他們不同而覺得不好，甚至我們也會以同樣的自我觀念去評估下一代，其實人類的每一個階段都是承襲了上一代最好的，然後轉換成適合現在的模式，依然很好，物競天擇、適者生存，只是方式變得不同而已。

32. Each Generation is Better Than the Last?

Have you heard this before?

"This generation is better than the last!"

"The previous generation was outdated, the next generation can't endure hardship, our generation is the best!"

When we say this to our children, it reminds me of how my parents said the same thing to me when I was young. I believe my grandparents said similar things when my parents were young, and perhaps I will say the same to my children when they grow up.

Each generation moves up and each continues down, seemingly saying the same things. What's the result? Humanity is not progressing, evolving, and improving?

Why does this generation believe it is the best? It turns out that we think we have inherited the strengths of the previous generation, combined with our own efforts and improvements, so we believe we are the best. We hope the next generation will continue our advantages but often feel that their views, attitudes, and methods differ from ours, leading us to believe they are regressing.

In reality, we are more advanced than the previous generation. Why are we perceived as inferior? The previous generation's mindset and successful models were deeply entrenched, so they might see our different thinking and habits as inferior. We also use similar self-concepts to judge the next generation. In fact, each human stage inherits the best of the previous generation, adapting it to the present mode, and it remains good. Evolution and survival of the fittest mean the methods change but are still effective.

用這樣的思考角度去看待下一代，他們能夠延續我們的優點，而且不會墨守成規、一成不變，懂得調整成適合那個時代的方法，當然也是最優秀的，這樣代代相傳下去，人類當然是越來越進步，當然不會一代不如一代！

　　每個時代的間隔，少則1年多則5年，思想、行為會產生觀念上的差異，生命的延續、經驗的傳承，見證了一代更勝一代，因此，無論身處哪個年代，都是最優秀的，這樣的思維，讓心境倍感溫馨。

　　接納任何年代的思想觀念和行事風格，沒有好壞、落伍或新潮怪異，任何一個年代，都有它最恰當的生存模式和適應性，絕對最適合那個年代的當事人，那當然就是最好的！

Viewing the next generation from this perspective, they continue our strengths and adapt to their era, making them excellent too. As generations pass, humanity naturally progresses, and no generation is worse than the last!

The gap between eras may be 1 year to 5 years, leading to differences in thought and behavior. The continuity of life and transmission of experience witness each generation surpassing the last. Thus, regardless of the era, each is the best in its way, bringing warmth to our mindset.

Accepting ideas and methods from any era, without labeling them as good or bad, outdated or trendy, is the right approach. Each era has its most suitable mode of survival and adaptation, making it the best for its time!

33. 增廣見聞

　　由於經常出國洽商，朋友覺得我的見聞會比他們廣，然而我有不一樣的想法：經常出國，未必見識廣。

　　出國次數的多少和見識廣不廣，沒有絕對關係，而是去的地方的多寡和瞭解的深淺有關。舉幾個例子：

- 一年去日本 10 次，對日本就非常熟悉嗎？未必！

  如果是去洽商哪裡都沒去，那麼行程應該是機場搭車到飯店，再從飯店搭車洽商，之後回飯店。

  問他日本哪裡好玩，應該就是機場、飯店，其他就不知道了，所以，即使經常出國，如果只是單純商務行程，沒有四處走走，見識未必廣。

- 兩位朋友經常出國，一位跑了日本 20 個城市，另一位跑了 20 個國家 20 個城市。或者是，其中一位跑了亞洲 20 個國家，另一位跑了全世界 20 個國家，那麼，哪一位閱歷豐富呢？這可能要從我們想要瞭解什麼樣的內容去做比較，才能做論斷。

- 一位朋友去日本 1 次，另一位去了 10 次，去 10 次的那位對日本比較熟悉嗎？我的想法：還是未必。

　　首先，必須瞭解 1 次和 10 次的內容，才能清楚誰才是符合我們所希望的「見識廣」。一位去了日本 1 次，住了 1 年；另一位去了 10 次，每次 3-5 天。想瞭解日本，我想我會請教去日本 1 次的那一位。

33. Expanding Knowledge

Due to frequent business trips abroad, friends believe I have a broader perspective. However, I have a different view: frequent travel abroad doesn't necessarily equate to broad knowledge.

The number of trips abroad does not directly correlate with broadness of experience; it's more about the quantity and depth of understanding of the places visited. Here are a few examples:

- Going to Japan 10 times in a year doesn't necessarily make you very familiar with Japan. If the trips are purely business, the itinerary might just be the airport, hotel, and business meetings, with little exploration of other areas. So, frequent travel for business doesn't guarantee broad knowledge.

- One friend visited 20 cities in Japan, another visited 20 cities in 20 different countries. Or one traveled to 20 Asian countries, while the other visited 20 countries worldwide. Which one is more experienced? It depends on what you want to understand to make a comparison.

- One friend visited Japan once and stayed for a year, while another visited 10 times, each for 3-5 days. To understand Japan, I would consult the person who stayed for a year.

So, "broad experience abroad" needs to be explored for depth. Relative and absolute broadness of experience are both broad, but the difference lies in the type of information you seek and how well you understand local

所以,「出國見識廣」這句話,還是要探究其中的深入性。其實,相對的見識廣和絕對的見識廣,都是見識廣泛,差別在於我們想要瞭解什麼情況下什麼樣的訊息,去的地方多而且又能深入瞭解當地人文風情,那就真的見識廣。

　　瞭解一件事情的真相,可以運用反向思考的方法,去探究內在的實質面和真正的內涵,而不是只看表面現象,用比較客觀的深度和廣度去解釋它和推斷內在意義,這樣才不會錯失了判斷人事物的真確性。

　　所以,如果朋友問我哪個國家、哪些城市好玩,我的答案可能是:機場!

cultures. If you visit many places and deeply understand local customs, that's true broad experience.

To understand the true nature of things, use reverse thinking to explore the internal substance and real meaning, not just surface phenomena. Explain and infer with objective depth and breadth to avoid missing accurate judgments of people and situations.

So, if friends ask me which countries or cities are fun, my answer might be: the airport!

34. 善良

　　我聽過這麼一句話：放心，我是某某機構志工，所以我心地善良。

　　這句話似乎這樣說比較能夠說服我：我心地善良，所以是某某志工，而不是，我是某某志工，所以心地善良。例如：我是出家人，所以心地善良。和：我心地善良，所以是出家人。總覺得真誠度不一樣。

　　「我是某某志工，所以我心地善良」。有種被動心態和感覺，也就是利用一些大家所認知代表善良的名稱、機構、頭銜或現象，讓大家認為善良，然而有可能不是真誠發自內心，而是把一些善良的現象加諸在自己身上讓大家以為善良，然而，真的善良了嗎？或許真的是真誠的善良，也有可能只是拉攏關係或某種目的過程而已。

　　以前聽過一位公司的業務，他為了推廣產品而加入某慈善團體，藉此取得信任，然後推銷自家產品，他的口頭禪就是：放心，我也是某某機構志工，都是心地善良，不會騙人，買我的絕對放心。結果他一共加入3個慈善團體，表面上熱心配合活動，私底下藉此名義銷售產品謀取暴利，欺騙了很多善良的老實人。

　　當然，這只是在真誠和被動上感覺不同，未必代表好或壞的心態。即使被動，對某些人來說，如果因為有了「我是某某志工，所以心地善良」觀念的框限而可以約束一些行為也是好的，這也是參加好的組織、團體可以讓人向善的力量。

　　善良是發自內心的本性，會無時無刻散發這樣的氣息，周遭

34. Kindness

I've heard a saying: "Rest assured, I'm a volunteer for such-and-such organization, so I'm kind-hearted."

This statement seems more convincing when phrased like this: "I'm kind-hearted, so I am a volunteer for such-and-such organization," rather than "I'm a volunteer for such-and-such organization, so I am kind-hearted." For example: "I'm a monk, so I am kind-hearted," versus "I am kind-hearted, so I am a monk." It feels like the sincerity is different.

The statement "I'm a volunteer for such-and-such organization, so I am kind-hearted" gives a passive impression. It suggests using recognized names, organizations, titles, or phenomena that represent kindness to make others believe in one's kindness, which may not be truly sincere or heartfelt. It could be that such kindness is just a facade to build relationships or achieve certain goals. However, genuine kindness could indeed be present, or it could be a method to leverage some other purpose.

Previously, I heard a salesperson who joined various charity groups to promote their products and gain trust. Their catchphrase was: "Don't worry, I'm also a volunteer for such-and-such organization, so I'm kind-hearted and won't deceive you. You can absolutely trust me to buy my products." As a result, they joined three charity groups, seemingly enthusiastic about activities, but used this facade to sell their products and deceive many honest people.

Of course, the difference between the passive and active approaches is just a matter of perception. Even if passive, if having the "I'm a volunteer for

的人也會感受到，善良的本性無需透過任何名稱、頭銜來裝飾，這才是善良的本質。

　　我會從一些小細節觀察，上面提到的第一種說法，表現出來的行為、態度如何？第二種說法，又給我什麼樣的感覺？善良，無論是本性或是後天修為，都應該是發自內心的行為，不管有沒有加諸任何的稱謂、團體或組織，都跟善良的本質無關。

　　清楚明白所碰到的善良，是為善不欲人知或偽善欲顯人知，後者未必會是傷害，差別在於那種真誠的溫暖和感受不同罷了。

such-and-such organization, so I am kind-hearted" mindset helps to restrain certain behaviors, it is beneficial. This is the power of participating in good organizations or groups to guide people towards goodness.

Kindness is an innate nature that radiates constantly. Surrounding people can feel it, and the essence of kindness doesn't need any name or title to embellish it. This is the true nature of kindness.

I observe from small details: How does the behavior and attitude in the first statement come across? What feeling does the second statement give me? Kindness, whether innate or cultivated, should be an internally driven action, irrespective of any titles, groups, or organizations, as these are unrelated to the essence of kindness.

Understanding the kindness we encounter involves discerning between genuine kindness, which desires not to be known, and false kindness, which seeks to be noticed. The latter may not necessarily be harmful; the difference lies in the sincere warmth and feelings conveyed.

35. 不如意，十之八九？

　　這是大家耳熟能詳的一句話：人生不如意，十之八九。

　　這句鼓勵的話，用來勉勵人們積極努力去面對絕大多數的困難險阻，勇敢面對那十之八九的不如意，而經由努力奮鬥、挑戰困難、克服問題後所獲得的成功，讓人更懂得珍惜。只是，當我們知道眼前充滿困難跟挑戰，和發現眼前一片希望與朝氣，心情的感受和奮勇向前的動力是不一樣的，結果即使相同，充滿荊棘心情的努力過程會倍覺艱辛。

　　聊到這個話題時，我會反向思考：如果人生不如意十之八九，那麼相對的，人生如意有十之一二。是的，這是多麼棒的十之一二！也就是說，80%的不如意，還有20%的如意；90%的不如意，就有10%的如意，就算99.999%的不如意，還是有0.001%的如意！人生沒有100%的不如意，所以，人生沒有完全困難的事！

　　或許某些人，正在經歷這樣的過程：

　　生活中，除了工作，常常只有自己一個人，走在夜燈下，覺得好孤單；看見別人成雙成對，覺得好寂寞；自己一個人默默在餐廳用餐，覺得好淒涼；和朋友聚會後的散會，夜闌人靜時，有種被剝離、孤立的感覺；……，總覺得好多事都不如意。

　　換個角度，或許某些人，也正在經歷這樣的過程：

　　生活中，除了工作，常常只有自己一個人，走在夜燈下，覺得好自在；看見別人成雙成對，覺得好愉快；自己一個人靜靜在餐廳用餐，覺得好輕鬆；和朋友聚會後的散會，夜闌人靜時，有

35. Unfulfilled Expectations

This is a familiar saying: "Life is not always as we wish, eight or nine times out of ten."

This encouraging phrase is used to motivate people to face the majority of difficulties and obstacles, and to bravely confront those eight or nine parts of unfulfilled expectations. By striving and overcoming challenges, one can better appreciate the successes achieved. However, knowing that there are numerous difficulties and challenges ahead can affect our mood and motivation, making the effort feel more arduous despite the outcome being the same.

When discussing this topic, I consider: If life is unfulfilled eight or nine times out of ten, then conversely, there is one or two parts of life that are fulfilling. Indeed, this one or two parts is wonderful! In other words, with 80% of unfulfilled expectations, there is still 20% of fulfillment; with 90% of unfulfilled expectations, there is 10% of fulfillment, and even if there is 99.999% of unfulfilled expectations, there is still 0.001% of fulfillment! Life is not 100% unfulfilled, so there is no completely difficult matter in life!

Some people may be experiencing this process: In life, aside from work, they are often alone, walking under night lights, feeling lonely; seeing others in pairs, feeling lonely; dining alone in a restaurant, feeling desolate; feeling isolated and detached after gatherings with friends; ⋯, everything seems unfulfilled.

Looking at it from another angle, some people may also be experiencing: In life, aside from work, they are often alone, walking under night lights, feeling content; seeing others in pairs, feeling happy; dining alone in a restaurant,

種寧靜、放鬆的感覺；⋯⋯，覺得好幸福、好開心。

其實，當我們的思緒圍繞著那如意的十之一二時，心境會是愉悅、正面、陽光、積極的，所有的思緒、情緒，會因此而充滿正向能量和活力，即使只是那麼一點點、一點點的感覺，也可以把那種感覺留在心裡，它會一直迴盪心靈、反覆回味，也因為整個心境的轉變，即使面對那不如意的十之八九時，會感覺不再是那麼的不如意，這就是一種心境的轉念，以不同的心情（積極或消極）面對同樣的困難，結果會不一樣。

feeling relaxed; feeling calm and relaxed after gatherings with friends; ⋯, feeling happy and content.

In fact, when our thoughts focus on that one or two parts of fulfillment, our mindset will be joyful, positive, sunny, and proactive. All thoughts and emotions will be filled with positive energy and vitality. Even if it is just a small bit of feeling, it can remain in our hearts, echoing and being remembered. Due to this change in mindset, even when facing the eight or nine parts of unfulfilled expectations, it won't feel as unfulfilled. This is a kind of mental shift—facing the same difficulties with either a positive or negative attitude will lead to different outcomes.

36. 學歷？經歷？

　　學歷（證照、高中、大學、碩士、博士文憑），是人們設定通過某個學習階段所給予的肯定和證明，

　　是一種知識累積、榮譽感、成就感、自我肯定和自信的呈現，尤其經由書本提供的知識和有計劃性的階段學習，可以很有系統的將知識完整的累積下來，學歷，是書本知識程度的肯定，完整的學習而後運用在生活上、工作上，是很好的一種學習方式。

　　經歷，是在日常生活中各種狀況的經驗累積，畢竟「社會大學」學海無涯，我們也聽過：不經一事，不長一智。有些層面的領域或狀況，非書本知識可以學習得到或如書本所言的內容而已，面對人生千變萬化的生活形態如何應對，經驗的累積變得重要，這和學歷得來的知識不盡相同，尤其是親身經歷而後學到的經驗，每個人未必一樣，以自己的經歷所得到的結果，會成為自己深信不疑的經驗，對每個人來說，都是很重要的。

　　某些人的成就來自於高學歷，因此，這樣的過程會成為他們認定的成功模式，並以此來鼓勵別人，希望別人也可以用知識累積而來的高學歷的認可，成為日後成功的基礎。

　　某些人的成就是來自於經歷，因為經驗的累積很多並非來自於學歷的知識範圍，因此，他們會認定實際經驗勝過一切，以這樣的模式來鼓勵別人，希望別人瞭解實務經驗的累積，才是成功的重要基礎。

　　學歷比經歷重要？經歷比學歷重要？兩者都重要？兩者都不重要？都對！無論是學歷還是經歷，別人的經驗都可以參考甚至

36. Education? Experience?

Educational qualifications （such as certificates, high school diplomas, university degrees, master's degrees, and doctoral diplomas） are a form of recognition and validation for completing a specific stage of learning. They represent a form of knowledge accumulation, honor, achievement, self-affirmation, and confidence. Structured learning through books and planned stages allows for systematic knowledge accumulation. Educational qualifications validate one's academic knowledge, and applying what is learned in daily life and work is a great way to reinforce that learning.

Experience, on the other hand, is the accumulation of knowledge gained from various situations in daily life. As the saying goes, "Life is a never-ending school." We've also heard, "You grow wiser with every experience." Some aspects of life cannot be learned from books or directly correspond to what books teach. Facing life's unpredictable challenges requires an accumulation of experience, which is different from the knowledge gained through formal education. The lessons learned through firsthand experiences are unique to each person and are often deeply ingrained as personal truths.

Some people's achievements stem from their high educational qualifications, making their journey to success through academia a model they believe in and use to inspire others. They encourage others to seek the recognition that comes with a solid education as a foundation for future success.

Others derive their success from experience. Since many valuable lessons come from practical experience rather than academic knowledge,

學習，至於哪一個才是最恰當的，無法用相互比較的方式來評價，還是以符合自己的生活環境和模式最重要！

仔細想想，其實，有人因高學歷而成功或不得志，有人因經驗豐富而成功或四處碰壁，有人因高學歷和經驗豐富而成功或未遇知音、伯樂而怨懟，有人什麼都沒有依然可以隨遇而安過日子或鬱鬱寡歡，這也證明任何人告訴我們哪一個才是最重要的時候，那些都是他們因此成功的方法，然而適不適合運用在自己身上，還是要以自己的狀況為準，無論學歷、經歷哪一個重要，找出符合自己的模式，那才是最「重要」的！

對自己有信心、瞭解自己的需求，尤其是認同、接受、喜歡自己的學經歷現況，以自己的需要去平衡學經歷的需求，不羨慕、不比較、不盲目、不強迫，這是對自己最好的安排。學歷、經歷，都是一種學習的過程，無論目前正在求學（學歷）的過程或在工作（經歷）的過程或同時存在，重要是在於學習的態度，學習過程中，態度決定了所有知識累積的多寡，有了積極的態度，在學經歷領域都能學富五車。

學歷、經歷，是人們在自己生活的環境中所設定的一種能力的認定，只是標準為何？相信我們都喜歡學經歷豐富的人生，「學」歷的豐富，未必完全來自書本，任何一種學習方式，都可以豐富自己的「學」歷。「經」歷的的豐富，也未必一定要凡事親身經歷來累積甚至是慘痛經驗後才學到教訓，經由觀察、體會、領悟，一樣可以豐富自己的「經」歷。

相信自己、愛自己，自己的學歷、經歷，是最符合自己的！

they tend to prioritize real-world learning. They encourage others to understand that experience is crucial to achieving success.

Is education more important than experience? Is experience more important than education? Are both important? Or are neither crucial? The answer is: all perspectives are valid! Whether it is education or experience, learning from others is always beneficial. The key is finding what aligns best with your circumstances and lifestyle, rather than comparing the two.

Consider this: some people succeed with high educational qualifications, while others don't find fulfillment despite their degrees. Some achieve success through rich experiences, while others face setbacks despite their practical knowledge. Some may have both education and experience but still feel unrecognized or underappreciated, while others, with neither, manage to live contentedly or struggle with dissatisfaction. This illustrates that when someone tells us which path is more important, they are merely sharing what worked for them. Whether it suits you depends on your unique situation. What truly matters is finding the approach that fits you best.

Confidence in yourself, understanding your needs, and especially accepting and embracing your current educational and experiential background is crucial. Balancing your academic and experiential needs based on your own requirements—without envy, comparison, blind pursuit, or forcing things—leads to the best outcomes for yourself. Both education and experience are learning processes. Whether you're currently pursuing your studies (education), working (experience), or doing both, what's essential is your attitude toward learning. An active and positive attitude during this journey determines how much knowledge you accumulate, enabling you to excel in both fields.

Education and experience are abilities defined by the environment we live in. But what are the standards? We all value a rich life of learning and experiences. A rich "education" doesn't have to come solely from books—any form of learning can enhance your educational background. Similarly, a rich "experience" doesn't require firsthand encounters or painful lessons; it can also come from observation, understanding, and insight.

Believe in yourself and love yourself—your education and experience are the most suitable for you!

37. 幽默回應

　　年齡是女性在乎的秘密，也經常成為話題。一位學經歷豐富、年近 50 歲頗受歡迎的典禮主持人，來賓無論年齡多少，大家都習慣稱呼她阿美姐，有時候她也會拿來調侃來賓說：「你年紀比我大耶，不要叫我姐姐」。在那種場合下，這是個有趣的說詞，因為，第一：她的年齡確實比來賓小，被年紀比自己大的稱呼為姐姐，哪位女性心裡不嘀咕呢？第二：「阿美姐」這三個字，幾乎已成為她不動的招牌。那麼，要如何幽默回應才能兩全其美，氣氛更顯輕鬆愉快呢？一般回應大致有以下幾種：

- 「妳這麼優秀，大家都叫妳阿美姐阿，叫習慣了啦！」

　　（這句話雖然似乎在捧她，只是感覺還是沒有解開年齡大小的結）

- 「對對對，下次要叫妳阿美妹才對。」

　　（這句話感覺很奇怪，尤其招牌的「姐」變成「妹」，非但不習慣，也有點被貶抑的感覺）

- 「我年紀比妳小喔。」

　　（這是最白目的回答！明明年齡比她大，還如此回應，雖然現場氣氛還是嘻嘻哈哈，只是非常不幽默）

　　我是這麼說：「妳博學多聞，所以叫妳阿美姐阿，雖然妳才「18」歲，我實在很嘔，這都是妳害的啦！」，此話一出，她開心的笑了，氣氛更勝前面三種說法。

　　這句話術，我要告訴她，第一：她的豐富閱歷，所以尊稱她「阿

37. Humorous Responses

Age is a secret that women often care about and frequently becomes a topic of discussion. A well-known and highly respected emcee in her late 40s, who is popular regardless of the guests' ages, is usually referred to as "Sister Mei" by everyone. Sometimes, she uses this nickname to tease guests by saying, "You're older than me, so don't call me 'sister'." In such situations, this is a fun remark because, first: her age is indeed younger than that of the guests, and which woman wouldn't question being called 'sister' by someone older? Second: "Sister Mei" has almost become her permanent trademark. So, how can one respond humorously to balance both sides and make the atmosphere more relaxed and enjoyable? General responses might be:

- "You're so outstanding that everyone calls you Sister Mei, we've just gotten used to it!" (This might seem like a compliment, but it doesn't really address the age issue.)

- "Yes, yes, next time we should call you Sister Mei instead." (This response seems odd, especially since changing 'sister' to 'younger sister' feels both unfamiliar and a bit demeaning.)

- "I'm actually younger than you!" (This is the most blunt answer! Even though the atmosphere might still be lighthearted, it's not very humorous.)

Here's how I responded: "You're so knowledgeable and outstanding that we call you Sister Mei, even though you're only '18,' it really bothers me! It's all your fault!" When this was said, she laughed happily, and the atmosphere was even better than the previous three responses.

This response shows her wealth of experience is why she is respectfully called

美姐」,「姐」字和她的年齡無關。第二:雖然才「18」歲,刻意說出她可能喜歡的年紀,然後說出如此年輕就能這麼優秀,我年紀比她大還稱呼她「姐」,感覺實在很嘔,是她「害」我叫她「姐」的。既能化解年齡尷尬,也能讓她感到優秀,而我也沒有貶低自己,這樣的幽默,沒有誰高誰低,讓大家的心情都受益。

釣魚是我最喜愛的休閒娛樂,享受一竿在手、偷得浮生半日閒的樂趣,尤其置身大自然的寧靜與放鬆,可以讓心境得到徹底的釋放。有時候在釣魚的地方,會遇到未曾謀面的釣友,也可能從此不再相遇,雖然彼此不認識,依然可以沒有負擔、沒有利害關係的天南地北的「吹噓」著自己釣魚的豐功偉業,這是一種非常奇妙又愉快的互動。

有一次在水庫釣魚,我的收穫頗豐,一旁的幾位釣友漁獲卻寥寥可數,閒聊中,其中一位釣友說:「你釣的魚都沒長眼睛啦!」(意思是:那些魚都瞎了眼,才會被你釣起來),要怎樣回話呢?一般人可能這樣回答:

- 「今天運氣好啦。」(感覺太謙虛)
- 「沒什麼啦,隨便釣一釣而已。」(感覺有點自大)
- 「我就是專門釣沒眼睛的魚!」(感覺太僵硬)

我這麼回答他:「沒辦法啦,魚眼睛都被你釣走了,我只好釣魚啊」,只見那位釣友開心的哈哈大笑。

這句話,捧了他也捧了我,即使他的魚獲比我少,這樣的幽默回應,和上面三種回應話語比較,相信氣氛會更輕鬆愉快,也會讓他感受到我正向又有趣的話術。

我們都喜歡幽默的話語,在對話的一來一往中,如果能夠相得益彰、相互提升彼此的優點或以積極正向的話語回應,在幽默中不失誰高誰低的感覺,那會是最棒的感覺。氣氛不佳的場合,有時候適當的幽默,可以減少尷尬或減緩緊張的氣氛,甚至一句幽默回應,可能就化解了某些爭論。愉快的場合,再來一句恰到好處的幽默,心情會更加的愉悅。

幽默別人的同時,也試著一起幽默自己,讓彼此都能感受到幽默的氛圍,那就是最棒的幽默!

"Sister Mei," and that the "sister" title is unrelated to her age. By deliberately saying she is "18," I am acknowledging her youth and excellence, and expressing how it bothers me to call her "sister" given my older age. This humor not only defuses the awkwardness about age but also makes her feel valued, without belittling myself. Such humor makes everyone's mood better and is mutually beneficial.

Fishing is my favorite leisure activity. I enjoy the pleasure of holding a rod and stealing a half-day of tranquility in nature, which allows my mind to be completely relaxed. Sometimes at fishing spots, I meet fellow anglers whom I might never meet again. Even though we don't know each other, we can still boast about our fishing achievements from all over, without any burden or conflicts. This is a very wonderful and enjoyable interaction.

Once, while fishing at a reservoir, I had a bountiful catch, while the nearby anglers caught very few. During a chat, one angler said, "The fish you caught must be blind!" (Meaning: those fish must be blind to be caught by you.) How should I respond? Typical responses might be:

- "Today's luck is just good." (This response feels too modest.)
- "It's nothing, just caught a few by chance." (This response seems a bit arrogant.)
- "I specialize in catching fish without eyes!" (This response feels too stiff.)

I replied: "There's nothing I can do, the fish's eyes must have been caught by you, so I had to catch the fish." That angler laughed heartily.

This response both compliments him and praises myself. Even if his catch was less than mine, this humorous reply makes the atmosphere lighter and more enjoyable, and makes him feel my positive and interesting communication style.

We all appreciate humorous words. In conversations, if we can respond in a way that complements and uplifts each other, it creates the best atmosphere. In less favorable situations, appropriate humor can reduce awkwardness or ease tension, and sometimes a humorous reply can resolve certain disputes. In pleasant situations, a well-placed joke can enhance the mood even further.

Humor, when directed at others and oneself, creates an environment where everyone can experience the joy of humor. That's the best kind of humor!

38. 沒空的醒思

人與人的相處，曾經問過也被問過：現在有沒有空？等一下有沒有空？晚上有沒有空？明天上午有沒有空？也都說過這樣的話：沒空耶。

「沒空」，其實代表了很多的意思：

- 當下真的分身乏術，也可能是疲累，現在的確沒空；或許幾分鐘、幾小時，等這事情忙完或休息之後就有空，這是真的沒空。
- 不是很忙，只是不想參與或不在意別人的事情，所以沒空，這是藉口的沒空。

我們也聽過這樣的話：為什麼他經常沒空？摒除上面第一個的情形，可以從心理層面去瞭解一個人為什麼會這麼說，他的想法是什麼。

如果是藉口，就是在乎、不在乎的區別而已。意思就是：「在乎的事情，沒空也變成有空；不在乎的事情，有空也變成沒空」。這句話可以用幾個例子印證：

- 男女都曾抱怨過，女性又比較多。婚前經常接送上下班，婚後就變得沒空，難道婚前不忙，婚後很忙嗎？其中的感覺，多數在於在乎多少的程度罷了。

38. Time Management Reflections

In interactions with people, we've all asked or been asked: "Do you have time now?" "Do you have time later?" "Do you have time tonight?" "Do you have time tomorrow morning?" We've also said things like: "I'm not available."

"Not available" actually represents many things:

- At the moment, being genuinely overwhelmed, possibly tired, and indeed not available; perhaps in a few minutes or hours, after finishing this task or resting, there will be time—this is genuine unavailability.

- Not really busy, just unwilling to participate or not interested in someone else's matters, so it's an excuse for being unavailable.

We've heard people say: why is he always unavailable? Excluding the first scenario, we can understand a person's reason for frequently saying "not available" from a psychological perspective; it's merely a matter of whether they care or not.

If it's an excuse, it's just a matter of care and indifference. It means: "For things I care about, being unavailable turns into being available; for things I don't care about, even if I have time, it turns into being unavailable." This can be illustrated with several examples:

- Both men and women have complained, with women more often. Before marriage, they often drop off and pick up from work, but after marriage, they become unavailable. Wasn't it busy before marriage

- 某些業務員推銷產品，成交前，主動噓寒問暖，一通電話馬上到，什麼麻煩事都可以立即解決，成交後，需要協助的電話卻可能屢催不到。難道成交前不忙，成交後很忙嗎？其實，就是在不在乎而已，因為，那些業務員還有一些成交前的「有空」要忙。

某些情形之下，我們會用「沒空」來當藉口、推拖之詞，用來推掉或逃避事情，當然，如果心裡清楚是沒必要參與的事情，用「沒空」的說話藝術來當擋箭牌，也是很好的一種推辭。

例如：晚上有個普通飯局，雖然晚上有空，然而不想參加，就用「沒空」來推辭。如果是重要飯局，即使忙碌也要「有空」，心裡清楚明白如何拿捏「有空、沒空」，就是這個道理。

「有空」或「沒空」的心態，沒有絕對的好或不好，完全以當時的事件來衡量。「有空」是積極、正向的態度，如果「沒空」的藉口多了，會產生消極、逃避、負面的態度。我們的確可能因為忙碌而沒空，然而，依然可以把眾多事情按照輕重緩急的前後順序安排，把在乎、關心的心思放在心中而變得有空。

and now busier after? The feeling often relates to the level of care.

- Certain salespeople, before closing a deal, are proactive, warm, and can solve any trouble immediately, but after the deal, it's challenging to get their help even with repeated calls. Were they not busy before, and busy afterward? It's just that those salespeople have other "available" tasks before closing the deal.

In some situations, we use "not available" as an excuse or a way to avoid something. Of course, if one clearly knows it's unnecessary to participate, using "not available" as a polite way to decline is also a good strategy.

For example: if there's an ordinary dinner invitation, although I am free that evening, I don't want to attend, so I use "not available" to decline. If it's an important dinner, even if busy, I'll make time, clearly understanding how to balance "available" and "not available"—this is the point.

The attitude of "available" or "not available" isn't inherently good or bad, entirely depending on the situation. Being "available" is a positive and proactive attitude. If "not available" becomes an excuse frequently, it leads to a negative, evasive, and passive attitude. We may indeed be genuinely busy, but we can still prioritize and arrange things according to importance, keeping care and concern in mind to make time.

39. 美食、豪宅

　　早年和朋友去東南亞某生活水平很簡單的國家考察兼瞭解風土民情，在驅車前往當地友人家裡拜訪時，他似乎先給我打預防針，要我先有心理準備。

　　他說：等一下我的朋友會請我們在家裡吃火鍋，不過你看到會是一整鍋的菜和「草」而已，除了菜就是菜沒有一點肉，他們吃肉比登天還難，而且常年吃菜的結果，也不太習慣吃肉了，你可別介意啊。

　　我回答：喔，沒問題的啦。

　　其實我心裡是想：真的還假的？一堆的菜和「草」？那一定有很多是我沒見過的菜和「草」囉，哇！那肯定是頓豐盛的野菜大餐了！太棒了！喜出望外的想馬上見識見識，大開眼界！

　　聽朋友說完那句話之後，我整個心早就充滿期待，開心的不得了，好奇又愉快的準備迎接不曾體驗過的野菜風味餐！

　　眼前十多種的菜、草、菇類、水果，幾乎真的不曾見過，無論是生食或川燙，沒想到口味那麼的爽口，未曾品嚐過的那些菜的味道，口齒清香、回甘餘韻，真的好棒。我猜得到的，大概只有芭蕉、芒草心、野蕨類、樹薯、箭竹筍、野薑，而生平第一次喝到香茅茶，就是他朋友隨手摘來沖泡的，為了我的到來，這位朋友用心準備，拿出豐盛的各種野菜來招待我，是我生平最難忘的素食美食大餐！

　　曾經和朋友在中美洲，到河邊拜訪他的朋友，準備找他駕船遊河及探訪馬雅遺跡，到他家時，房子雖然是黏土加石頭蓋的，

39. Food and Luxury Homes

Years ago, when visiting a Southeast Asian country with a very simple lifestyle, I was warned by a friend to prepare myself.

He said: "My friend will invite us to his home for hot pot, but you'll see a whole pot of vegetables and 'grass' only; there's no meat at all. They rarely eat meat and aren't accustomed to it anymore, so don't be offended."

I replied: "Oh, that's fine."

Actually, in my mind, I thought: Really, just vegetables and 'grass'? That must mean many of these are vegetables and 'grass' I've never seen before. Wow! That should be a lavish wild vegetable feast! I was thrilled to experience this novel feast.

When the time came, there were more than ten types of vegetables, grasses, mushrooms, and fruits that I had never seen before. Whether raw or blanched, the taste was surprisingly refreshing. The flavors of these vegetables were unique and pleasant, making it the most unforgettable vegetarian meal I've ever had.

Once, while visiting a friend in Central America, I was curious about the stones used in his house's construction. He casually mentioned that they were agate and quartz, and my friend said they were collected from the riverbed where agate was abundant and cheap.

I thought: What, no money? So you build a house with agate and quartz??? This logic was unimaginable to me. Living in an agate house, if agate truly has some health benefits, it's no wonder his friend is so healthy

我總覺得房子的那些石頭怪怪的，石頭顏色有淡褐、半透明、淡藍、微黃、暗紅、暗淺綠、黑……，我好奇的問那是什麼材料，他朋友很自然又直接的說：瑪瑙和石英。我朋友說，因為他比較沒錢，所以石頭就從河裡拿，那條河隨地都是瑪瑙，不值錢的。

我想：天啊，沒錢？所以拿瑪瑙和石英蓋房子？？？這樣的邏輯，在我以往的認知裡，根本是想都想不到的。住在瑪瑙屋裡，如果真如文獻記載瑪瑙的一些功效，難怪他朋友身體這麼好，根本很難很難生病了。看他住得健康、住得開心，什麼才是豪宅？從那時候起，在我心中有了另一種視野。

美食、豪宅標準是什麼？以金錢、物品價值來衡量，豪華盛宴、富麗堂皇的確讓人賞心悅目、心情愉快，只是如果單以這種方式來追求和接觸，恐怕會失去對很多事情理解的機會及體悟。快樂未必來自於表面看見的富裕或貧窮現象，有人因富裕而不喜歡甚至不接觸其他層面的生活，有人因貧窮而不習慣甚至有排斥富裕的心態，其實，真正的接納，是來自於心情上的認同、滿足。

以接納的心情去喜歡、接受、體驗所有的生活模式，也是一種同理心的表現，更是自我認同的展現，無論什麼生活層次，都能夠感到知足和快樂，那樣的心情，讓自己無論身處什麼環境，都會輕鬆而愉快。可以品嚐各國食物、路邊攤、可以五星米其林、滿漢全席；可以別墅、莊園、可以茅屋土牆，世界各個角落，都有屬於那個區域所認可的「美食、豪宅」，隨遇而安、隨興喜悅，讓自己的心情什麼都接受、什麼都好、什麼都開心，會因此變得簡單而自在。

「美食、豪宅」無限寬廣，心情對了，什麼都好！

and rarely gets sick. Seeing his healthy and happy living, I had a new perspective on what constitutes a luxury home.

What defines "food" and "luxury homes"? Measuring by money or material value, luxury feasts and lavish mansions are indeed pleasing and uplifting. However, pursuing and experiencing only through these means might lead to missing out on understanding and appreciating many other things. Happiness doesn't necessarily come from visible wealth or poverty. Some people dislike or avoid other aspects of life due to their wealth, while others reject or are uncomfortable with wealth due to poverty. True acceptance comes from emotional recognition and satisfaction.

To appreciate, accept, and experience all modes of living with an open heart is also an expression of empathy and self-acceptance. Regardless of one's living conditions, feeling content and happy is what makes life simple and free. One can enjoy various foods and living spaces, from street food and five-star Michelin meals to villas, estates, and simple mud huts. Every corner of the world has its own "food" and "luxury homes," and embracing and delighting in all of them can lead to a simple and pleasant state of mind.

"Food" and "luxury homes" are infinitely broad; with the right mindset, everything is good!

40. 認知層次

曾經聽過這類的報導:「某人用 100 萬買了一個名牌包」、「某車牌被某人以 200 萬標走」……,聽到這些報導時,通常會有一些負面評價,例如:奢侈、浪費、炫富……。有些人會說:如果有 100 萬,我會拿來出國旅遊、吃大餐、買車子、存在銀行生利息、投資股票、做生意……。認為 100 萬可以做很多事,用來買一個包包或首飾或什麼的,太浪費了。

假若先摒除奢侈浪費的想法,針對價值能力而言,或許也可以是另外一種認知層次的擴充。

比如 A 君有 100 萬,問他會做什麼而不會做什麼時:

問:「如果總財產有 1 萬(這裡指的是現金),你會想出國旅遊、吃大餐嗎?」。

答:「怎麼可能,根本不夠啊」。

問:「如果總財產有 10 萬,你會想出國旅遊、吃大餐嗎?」。

答:「當然不會」。

問:「如果總財產有 100 萬,你會想出國旅遊、吃大餐嗎?」。

答:「應該會」。

問:「如果總財產有 1 億,要你買個名牌包包或首飾,覺得如何?」。

答:「沒問題啊」。

問:「所以囉」。

40. Cognitive Levels

We often hear reports like, "Someone spent 1 million on a designer bag," or "A license plate was auctioned for 2 million." These reports typically receive negative reactions such as being deemed extravagant, wasteful, or flaunting wealth. Some people might say, "If I had 1 million, I'd use it for travel, dining out, buying a car, saving it in the bank for interest, investing in stocks, or starting a business." They believe that 1 million could be used for many things and spending it on a bag or jewelry is too wasteful.

If we set aside the idea of extravagance and wastefulness, we can see it from a different cognitive level regarding value and capability.

For instance, if Person A has 1 million and is asked what they would or wouldn't do:

Asked, "If your total assets were 10,000, would you want to travel abroad or dine out?" Answer: "No way, it's not enough."

Asked, "If your total assets were 100,000, would you want to travel abroad or dine out?" Answer: "Definitely not."

Asked, "If your total assets were 1 million, would you want to travel abroad or dine out?" Answer: "Probably."

Asked, "If your total assets were 100 million, what do you think about buying a designer bag or jewelry?" Answer: "No problem."

Asked, "So?" Answer: ???!!! （Understands the point.）

Without personal experience, even with thorough planning and

答：？？！！（明白我要表達的意思了）。

　　沒有親身參與一件事，即使想得面面俱到、規劃完整，也可能很難完全明白真相，如同總財產100萬的人，無法理解總財產有1億的人的想法和能力，當我們在思考或評論一件事時，或許只是在自己的認知範圍內下判斷或結論而已，未必是完整的事實，如果就以此下定論，會讓自己侷限在一個自我認知的框架內，錯失了客觀瞭解人世百態的機會。

　　如上對話的例子，能力在什麼層次，會說出什麼想法，而當能力提升時，想法就不一樣了，甚至推翻了之前的想法，然而之前自己信誓旦旦的評論，奉為圭臬的思想，怎麼就全盤否認了呢？

　　這就像自己是員工時的想法或批評，成為主管時可能不同了，主管時的想法或批評，成為總經理或老闆時又可能不一樣，從員工升為主管再成為總經理或老闆和直接成為總經理或老闆，對事情的想法又不一樣，如同金字塔般因為層次及高度的不同，對事情理解的程度自然不同。

　　有人跟我說，如果我有100萬（這裡以金錢數字舉例，未必就是針對金錢而已），我會做什麼什麼，才不會去做什麼什麼。我的直覺是，他的能力和認知，應該就在這「百萬」上下的範圍，不是「千萬」的領域。這就像有人說如果我是總經理、老闆，我會做什麼不會做什麼，事實上，他不會是總經理、老闆，那些如果的說法，和現實狀況勢必有差異，如果我們因此聽信或認同他的想法，可能就錯失判斷真相的機會。

　　這似乎在提醒我，以我目前的認知現況去看待世間的人、事、物時，如果有自己感到不滿意的地方，也不要一概否定或批評，而是要用心體會別人這麼做的動機或能力是什麼，感受自己不知道的領域和層次，之後無論認同或否定，也會明白為什麼，這樣的成長，會讓自己以平常心、無所謂的心態，去接納人世間各種不同生活模式的人們。

　　無論現在的我，具備了哪些認知的水平，也要抱持著接納的態度，而不是以自己的認知和喜惡，去否定自己不喜歡的人、事、物，以同理心的態度去瞭解別人為什麼如此，因清楚事實而反對與不清楚而反對，前者會讓我們的視野更寬廣，尤其會在與任何人的相處上，愈加的輕鬆、自在、圓融。

consideration, one might find it difficult to fully grasp the truth. Just as a person with 1 million may not understand the thoughts and capabilities of someone with 100 million, when we think about or critique something, we might only be making judgments or conclusions within our own cognitive framework. This might not reflect the complete truth, and if we make judgments based solely on our own understanding, we could miss out on opportunities to objectively understand various aspects of life.

In the dialogue example, thoughts and opinions change with different levels of capability. As one's capability increases, their thoughts change and may even overturn previous ideas. This can be compared to how one's views as an employee, supervisor, or CEO can differ based on their position and perspective. Moving up the hierarchy, the understanding of issues naturally evolves.

Someone might say, "If I had 1 million, I would do this and not that." My intuition is that their capability and understanding are likely within the "million" range, not the "ten million" range. For example, someone might say, "If I were a CEO or boss, I would do this and not that," but in reality, they may never become a CEO or boss. If we rely on their hypothetical statements, we might miss the chance to accurately judge the situation.

This suggests that when we view people, events, and things with our current cognitive level, if we are dissatisfied, instead of dismissing or criticizing, we should understand the motivations or capabilities behind others' actions. By doing so, we can accept various lifestyles with an open mind.

Regardless of our current cognitive level, we should maintain an attitude of acceptance rather than rejecting what we dislike based on our own preferences. Understanding why others act the way they do, whether we agree or disagree, will broaden our perspective and make interactions with others more relaxed and harmonious.

41. 不自覺的負面激勵

　　每個人的情緒難免都會有高低起伏、積極、消極的時候，差別在於比例的多寡，某些人由於長態性忙碌、壓力、煩悶的關係，不知不覺中，有些看似鼓勵的話，感覺似乎還是隱藏了負面的觀點，因此，在接收激勵話語的同時，也吸收了負面思維，這樣的感覺，即使知道是鼓勵的話，在心情上還是難以全部感受到激勵，甚至原本被激勵的心情又沉了下來，無法把好的情緒和氣氛整個提昇起來，那是很可惜的。

　　這裡所提到的「負面」想法，並不是指偏激、消極的觀念和行為，而是面對生活所發生的人事物時，比較會先往困難、不容易、沒辦法、……的方向思考，潛意識裡已經不自覺的先給自己設立了重重關卡，這樣的思緒所牽引出來的「激勵」，難免會令人感到壓力或覺得無法完成。

　　幾年前，有這麼一件令人開心的報導：

　　「「雖然」郭泓志打出了代表台灣的第一支全壘打，「但是」今天優異的投球內容，更讓郭泓志感到開心」，多麼振奮人心的一則新聞！

　　如果我是記者，報導會這麼寫：

　　「郭泓志打出了代表台灣的第一支全壘打，「而且」今天優異的投球內容，更讓郭泓志感到開心」。上面兩句話，感覺有什麼不一樣呢？

　　一位主管讚美同事：「妳這嫣紅的口紅好好看，「不過」這件靛藍色衣服也很棒喔！」

41. Unintentional Negative Reinforcement

Everyone experiences fluctuations in emotions, with times of high and low, and periods of optimism and pessimism. The difference lies in the extent of these fluctuations. Some people, due to chronic busyness, stress, or frustration, may unconsciously convey negative viewpoints even in seemingly encouraging words. As a result, while receiving motivational messages, they might also absorb negative thinking, which can dampen the intended encouragement and affect their mood.

The "negative" thoughts mentioned here are not extreme or pessimistic, but rather a tendency to focus on difficulties and obstacles when facing life's events. This subconscious tendency sets up barriers and makes the received "encouragement" feel pressured or unachievable.

A few years ago, there was a heartwarming report: "Although Guo Hongzhi hit the first home run for Taiwan, today's excellent pitching content made him even happier."

If I were the reporter, I would write: "Guo Hongzhi hit the first home run for Taiwan, and today's excellent pitching content made him even happier."

The difference in sentiment is noticeable.

A supervisor might compliment an employee: "Your bright red lipstick looks great, but this indigo dress is also nice!" I would say: "Your bright red lipstick looks great, and this indigo dress is also nice!" (or: "Your bright red lipstick looks great; this indigo dress is also nice!")

The phrases "although... but" often include negative connotations (e.g.,

我會這麼說：「妳這嫣紅的口紅好好看，「而且」這件靛藍色衣服也很棒喔！」

　　（或：「妳這嫣紅的口紅好好看，這件靛藍色衣服也很棒喔！」）

　　「雖然……但是」，在鼓勵別人時，經常不知不覺說了負面的字眼（例如：雖然、但是、可是、不過、無法……），表面看起來好像是開心的心情，其實，內在及潛意識還是隱藏了一些負面情緒與壓抑，只是自己可能並不知道。

　　「……而且」，這是正向鼓勵的方法之一。當聽到全然正向鼓勵的話時，心情會更加的倍感舒暢，上面的兩個例子，感受會不一樣。

　　那些負面的字眼和思維，沒有什麼絕對的不恰當，然而如果可以轉個念，用更愉快的字眼，相信別人在接收到以及自己口中說出時，都會感受到那股「全面」正向的激勵。鼓勵別人，如同鼓勵自己；激勵別人，先激勵自己。負面思維會長大，正面思維也會長大，只要其中一個長大，另一個就會變小，一句激勵人心的好話，會導向正面、會提昇行動力，是相當棒的鼓勵。

although, but, however) which, even if meant to be encouraging, may still carry underlying negativity. Conversely, "and" is one way to provide positive reinforcement. Hearing purely positive encouragement can uplift mood more effectively.

    Negative words and thoughts aren't inherently inappropriate, but if we can shift our thinking to more positive expressions, it will benefit both the recipient and ourselves. Encouraging others is like encouraging ourselves; positive reinforcement will grow, while negative thinking will diminish. A motivating comment can drive positive action and is an excellent form of encouragement.

42. 開心「當下這一秒」

　　經常保持愉快心情好像不是件簡單的事？一天當中，有可能因為發生一些不如意的事而讓心情受到影響，如果心情經常被瑣事、煩事、負面的情緒包圍，想要「經常保持愉快」自然不容易，畢竟內在的心情、觀念、想法如果沒有轉變，外表的開心只是暫時而已，不是發自內心的喜悅當然很快就會回到原點。

　　其實，人們一生所必須面對的事情，除非是生命結束，有很多事情的發生和存在的問題是不會結束的，只是換了環境、換了不同的人事物，然而，不同的環境、不同的人事物，依舊會產生不同的問題（例如：換個工作環境），因此，在解決問題時，轉換環境或許是個暫時不錯的方法，而如果可以讓心情保持愉快，那麼，無論身處什麼地方，都能夠擁有喜悅的心情。

　　愉快的感覺，我會先從小地方一點一滴開始累積，在不知不覺中讓自己天天開心。

　　開心「這一秒」，只要「一秒」，會覺得容易多了！就好像活在當下的想法，把這個觀念具體化，就是「這一秒」。讓心情保持在開心當下的一秒鐘，只要把握住「這一秒」就好，一秒只在瞬間而已，當心裡這麼想時，心情會頓時感覺豁然開朗而輕鬆。

　　一秒很快過去，接著下一秒立即到來又瞬間過去，然後下一秒馬上來臨，簡單、平靜、愉快的心情就一直停格在「當下這一秒」，心情永遠不動的「這」一秒，去應對時間跳動而不斷累積的「那」一秒，時間已過了好幾秒，甚至數分鐘、數小時，不知不覺中，才發現原來已經整天好心情了。

42. Happiness in the "Present Moment"

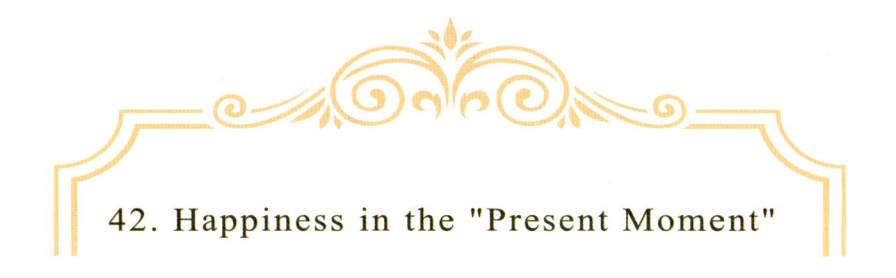

Maintaining a cheerful mood seems to be a challenging task. Throughout the day, various unpleasant events can influence our emotions. If we frequently find ourselves surrounded by trivial issues, annoyances, and negative feelings, keeping a positive attitude becomes difficult. After all, if our internal mood, beliefs, and thoughts don't change, any outward happiness is merely temporary and not a genuine joy.

In reality, many challenges in life persist unless we reach the end of our lives. Numerous events and existing problems won't cease; they simply change with our environment and the people and things around us. However, different settings and circumstances will still bring about new issues （for instance, changing jobs）. Therefore, when addressing problems, switching environments might be a good temporary solution. If we can maintain a cheerful disposition, we can experience joy no matter where we are.

I begin to accumulate happiness from small things, gradually making myself happy every day.

Feeling happy "this second" feels easier with just "one second." It's akin to living in the present; concretizing this idea translates to "this second." By keeping our mood in a joyful state for just a moment, we need to focus on "this second." A second is fleeting; when we think this way, our mood can instantly feel light and clear.

A second passes quickly, followed immediately by the next second, and so on. Simple, peaceful, and joyful feelings can remain frozen in "this second." Time continues to flow, accumulating those other seconds. After

面對生活的種種，不容易事事順遂，只要讓心情擁有「開心當下這一秒」，即使碰到了一些在所難免的煩惱，也會因為心中一直擁有開心的「這一秒」，會讓當下愉悅的心情化解掉暫時而來的不如意，已經發生的困難是無法改變的事實，選擇用輕鬆的心情或緊繃的情緒去面對困難、解決問題，過程和感受絕對不一樣，相信我們都喜歡也期待自己可以用愉悅心情的面對。

　　「一秒」的觀念其實很簡單，就是心中隨時存在著輕鬆、簡單的想法。

several seconds, or even minutes or hours, we may find we've experienced a whole day of good moods without realizing it.

In the face of life's various challenges, not everything will go smoothly. If we allow our mood to possess "this happy second," even if we encounter unavoidable troubles, holding onto that joyful "this second" can help alleviate any temporary dissatisfaction. The difficulties that have already occurred are unchangeable realities. Choosing to face challenges with a relaxed or tense attitude will lead to entirely different processes and feelings. We all appreciate and look forward to facing life with a joyful heart.

The concept of "one second" is quite simple; it is simply a state of mind where we always have easy and light thoughts.

43. 生存韌性

　　如果可以三餐溫飽真的要滿足、惜福，我們覺得理所當然、幾口就輕鬆吃完的一餐，在地球其他角落，還有很多的生命費盡心思、用盡氣力，只為了找不到這一餐。

　　如果現階段的生活、工作、家人、基本收入，每天的日子平平順順，那也真的要感到滿足、幸福，畢竟，每天有多少人只求一個基本的平順、幸福而不可得。大富大貴、汲汲營營累積財富的標準無法相互比較，全在於心境的知足，滿足於自己的現況，就是富裕、就是韌性的展現。

　　地球上有很多的生命，無論是動物、植物、昆蟲，幾乎都在艱困的環境中生存，也都能夠找到生存的方法，見證了生命的毅力和韌性，觀察著、思索著那些生命用心生存的各種方式，是激發自我潛能的重要動力。

　　大象為了喝水，可以在高溫烈日下長途跋涉上百公里甚至數星期之久；岩石峭壁的堅硬石塊，可以長出樹木、花草；黃沙滾滾、草木不生的土地，可以因一場雨而綠意盎然、生氣蓬勃；一隻掉入溪流的小蟲，就好像人掉進尼加拉瓜大瀑布，它本能的奮力掙扎、游向岸邊。這些展現生存韌性的例子是多麼的振奮人心！

　　一位朋友聊起他在偏僻的海邊服役時，有幾次食物只剩麵粉和水，柴火因管制無法隨時取用，為了止飢，他直接拿麵粉加水，食指當筷子攪拌後喝下肚，肚子沒了飢餓感，填飽肚子的任務就完成了。如果沒有水，口含著麵粉一樣可以下肚，在任何環境下，目的是解決飢餓感，摒除自己對於食物的喜好，感受胃要的是什

43. Resilience in Survival

If we can have three meals a day and be satisfied, we should feel grateful and appreciate it. A meal that we find easy to finish might be a struggle for others in different parts of the world who cannot find this meal.

If our current life, work, family, and basic income are stable, we should feel content and happy. Many people only seek basic stability and happiness but cannot attain it. The standards of wealth and accumulation differ, but contentment in one's situation reflects richness and resilience.

Life on Earth, whether animal, plant, or insect, survives in challenging environments and finds ways to thrive. Observing and reflecting on how different lives survive is a powerful motivator for self-potential.

Elephants travel hundreds of kilometers under the scorching sun to find water; trees and plants grow in rocky cliffs; barren land turns green with just one rain; a small bug struggling in a stream fights as if it's falling into Niagara Falls. These examples of survival resilience are truly inspiring!

A friend shared how, during service at a remote seaside location, food was only flour and water, and firewood was not readily available. To satisfy hunger, he mixed flour with water and used his finger as a spoon. Even without water, he could eat flour directly. This demonstrates survival resilience by focusing on the goal of alleviating hunger, regardless of food preferences.

Survival resilience is an active attitude and motivation to adapt to any environment with the most suitable methods, rather than adhering to

麼，接納了任何可以解決饑餓感的食物，這就是生存的韌性。

　　生存韌性，是一種積極的態度和動力，在什麼樣的環境底下，就用最恰當的方式去應對，而不是用一些自我設限的原則或喜好厭惡的態度，去面對外在環境的變化，就如同自我成長領域裡所代表的接納度，也等同於同理心的境界。

　　順著逆境就能設法走出逆境，如同順水推舟、水到渠成的觀念，這就是生存的韌性。

self-imposed limitations or dislikes. It represents acceptance and empathy, similar to personal growth and understanding others.

Going with the flow in adversity can help navigate through it, akin to the concept of "smooth sailing." This is the essence of survival resilience.

44. 相信的迷思

　　學習、模仿或複製別人成功經驗，對於生活上某方面的需求而言，是捷徑也是不錯的方式，可以省去摸索的時間甚至失敗的結果，因此，成功的訊息或例證，就成為大家關注、相信而去搜尋的資訊，如果覺得可行，就會運用在自己身上，期待別人成功的結果也能夠發生在自己身上。

　　因為相信而模仿、複製，因此得到成功，從此會深信不疑「相信」是很棒的方法，然而，如果相信的結果是失敗，有時候會認為是自己的問題，其實，世事千變萬化，並非一個觀念就可以適用所有的事情，別人呈現在我們眼前的是一個結果的現象，然而過程是什麼，或許才是我們必須瞭解的重點，在「相信」之前，要先推敲「相信標的物」是什麼，才不會因此陷入相信的迷思，有些可以相信，有些必須瞭解其中的真實性。

　　時下很多商品的文宣、廣告，為了引起注意、增加吸引力或大大提高商品的知名度，找了知名、相關頭銜人士或符合商品效益的人替商品代言，強調商品使用後的優點，希望大家經由對知名人士和形象的喜愛、崇拜、信任，進而認同代言的商品，最終目的就是創造商品的銷售量和收益，如果買賣雙方都受益，那當然是最好的結果。

　　某些廣告，找來身材姣好、穠纖合度、凍齡美貌、具備外形吸引力的人士，為減重、美容代言，說明使用後的好處，讓消費者「相信」會因為使用他們代言的商品後，也能和他們一樣，然而，這些或許只是廣告的表面現象而已，我會有一些反向思考的想法和推敲其中的可信度：

44. The Myth of Belief

Learning, imitating, or copying the success of others can be a shortcut and an effective way to meet certain life needs. It can save time spent on exploration and even prevent failure. As a result, successful messages or examples become information that people pay attention to, believe in, and search for. If something seems feasible, they apply it to themselves, hoping that the success of others will also happen to them.

When someone succeeds by believing, imitating, or copying, they will firmly believe that "belief" is a great method. However, if the result of that belief is failure, they might sometimes think the problem lies with themselves. In reality, the world is ever-changing, and no single concept can apply to everything. What others present to us is merely the phenomenon of a result. Perhaps it is the process we need to understand. Before believing, we must first scrutinize the object of our belief to avoid falling into the trap of blind faith. Some things can be believed, while others require us to understand their authenticity.

Nowadays, many product advertisements and promotions are designed to attract attention, increase appeal, or significantly boost the product's popularity. They invite well-known, credentialed individuals or people who align with the product's benefits to endorse it. These advertisements emphasize the advantages of using the product, hoping that people will, through admiration, worship, or trust in the celebrity, recognize the endorsed product. The ultimate goal, of course, is to boost sales and revenue. If both the buyer and seller benefit, that's the best result.

- 知名人士強調商品的優點，無論商品敘述的多麼美好，他是身歷其境、確實用過或確實獲利而後代言？還是純粹只是商業利益代言？如果是前者，那些優點的真實性、當時的環境因素、客觀性和可信度有多少？是不是適合、符合自己需要？如果是後者，那麼就比較沒有參考價值了。

- 坊間減重、美容代言，都是由身材玲瓏有緻的女子展現好身材和容貌，讓我們看到之後因羨慕、期待而產生「我要跟她一樣」的想法，進而相信那些代言人的說詞而消費購買，然而，我還是會先回到問題的原點去思考：那些代言人之前有多胖或不好看在哪裡？是使用多久而有現在的身材和容貌？從肥胖到停止使用那些產品之後，目前這樣的身材，維持多久了？還是，只是找來身材好或美麗的人代言而已？這類型的產品，如果沒有親身經歷再代言，難免讓人感覺不實際。

相信，和產品對自己是否真的有幫助和實際需要有關，應該和代言者的名氣、長相、外形無關，如果只因為那些表面和外在的現象而相信，就會陷入相信的迷思。有些「相信」即使事後發現不適合也無傷大雅，例如：民生用品、衣服等等，有些「相信」就必須慎重，例如：理財、投資、用在自己身體的藥物（例如：某些民間所謂的醫療秘方和醫術、減重藥品、運動或醫療器材等等）、保養品、整形美容手術等等。

任何資訊，我們都可以當做參考，也可以相信都是好的，因為，或許確實有人因此受惠而願意分享，然而，每個人的狀況和環境因素可能不同，因此結果未必一樣，所以，在相信之後，還要理性的去瞭解背後的真實性，是否合乎常理、是否符合自己需要，這樣的相信，才是最踏實的。

相信自己的需要，清楚明白自己的選擇，是自我肯定、自信的展現，真的愛自己，會愛上自己的「相信」！

Some ads feature people with excellent figures, perfect proportions, ageless beauty, or physical attractiveness to endorse weight-loss products or beauty treatments, making consumers "believe" that by using the same products, they can achieve the same results. However, this may just be the surface of the advertisement. I tend to think critically and question the credibility of these claims:

- When a celebrity emphasizes the product's advantages, no matter how wonderful the product seems, did they actually experience it? Did they truly use it and benefit from it, or is it purely a commercial endorsement? If it's the former, how authentic are those advantages, considering the environmental factors, objectivity, and credibility? Does it suit my needs? If it's the latter, then it holds less reference value.

- Many weight-loss or beauty product endorsements feature women with shapely figures and attractive appearances, causing envy and making us think, "I want to look like her." This leads us to believe in the spokesperson's claims and make purchases. But I still return to the basic question: how overweight or unattractive were these spokespeople before? How long did it take to achieve their current look? How long have they maintained their figures after stopping the use of those products? Or were they simply chosen for their beauty and good figures to endorse the product? If the spokesperson has not personally experienced the product, it inevitably feels unrealistic.

Belief, and whether a product truly benefits and meets one's needs, should not be tied to the spokesperson's fame, appearance, or shape. If belief is based solely on surface appearances, one risks falling into the myth of belief. Some "beliefs" may not be harmful even if they turn out to be unsuitable, such as consumer goods or clothing. However, some beliefs require serious consideration, such as finance, investment, medicine （e.g., folk remedies, weight-loss drugs, exercise or medical equipment）, skincare products, and cosmetic surgery.

We can treat all information as a reference and believe that it is good because someone may have genuinely benefited and shared their experience. However, everyone's circumstances and environmental factors may differ, and the results may not be the same. Therefore, after believing, it's essential

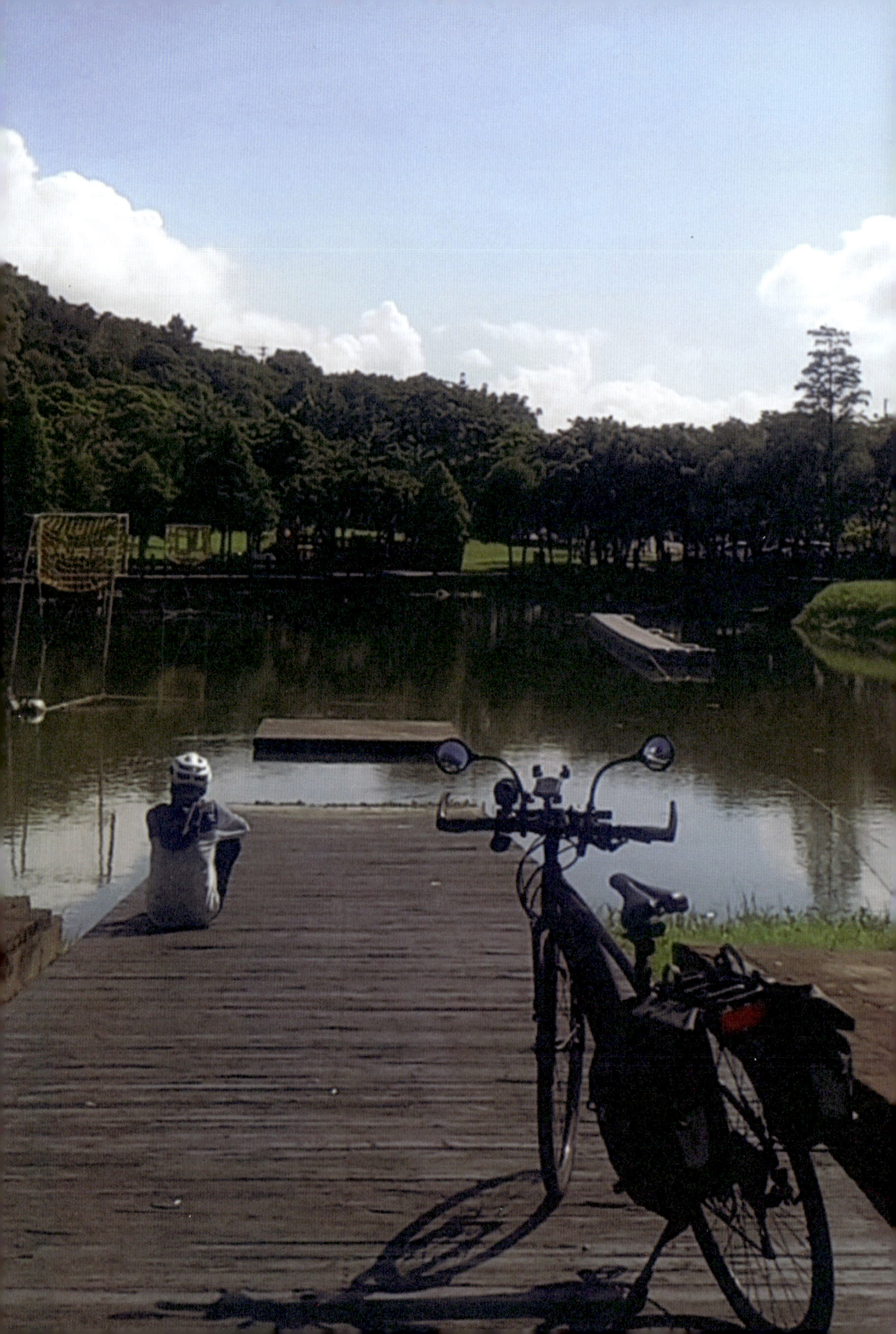

to rationally understand the authenticity behind it: does it make sense, and does it meet your needs? Only this kind of belief is truly solid.

Believing in your own needs and understanding your choices clearly is a manifestation of self-affirmation and confidence. Truly loving yourself means loving your "belief"!

45. 沒有困難只有方法

　　生活周遭不是每一件事都能順利圓滿，或按照自己的想法完成，所以有了「困難」的觀念。一旦有了困難的想法，潛意識多多少少會產生排斥或逃避的心態，思緒也會被困難的情緒圍繞，變造很難冷靜和清晰的去思索問題，即使依然面對問題設法解決，過程會產生壓力、煩躁、不愉快的負面情緒。

　　「沒有困難只有方法」，面對事情時，運用靈活的思緒可以源源不絕的想出方法，並且從中找到最恰當的方案，這是面對事情的正向態度，所有事情都可以找到其他各種的替代方法。

　　從小酷愛釣魚的我，因釣魚而體會一些「解決問題」的方法，這樣的領悟和態度，在日後運用到其他方面，道理是互通的。

　　「情境一」

　　國中因未滿 18 歲不能騎機車，搭公車要花錢，為了省錢，我總是全副武裝的背滿釣具，騎自行車到溪邊釣魚，單程路途大約 5~6 公里。有一天自行車被偷了，要釣魚怎麼辦？

- 跟同學借？萬一又被偷怎麼辦？而且借來借去很麻煩。
- 再買一輛？當時中古自行車約新台幣 1000 元左右，價格不便宜，即使跟父母說也沒辦法幾星期內就再買一輛。
- 搭公車？來回要新台幣 10 元，經常搭也是一筆不小的開銷，因為那個年紀，一星期可能會釣 5-7 天的魚，能省就省。

45. No Difficulty, Only Methods

Not everything in life can proceed smoothly or be completed according to one's wishes, so we develop the concept of "difficulty." Once the notion of difficulty arises, subconscious resistance or avoidance may occur, and our thoughts become overwhelmed by the emotions of difficulty, making it hard to calmly and clearly think through problems. Even if we face the issue and try to resolve it, the process can lead to pressure, frustration, and negative emotions.

"There is no difficulty, only methods." When facing challenges, flexible thinking allows us to continuously come up with solutions and find the most appropriate one. This is a positive attitude, as every problem can have various alternative solutions.

Since childhood, I have loved fishing, and through fishing, I've learned methods to "solve problems." This understanding and approach have been applicable to other areas of my life, as the principles are interconnected.

"Situation 1"

In middle school, I wasn't yet 18 and couldn't ride a motorbike, and taking the bus cost money. To save money, I always rode my bike, fully equipped with fishing gear, to the river, which was about 5 to 6 kilometers away. One day, my bike was stolen. What now?

- Borrow from a classmate? What if it gets stolen again? Borrowing is troublesome.
- Buy a new one? A used bike cost about NT$1,000 at the time—not cheap. Even if I told my parents, they wouldn't be able to buy one for

經過思索與衡量各種想法，最後，我選擇兩條腿用走的。決定用走的原因：

- 不搭公車省錢是最高原則。
- 買中古自行車，慢慢再跟父母商量。
- 5~6公里路程，當時年紀走路一般速度1小時約3~3.5公里，快步走1小時約4~5公里，我走1小時多就可以到溪邊，這是最划算的方法。

於是依然背著全副武裝的釣魚裝備走到溪邊釣魚。下雨有雨衣，流汗有毛巾，口渴有帶水，目標很明確—到溪邊釣魚，至於用什麼方法都行，所以我找到了當時最恰當的方法。

「情境二」

海邊釣魚，因未滿18歲不能騎機車，單程路途約45公里，只有搭公車一途，然而因為以下一些因素的考量，有時候會選擇騎自行車更方便：

- 即使趕早上第一班公車，到海邊最快也將近早上9點。
- 海釣必須看潮水，滿潮前約2~4小時開始垂釣效果最好，萬一滿潮是早上9點，至少要趕在7點前抵達。
- 夏天，海邊通常早上10點以後會吹起海風，有時候風太大會影響釣況，搭公車最快9點到，如果在8點之前抵達會更好。
- 夏天清晨約4：30~5點天色漸漸轉亮，如果可以配合潮水在清晨4：30之前垂釣，不但涼爽、舒服，魚也多。

既然我想要4：30到達，公車都是早上5：30才發車，勢必來不及！路程約45公里，騎自行車約要

2小時，因此我必須清晨2：30分左右出發，所以鬧鐘設定清晨2點起床，在自行車上綁上釣魚冰箱、綑著釣竿，背著全副裝備騎往海邊。我的目標很明確—天亮前抵達海邊，以當時的年齡，我找到了當時最好的方法。

只有方法沒有困難，一旦面對問題，心中馬上浮現：要的是什麼？目標是什麼？要如何選擇才是最符合需要的？思索哪個方法是最恰當的？然後朝目標前進，途中遇到什麼狀況再隨機應變

me in just a few weeks.

- Take the bus? A round trip cost NT$10. Frequent bus rides would add up since, at that age, I would go fishing 5 to 7 days a week. I had to save money where I could.

After thinking it over, I decided to walk. Here's why:

- Saving money by not taking the bus was my top priority.
- I could gradually convince my parents to buy a second-hand bike.
- The distance was about 5–6 kilometers. At that age, I could walk 3–3.5 kilometers per hour at a normal pace or 4–5 kilometers per hour walking quickly. It would take me a little over an hour to reach the river, making walking the most economical option.

So, I continued to walk to the river fully equipped for fishing. If it rained, I had a raincoat; if I sweat, I had a towel; if I was thirsty, I brought water. My goal was clear—get to the river for fishing, and the method didn't matter as long as it worked. I found the most appropriate solution at that time.

"Situation 2"

When fishing by the sea, I couldn't ride a motorbike because I wasn't 18 yet, and the trip was about 45 kilometers. The only option was to take the bus. However, considering several factors, sometimes cycling was more convenient:

- Even if I caught the first bus in the morning, I wouldn't reach the sea until almost 9 a.m.
- The best time to fish is 2–4 hours before high tide. If high tide was at 9 a.m., I had to arrive by 7 a.m. at the latest.
- In the summer, the sea breeze would start blowing after 10 a.m., sometimes making fishing conditions difficult. The bus wouldn't get me there until 9 a.m., so arriving before 8 a.m. would be better.
- In summer, dawn breaks around 4:30–5 a.m., and if I could start fishing before then, it would be cooler, more comfortable, and more fish would be around.

Since I wanted to arrive by 4:30 a.m., but the buses didn't start running until 5:30 a.m., I knew I would be late! The trip was about 45 kilometers, which would

與調整，面對人生的種種變化，應對也是如此。這樣的思考模式和行動力，就是自我肯定、相信自己的人格展現。

take me around two hours by bike. So, I set my alarm for 2:00 a.m. and rode my bike with my fishing gear strapped on. My goal was clear—arrive at the sea before dawn. At that age, I found the best method available.

There are only methods, no difficulties. Once faced with a problem, the question immediately becomes: what do I want? What is the goal? Which option best suits my needs? Then, I think about which method is the most appropriate and move toward the goal, adjusting as I encounter situations along the way. Life is much the same. This mindset and action reflect self-affirmation and belief in oneself.

46. 所有生命

　　生命的定義是什麼？我覺得：「存在，就是生命」。因此，會長大、會動、有反應和存在於時空裡的所有物類，都是生命，人類區分出來的動物、植物、昆蟲甚至塵土、物類，這些都是存在的事實，只是呈現出來的生命模式不同而已。

　　生命的表現和存在，無法用血液顏色、有沒有叫喊聲、會不會跑動、神經反應的方式這些觀點去論斷。如果以人類的觀點去論定地球甚至宇宙的生命存在模式，那是非常狹隘的。

　　紅色血液的流失，讓人類產生恐懼、害怕，所以覺得那是生命存在的現象。然而，植物、昆蟲，甚至蝦子、螃蟹、章魚，血液是透明的，如果蝦子、螃蟹、章魚是生命，那麼透明血液的植物、昆蟲呢？人類把生物體內的紅色物資，稱為血液；透明，稱為液體，其實，這些「流動的物質」，都是維持生命存在的現象，只是顏色不同而已。事實上，生命存在與血液顏色沒有絕對相應關係，無論血液呈現什麼顏色，都是生命。

　　音頻的關係，人類可以聽到某些動物的聲音，而這些動物所發出的聲音，因為人類聽得到，讓人類感覺是生命的反應。然而，絕大多數的魚類聲音人類聽不到，不過，人類依然認定牠們是生命，那麼，因為音頻關係而聽不到聲音的植物、昆蟲呢？或許只是因為它們的呼喊聲音，因為頻率的不同而讓人類聽不到，然而，無論音頻是不是聽得到，生命都是具體存在的。

　　人類會走動，知道有痛、緊張、恐懼的反應，所以，人類就認定和人類一樣會動、對神經和人類一樣有反應的物種，就是生

46. All Life

What is the Definition of Life?

I believe that "existence is life." Therefore, all entities that grow, move, respond, and exist in time and space are considered life. The classifications made by humans, such as animals, plants, insects, or even dust and various materials, all represent factual existence; they simply exhibit different life patterns.

The manifestation and existence of life cannot be judged solely by the color of blood, the presence or absence of sounds, whether something can move, or how it reacts neurologically. If we were to determine the patterns of life on Earth or even in the universe from a human perspective, it would be exceedingly narrow-minded.

The loss of red blood causes fear in humans, leading us to perceive it as a phenomenon of life. However, plants, insects, and even shrimp, crabs, and octopuses have transparent blood. If shrimp, crabs, and octopuses are considered life, then what about the transparent-blooded plants and insects? Humans refer to the red substances within living organisms as blood and the transparent ones as liquids. In reality, these "flowing substances" all contribute to the maintenance of life; they merely differ in color. In fact, there is no absolute correlation between the color of blood and the existence of life. Regardless of what color the blood is, it signifies life.

Due to audio frequencies, humans can hear certain animal sounds. The fact that humans can perceive these sounds gives the impression of a response to life. However, the sounds produced by the vast majority of fish

命。其實，即使植物不會走動，它的根一樣會不斷的延伸，枝、葉，不斷的生長，葉子會掉落，新葉子會不斷的長出來，這就是生命的具體象徵，只要是生命，都會有「痛」的感覺和反應，只因呈現的方式不同，我們人類感受不到而已，即便如此，也無法否定各類萬物以不同樣貌存在的事實。

空氣、水、溫度、塵土甚至宇宙的灰塵、隕石、星體和任何物類，都是生命存在的事實。

人類無法用自己的生命模式，去認定哪些生命模式的存在或不存在，而要用相同的態度去和所有的生命物類相處。所有生命都有它存在的價值和意義，用心體會它們存在的模式和我們有哪些的不同，用同樣珍惜人類的態度去珍惜它們。有了這份心思和細膩，心，會變得柔軟，情，會因而懂得珍惜。

兔子雲

are inaudible to humans. Nonetheless, humans still recognize them as life. So, what about plants and insects that emit sounds but are inaudible due to frequency differences? Perhaps their cries are simply beyond the range of human hearing. Regardless of whether these sounds can be heard, life exists concretely.

Humans move and experience reactions such as pain, tension, and fear, leading us to define as life those species that can move and respond neurologically like humans. In truth, even if plants do not move, their roots continuously extend, and their branches and leaves grow. Leaves fall, and new ones continually sprout. This is a concrete symbol of life. Any form of life experiences feelings and reactions to "pain," just expressed differently— humans simply cannot perceive it. Even so, this does not negate the fact that all things exist in different forms.

Air, water, temperature, dust, and even cosmic dust, meteors, celestial bodies, and any material are all manifestations of life's existence.

Humans cannot determine the existence or non-existence of life patterns based on their own mode of existence. Instead, we should interact with all life forms with a similar attitude. Every form of life has its own value and significance. We should earnestly appreciate the patterns of their existence and recognize our differences. With a mindset of cherishing all life forms as we do our own, our hearts become softer, and our emotions learn to appreciate.

47. 心情的旅行

　　面對每天每天幾乎一成不變的生活模式、工作形態，會很期待有個休息的日子，例假日、節慶長假、特休等等，成為可以安排遊玩、渡假、消遣的重要時刻，適度的休閒的確可以放鬆心情、釋放壓力，為機械式的生活和緊繃的心境做個潤滑調適。

　　仔細想想，每逢星期假日和特定的休假日，所有室內或戶外的休閒場合幾乎都是人山人海，讓原本安排好的休閒旅遊，因為塞車而煩燥、疲累；景點到處都是擁擠人潮的無形壓力；為了某些參觀或休閒而必須排隊又長長的人龍；住宿飲食的品質不如預期，反而感到疲憊和負擔。往往在休假結束後，心情、壓力非但沒有釋放，似乎感覺更加疲累、煩躁，對於這樣的「累休閒」，好像也無感的一直重覆循環著。

　　有一次全家安排了大湖鄉的採草莓，出發後卻因為高速公路上斷斷續續的塞車耗了 2 個多小時，抵達公館交流道到已經中午 12 點多，我依照塞車情況判斷，開到大湖鄉可能還需 40 分鐘~1 小時，如果繼續開，大概要下午 1~2 點才能抵達，如果中間休息一下吃個午餐，恐怕要 2~3 點才會到，通常遇到這種狀況會怎麼應對？繼續開車嗎？吃個午餐再走嗎？

　　如果繼續開車，下午 1~2 點抵達一定飢腸轆轆又疲累了，用餐後再採草莓，時間壓力讓休閒、放鬆的感覺已經沒有了。如果先吃午餐再往目的地，時間也一樣不很充裕，一樣沒有放鬆。旅遊的目的是什麼？不外乎就是希望放鬆、愉快。既然塞在路上，除非是已經安排的旅行團或一定要到達既定行程的一些因素，否則未必要堅持前往規劃好的目的地。

47. A Journey of the Mind

Faced with the almost unchanging daily routine and work schedule, one often looks forward to a day of rest. Weekends, holidays, and vacations become important times to plan for fun, relaxation, and leisure. Proper leisure can indeed help relax the mind, relieve stress, and smooth out the mechanical nature of life and tense emotions.

But if you think about it, during weekends and holidays, most indoor or outdoor leisure spots are packed with people. The well-planned getaway may be ruined by traffic jams, leaving you feeling frustrated and exhausted. The crowds at popular attractions create invisible pressure. The long lines for activities or sights, and the below-expectation quality of food and lodging, often leave you feeling burdened and more tired than before. Many times, after a vacation, rather than feeling refreshed, one feels even more drained and annoyed. This kind of "exhausting leisure" repeats itself without much change.

Once, my family planned a trip to Dahu Township to pick strawberries. We spent more than two hours stuck in intermittent traffic on the highway, and by the time we reached the Gongguan interchange, it was already past noon. Based on the traffic situation, I estimated it would take another 40 minutes to an hour to get to Dahu Township. If we continued, we might arrive around 1 or 2 p.m., and if we stopped for lunch along the way, it could be 2 or 3 p.m. before we reached our destination. In this situation, what would you do? Keep driving? Stop for lunch and then proceed?

If we had kept driving, we would have arrived hungry and exhausted by 1 or 2 p.m. After lunch, there wouldn't be much time left to pick strawberries, and the relaxation we had hoped for would have already

心中想到了公館鄉還有一個不錯的莊園，而且有可愛動物園區可以近身互動，當下提議更改行程，家人也一致贊成，於是方向盤一轉，中午12點多就享用了客家精緻美食，整個下午在莊園的美景、音樂、花草、小動物中輕鬆愜意的渡過，草莓行程呢？期待下次囉。

　　人們因為打拼事業、為了家庭生計，忙碌的日子似乎已經占據了每天的時間，好像很難有屬於自己的休閒時光，何妨試著把休假的心情融入到每天的生活裡，眼前的一景一物，其實天天都可以有屬於自己的心情休假日，心裡擁有一點一滴、隨時隨地的渡假心情，勝過刻意安排的實際旅行，當心中有了「心靈旅行」的喜悅，那麼，再次安排實際旅行時，將會有不同的想法、做法和感受。

　　寒冷的冬季裡，某個難得出現溫暖陽光的日子，依然很習慣又機械式的開著車在市區拜訪客戶，接近中午時分，陽光曬在駕駛座上倍感溫暖、舒暢，車子剛巧經過大安森林公園，等紅綠燈時眼光瞄了一下公園的綠樹花草，突然心情起了一個莫名的反應，我明白了我的心在告訴我什麼！

　　停妥車子，到超商買了杯熱咖啡、小飯糰、小盒水果盤，走進公園裡，找了一個太陽可以直曬的椅子坐了下來，享受著暖呼呼的冬陽、綠樹、花草及手中的輕食，偶爾跑出來閒晃的松鼠、鴿子、麻雀、飄逸舞動的葉樹、熙來攘往的人們，一個人輕鬆自在的渡過屬於自己的「午餐休假」時光。

　　午餐，未必是一成不變的囫圇吞棗、辦公室便當、自助餐點菜，偶爾隨機變動一下，即使只是短暫的時間，已經讓心情有了休假、旅行的感覺和真實的放鬆，一個人、一點點的時間，也可以讓自己有「渡假」的心情。

　　其實，心情對了哪裡都好，如果問我最喜歡什麼樣的旅行，我會說：在家渡假！

disappeared. If we stopped for lunch first, time would still be tight, and there wouldn't be much relaxation. What is the purpose of travel? Ultimately, it's to relax and enjoy. Given the traffic, unless you're part of a group tour or have some other must-visit reason, there's no need to stubbornly insist on sticking to the original destination.

I remembered that Gongguan Township had a nice estate with a petting zoo where you could interact with cute animals. I suggested we change our plans, and my family agreed. By 12:30 p.m., we were enjoying a delicious Hakka meal and spent the entire afternoon leisurely walking through the estate, surrounded by music, flowers, greenery, and adorable animals. As for picking strawberries? We'll save that for next time.

Many people are so busy with their careers and providing for their families that it seems hard to find any personal leisure time. But why not try integrating the mindset of a vacation into everyday life? Every view, every moment could be your personal holiday. Carrying a vacation mindset throughout your day, even a "mental vacation," can be more fulfilling than meticulously planning a physical one. With a joyful "journey of the mind," your next actual trip will bring new ideas, approaches, and feelings.

On a rare sunny winter day, while I was habitually and mechanically driving around the city visiting clients, the midday sun shone warmly on the driver's seat. I happened to pass Daan Forest Park, and while waiting at a red light, I caught a glimpse of the green trees and flowers. Suddenly, I felt an inexplicable reaction inside. I knew exactly what my heart was telling me!

I parked the car, bought a hot coffee, a small rice ball, and a box of fruit from a convenience store, and walked into the park. I found a bench bathed in sunlight and sat down, enjoying the warm winter sun, the greenery, flowers, and light meal in my hand. Squirrels, pigeons, sparrows, dancing leaves, and the flow of people passing by—it was a peaceful, leisurely lunch break just for me.

Lunch doesn't always have to be a hurried, routine affair, gobbled down at the office or from a cafeteria. Sometimes, just a small, spontaneous change can make even a short amount of time feel like a mini-vacation, a real moment of relaxation. One person, a little time—it's enough to feel like a vacation.

In the end, when your mind is at ease, any place can feel wonderful. If you ask me what kind of vacation I like best, I'd say: A holiday at home!

48. 對牠好嗎？

　　越來越多人開始願意飼養小動物，當成生活的潤滑劑、心靈的寄託，甚至是使命。狗、貓、兔子、鳥、魚、各種琳瑯滿目的動物，人們依照自己的喜好，選擇了喜歡的「寵物」和自己生活在一起。是什麼樣的原因，讓自己選擇這種「寵物」來飼養，可愛？孤單？流行？憐憫？彰顯身份？謀利……？

　　無論什麼想法之下飼養了牠，自己仔細想想，是否有用面對人類的同樣生命角度去照顧牠？還是只是「養」著來達到自己需求的目的而已（例如：陪伴、玩伴、賺錢號召等等）？卻根本忽略了動物也有自己的生命需求和照顧？

　　動物，原本是生活在野生大地，和飼主生活在一起之後，是幸？還是不幸？我們都知道：牠只是飼主的過客，飼主卻是牠的全部。因為被飼主選中，牠一生的吃喝拉撒睡、生活品質的好壞和型態，完全無法自己決定，飼主用什麼方式對牠，只能全盤接受，無從選擇，美其名「寵物」，是否等同於軟禁、玩物？

　　以人類自己的角度看待寵物，好像比在野外幸福的多（例如：有吃、有睡、有玩、安全又漂亮……等等），然而這是人類以自己的標準和生活模式而這麼認為，我們是否瞭解過寵物的感受呢？

　　因為寵愛與關懷，越來越多的飼主願意為自己的寵物去花費甚至比自己生活還多的費用，買高價飼料、漂亮打扮、高檔服飾和配件、豪華居住設備……，這真的讓人感到非常的溫暖和喜悅，能為自己所愛而付出，看到自己的寵物可愛又漂亮，心情是很愉悅的，

48. Are We Treating Them Well?

More and more people are raising pets, treating them as a soothing balm for life, a source of emotional support, or even a mission. Dogs, cats, rabbits, birds, fish—the variety of pets is vast, and people choose their companions based on personal preferences. But why do we choose a certain pet to raise? Is it because they're cute? Because we're lonely? Because it's trendy? Out of compassion? To show status? Or for profit?

Whatever the reason, we must ask ourselves: Do we care for our pets with the same regard we would show a human life? Or are we merely "keeping" them to fulfill our own needs （companionship, fun, profit, etc.）, while neglecting their true needs as living beings?

In the wild, animals are free to live as they please. Once they join a household, is that a blessing or a curse? We all know that to a pet, we are their entire world. They have no say over their food, shelter, and lifestyle; they must accept whatever their owner provides. Their life is determined by our choices, and they have no power to change it. Though we call them "pets," does this mean they are merely our playthings, even prisoners?

From a human perspective, it seems pets live a better life with us than in the wild—they have food, shelter, safety, and sometimes even luxury. But are we considering their feelings?

Out of love and care, many pet owners are willing to spend more on their pets than they do on themselves, buying expensive food, fancy outfits, and high-end accessories. This dedication is heartwarming. Yet if we could treat pets with the same empathy and care that we give to other people, we

如果我們能以寵物的角度去對待牠，如同人與人之間相處的照顧和同理心，真的寵了動物也寵了自己！

動物和人一樣，都有個性、脾氣，也會生老病死，只是語言不通或表達方式不同而無法暢行無阻的雙向互動，因此人們會忽略或不懂或不在意動物在生活行為上的反應或改變，很多動物生病、不舒服、疼痛，牠們不見得會用哀號來表答，或是以人們不理解的方式呈現（例如：趴著不動的時間變長或次數變多，誤以為休息；食量減少，以為又挑食……等等），讓人們不以為意而疏於照顧。

一隻體重約5公斤的狗，在1~2個月中慢慢瘦到約4公斤，主人很開心的說他的狗瘦了1公斤，減肥成功！我當下直覺是：是嗎？減肥成功嗎？我用另一個角度去思考這件事。

1~2個月內體重減少1公斤對人們來說沒什麼，動物呢？5公斤瘦到約4公斤，這是體重減少了20%！如同70公斤的人2個月內瘦到56公斤，體重一口氣下降14公斤（如果有從事減重計畫或許另當別論），我們會覺得是減肥成功？還是會去醫院詳細身體檢查呢？如果以人們的標準看待動物，恐怕已經錯失治療的時機，面對人們或動物的體重問題，應該以客觀又明確的百分比的比例來判斷，而不是用人們的體重標準來衡量。

因為對寵物的關心，越來越多飼主明白幾乎飼養的寵物壽命都比人短，以狗貓為例壽命大約10~22年，人類的1年約等於狗貓的5~7年，除了珍惜這短暫的緣份，是否也注意到寵物的健康照顧呢？對於寵物的關懷，我會這樣的思考著。

有了這個想法，我再繼續思索下去，人們如果急性腸胃炎、嚴重拉肚子、外傷、骨折、因生病而影響飲食或活動力……等等，會拖多久才去醫院檢查？馬上？半天（已經是狗狗的4天了）？1天（已經7天）？還是7天（已經49天）？甚至不管？還是讓症狀拖到自己好？我們會覺得現在沒空帶狗狗去醫院明天再說，而且狗狗才生病「1天」而已，應該沒關係。

上面的例證反向思考，如果是人，誰有能耐罹患例如急性腸胃炎、嚴重拉肚子甚至骨折潰爛等等症狀，等了7天才去醫院治療？然後可以順利又容易醫治？我們常聽過飼主說，怎麼寵物才生病沒幾天就走了？現在總算明白，其實是我們拖太久了！

would be truly honoring them—and ourselves.

Like humans, animals have personalities, temperaments, and they experience birth, aging, illness, and death. Because they cannot communicate with us in human language, we often miss the signs when something is wrong. A pet may not express pain or discomfort the way we expect, so we might overlook or misunderstand changes in behavior, thinking they are merely resting or being picky with food, when in fact they might be suffering.

For example, a dog weighing around 5 kg gradually loses weight over one or two months and now weighs only about 4 kg. The owner is pleased, thinking the dog has successfully lost weight. But my immediate thought was: Is that really the case?

Losing 1 kg in one or two months might not seem like much for a human, but for a dog, that's a 20% drop in body weight! That's like a 70 kg person suddenly dropping to 56 kg in two months. Would we consider that a successful diet, or would we go to the hospital for a thorough check-up? When we use human standards to evaluate animals, we might miss the crucial signs that something is wrong. We should use clear, objective percentages, not human weight benchmarks, to assess pet health.

Because pet owners care deeply for their animals, they understand that most pets have shorter lifespans than humans. For example, dogs and cats live around 10-22 years. One human year equals roughly 5-7 years for them. In addition to cherishing this short time together, are we also paying attention to their health?

Reflecting on this, I thought further. How long would a person wait before seeking medical attention for a condition like acute gastroenteritis, severe diarrhea, an injury, or a broken bone? Immediately? Half a day (which equals about four days for a dog)? One day (equivalent to seven days)? Seven days (equivalent to 49 days)? Would we just let it pass, hoping the problem resolves itself?

The reverse is true for pets. If a dog suffers from something like gastroenteritis or a broken bone, waiting a full day to seek medical help is like a person enduring such symptoms for a week. Delaying care can make treatment much harder. We've all heard owners say, "My pet was only sick

動物在野外，或許無法如同跟著飼主而食物不缺、裝扮漂亮、生活安全甚至長壽，然而，牠們可以行動自由，知道要找什麼吃來平衡飲食甚至治療疾病，會尋找地方躲避寒冬，不會因鍊條綁住、籠子關著而凍死、餓死，當飼主選擇了牠的同時，也已經決定了牠的一生用什麼方式渡過，而且別無選擇。

　　所有生命都平等、尊重且重要，尤其是選擇了和自己生活的寵物，因為牠而滿足、填補了人們的需求，我們更應該以牠們的生命角度去照顧、寵愛牠們，如同與不同的人用不同的同理心去互動，最能確實照顧、愉快相處、面面俱到。

　　當我們看著心愛的寵物用那種可愛、無辜、崇拜的眼神看著我們的時候，再次問問自己：「我真的對牠好嗎」？當然啦，所以，就以牠的立場去愛牠吧！

for a few days before passing away." Now we understand that it's not just a matter of days—the real issue was that we waited too long to act.

In the wild, animals might not have the comforts of living with humans, such as food, warmth, safety, and even longevity, but they do have freedom. They know how to find food to balance their diet or cure illness, seek shelter to survive the winter, and are not bound by chains or confined to cages where they might freeze or starve to death. When we choose a pet, we also decide how it will live its life, without giving it a choice.

All life is equal, deserving of respect and care. Especially when it comes to pets, whose presence fills a need in our lives, we should look after them from their perspective. Loving them as we love others, with empathy, ensures their well-being and happiness.

When we look into the innocent, adoring eyes of our beloved pets, we should ask ourselves: "Am I really treating them well?" Of course, we should love them from their point of view!

49. 成功

　　成功的人分享他的成功經驗，無論是否適合於自己，都有它的一番過程和道理。那麼，什麼才是成功呢？

　　追求成功，擁有因成功而來的那份成就感，誰都喜歡那種滿足感所帶來的喜悅。成功，可以是物質層面的成功，也可以是精神層面的成功，無論同時擁有或僅有其中之一都無妨，最重要是在那個成功的滿足點，也就是達到自己能力可以完成的滿足點而心滿意足，不會毫無止境的一直追求無邊無際的「大」成功。

　　物質層面的成功，是具象的目標，無需和任何人做比較，可以依照自己的能力、生活狀況及整個人生的想法去做規劃（例如：財富目標、醫療規劃），有了明確的目標，什麼時候達到了，就是成功的滿足點，往後的日子，會因為感到此生已無財力壓力（並非很有錢才算無財力壓力）、醫療（在第一篇［照顧自己健康］提過）等等的後顧之憂，會讓自己的心情平順而輕鬆，這就是屬於自己的物質層面的成功，是真正的成功。

　　精神層面的成功，是隱性的成長，沒有目標設定、沒有時間期限，是讓自己珍惜自己、愛自己的心靈層面的滿足。我們都希望自己可以情緒平穩、客觀面對一切，而這樣的想法之後去學習別人的成長經驗時，更要把那些方法慢慢體會，慢慢成為真正適合自己的方法，無論是向外學習或自我修煉，當自己內心感到滿足、感到平順，這就是屬於自己的精神層面的成功，是真正的成功。

　　物質層面的成功，比較容易有一個自我設立的標準，達到目標後，那種成就感是自我肯定，是開心的。精神層面的成功，或

49. Success

Successful individuals share their experiences, whether or not they fit others' situations, offering valuable insights and lessons. So, what exactly is success?

The pursuit of success brings a sense of accomplishment that everyone enjoys, along with the joy of fulfillment. Success can be either material or spiritual, and it doesn't matter if you achieve both or just one. What matters most is reaching a personal point of satisfaction, based on your abilities, without endlessly chasing boundless "big" success.

Material success is a tangible goal, without needing to compare yourself to others. It should align with your abilities, life circumstances, and long-term plans （e.g., wealth targets, healthcare）. When you reach that clear goal, that's your success point. From then on, life becomes smoother because concerns like financial pressures or medical worries （as mentioned in the first section on [Taking Care of Your Health]） are alleviated. This type of material success leads to a more relaxed and balanced state, which is genuine success.

Spiritual success, on the other hand, is an internal growth process. It has no set goals or deadlines but is more about achieving inner satisfaction and self-love. We all want to remain emotionally stable and objective in facing life's challenges. When learning from others' experiences, it's essential to adapt their methods slowly, transforming them into something that suits us personally. Whether through external learning or self-reflection, once our hearts feel content and at peace, that is our true spiritual success.

許難以訂定時間表，然而改變是在悄悄之中，而且時間越久，會覺得越來越好，心境會越來越知足、滿足，那種「成就」，是生命的成功。

成功，就是物質與精神的同步滿足及對比的平衡，兩者沒有高低的差異，也就是接受和滿足現在的自己，這就是人生的成功。

成功不在於比較，在於心靈的充實和滿足。無論是家財萬貫或家徒四壁、位高權重或市井小民、大老闆或薪水階級，這些都未必表示成功。

要清楚知道自己的個性和能力，可以選擇的是什麼樣的人生模式，即使只是三餐溫飽，然而心情愉快、充實、滿足、無憂無慮、自由自在，而且也享受、接受這樣的模式，那就是成功，因為，瞭解、接受、開心、自在的人生，才是真正的成功。

或許擁有財富、產業、權位，是一些人所羨慕或追求的，如果因此失去自己的時間、行動的自由、生活的隱私，甚至失去親情、感情、真心、真情，我想，那應該不是成功的人所想要擁有的。

每個人的成功都值得參考和學習，然而在努力不懈的過程，除了辛苦之外，其實是可以同時擁有放鬆與快與慢的心境的。努力衝刺固然重要，然而心境的滿足，才是真正重要，如果成功背後伴隨而來的是空虛、病痛或孤單，那是多麼的可惜，心靈是無法愉悅的！

觀察了週遭一些朋友的生活方式和想法，讓我發現成功的定義很簡單，其實就是心境上的滿足和幸福的感覺！

Material success often has a self-set standard, and reaching that goal brings self-affirmation and joy. Spiritual success, while more elusive and harder to schedule, grows over time, leading to greater contentment and fulfillment. That sense of achievement reflects a successful life.

Ultimately, success is about balancing material and spiritual satisfaction, with neither being superior to the other. It's about accepting and being content with who you are, which is the true essence of life success.

Success isn't about comparisons but about inner enrichment and fulfillment. Whether wealthy or poor, powerful or ordinary, an entrepreneur or a salaried worker—none of these alone define success.

Understanding your personality and capabilities, choosing the lifestyle that suits you, and enjoying that choice—even if it means just having enough to eat—brings contentment, joy, and peace of mind. That is success, because understanding, accepting, and enjoying life as it is represents true success.

For some, wealth, property, or power might be desirable. But if these come at the cost of time, freedom, privacy, or even relationships, emotions, and sincerity, I don't think that's what truly successful people would want.

Everyone's definition of success is worth studying. But during the journey toward success, while hard work is necessary, we should also cultivate a mindset of relaxation and balance. Pushing hard is crucial, but mental satisfaction is more important. If success brings emptiness, illness, or loneliness, how unfortunate that would be! The soul cannot feel joy under those conditions.

Observing the lifestyles and thoughts of friends around me, I realize the definition of success is simple—it's about feeling satisfied and happy in life!

50. 不完美的完美

　　絕對的完美，只在天堂，相對的完美，就在心房。完美或不完美，在於心境的轉念。真心的接受了現在的人事物，讓心情感到滿足，就是完美；如果內心感到不滿意、不滿足、不愉快，那麼無論表面表現的多麼美好，感覺不對，就是不完美。

　　我們會在某些不完美中，擁有另一種完美，也就是說，如果不是因為一些不完美的過程或磨練，就不會演變出後來的完美，可以這麼想：或許之前的完美變成了不完美，如果已經難以回覆為之前的完美，那麼，能夠認清事實懂得放下與轉念，接受這樣的不完美，可以讓我們發現另一個完美，拋開完美變成不完美的事實，我們會更開心的擁有不完美之後得到的完美，這就是心境轉念後對現況感到滿足的一種心情。

　　「上帝為你關一扇門，卻開了另一扇窗」、「失之東隅，收之桑隅」，因為不完美之後得到的完美，會令人份外珍惜，就好像以下的例子：

- 有些人在經歷負債累累、財富破產、經商失敗、感情挫折、人生挫敗等等重大打擊和嚴厲磨練後，沒有因此頹廢喪志，反而更加自我激勵、奮發圖強、突破逆境，在日後的商場和人際關係互動上，能夠謹慎、圓融、順利，有著因之前的不完美而獲得更為完美的現況和心境。

50. Perfect Imperfection

Absolute perfection only exists in heaven, while relative perfection lives in our hearts. Whether something is perfect or imperfect depends on how we shift our mindset. When we truly accept our current situation and feel content, that is perfection. If we feel unsatisfied or unhappy, no matter how good things seem on the surface, it's not truly perfect.

Sometimes, in moments of imperfection, we find a different kind of perfection. In other words, if not for certain imperfect processes or struggles, we wouldn't evolve into later stages of perfection. We can think of it this way: perhaps what was once perfect has now become imperfect, and if it can't return to its former state, recognizing, letting go, and changing our mindset can lead us to discover another form of perfection. By moving past the notion of what once was perfect becoming imperfect, we find more joy in the perfection that follows imperfection. This shift in perspective brings a new level of contentment.

"When God closes a door, He opens a window," and "One loss can lead to another gain." The perfection that arises from imperfection is often more cherished. Consider these examples:

- Some people, after experiencing significant setbacks such as financial ruin, business failure, emotional difficulties, or life challenges, don't fall into despair. Instead, they motivate themselves, work harder, and overcome adversity. Later, they become more cautious, adaptable, and successful in both business and personal interactions, having achieved a more perfect state of life and mindset due to their earlier

- 在親子問題、人際關係、夫妻感情中感到困擾、煩惱、徬徨無助，有人因此走上成長之路，重新認識自己、探索根源、尋求方法，之後得到了當下最佳的解決方式，即使某些情況未必可以完全解決，然而心情、視野因此變得更加豁達，不再拘泥於牛角尖，是人生的另一種收穫。

如果沒有不完美的挫折，就不會有自我成長與突破的想法和機會，更不會發現另一扇窗的廣闊美好，這種不完美，讓我們有了另一種完美。

接受不完美，就是完美。無論是什麼樣完美，心境經過轉換和改變之後，就會找到人生的另一片天空。

imperfections.

- Others may face challenges in parenting, relationships, or marriages, causing confusion, frustration, or helplessness. Some, however, embark on a journey of self-growth, rediscovering themselves, exploring the root causes, and seeking solutions. Even if not all problems are fully resolved, they gain a broader perspective and a more relaxed mindset, no longer stuck in futile struggles. This is another type of life achievement.

Without these imperfect setbacks, we wouldn't have the motivation or opportunity for self-growth and breakthroughs. We wouldn't discover the beauty of the wide-open window awaiting us. This imperfection gives rise to a different kind of perfection.

Accepting imperfection is, in itself, perfection. Whatever form of perfection it may be, once we shift and change our mindset, we find a new sky in life.

51. 生命存在

　　在追尋自我探索、心靈成長，期待自己擁有陽光、積極、自信、簡單、自在的人生時，我感覺到：瞭解自我真實存在的價值與可貴，是最重要的根本。

　　生命的出現只有一次，是一條線段，有開始和結束，只有「目前」，以前沒有我，以後不會再有我。

　　如果地球的年齡如科學家所說的 46 億年，那麼我的生命，是在等待了 46 億年後才終於出現，這是多麼漫長又漫長的等待，然而，我，只有出現一次的機會而已，一旦生命結束就永遠不會再出現，而 46 億年的 N 次方、N= 無窮大，會一直無限延伸下去，自己，只是有限的線段，線段停止後，永遠不會再出現。

　　至少自己總算明白，經過 46 億年的漫長等待，我終於出現了，即使願意再等個 46 億年，甚至 46 億年 ×2 或 ×3......，然而沒有機會了，不可能再出現一個我，所以，生命是多麼的難能可貴，還有什麼比自己生命存在更可貴呢？沒有了自己，其他也一起消失。

　　在短暫生命存在的時空裡，有太多太多美好的事物等著去欣賞、體會、感動，哪怕只是一粒沙、一棵樹、一滴水、一陣風。因為，如果生命 100 歲，也只有 100 年的時間可以接觸那些美好的事物，生命結束後，永遠永遠沒有機會看到，在生命存在的現在，更應該好好珍愛自己。

　　生命即使 100 歲，和 46 億年相比根本微不足道，尤其往後還有更多的 46 億年，地球、宇宙繼續存在，自己已經不再出現，在世界各國、地球、宇宙，甚至 46 億年的時空裡，自己的存在可能

51. Existence of Life

In the pursuit of self-exploration and spiritual growth, aiming to live a life filled with sunshine, positivity, confidence, simplicity, and freedom, I have come to realize that understanding the true value and preciousness of one's existence is the most fundamental principle.

Life only happens once. It is a line segment with a beginning and an end, and it exists solely in the "now." Before, I did not exist, and after, I will never exist again.

If the Earth is truly 4.6 billion years old, as scientists claim, then my life appeared after waiting for 4.6 billion years—a tremendously long wait. However, I only have one chance to appear. Once my life ends, I will never return. The span of my existence is finite, while the 4.6 billion years that lie ahead will continue to stretch into infinity. I am but a limited segment, and when that segment stops, I will never appear again.

At the very least, I understand now that after 4.6 billion years of waiting, I have finally appeared. Even if I were willing to wait another 4.6 billion years, or even multiply that by 2 or 3, there would be no second chance. It is impossible for "me" to reappear, which makes life all the more precious. What could be more valuable than my existence? Without me, everything else vanishes too.

In this brief span of life, there are countless beautiful things waiting to be admired, experienced, and appreciated, even as small as a grain of sand, a tree, a drop of water, or a breeze. If I were to live for 100 years, that would still only grant me 100 years to experience these wonders. Once life ends, I

連一粒微小的灰塵都不如,如此短暫又渺小的生命,是選擇讓自己珍惜,還是在紛紛擾擾中耗盡而結束?

　　生命的可貴難以言喻,想想生命的出現僅有一次,要善待自己、關愛自己、照顧自己、做自己,如果沒有了自己什麼都是虛幻的。同樣的,用這樣的心情去面對其他生命,會懂得尊重和關愛,那種心情,是多麼溫暖、喜悅。

　　在書裡,提到了很多正面思考、陽光、自信、積極、成長各方面自我修煉的想法,而其中最基本的根源,就是源自於對「生命存在」的認知、體悟與感動。

　　領悟了自己生命的可貴,心,就會柔軟細膩;情,就會感動深刻。也就是:用感動的心,感受生命存在的一切。

will never have the opportunity to witness them again. Therefore, while life exists, I must cherish myself.

Even if life lasts for 100 years, it is insignificant compared to 4.6 billion years, especially considering that many more billions of years will follow. The Earth and the universe will continue, but I will no longer exist. In the vastness of the universe, I may be less significant than a speck of dust. In this short and fleeting life, will I choose to treasure myself or let it dissipate in the chaos?

The preciousness of life is beyond words. When I reflect on how life only appears once, I know I must treat myself well, love myself, care for myself, and be myself. Without "me," everything else is just an illusion. In the same way, when I approach other forms of life with this understanding, I will learn to respect and care for them. Such feelings are warm and joyful.

In books, I have come across many ideas on positive thinking, confidence, personal growth, and self-cultivation, but the fundamental root of all these concepts comes from the understanding and appreciation of "life's existence."

Once we realize the preciousness of our own life, our hearts become softer and more delicate; our emotions are more profound. In other words, we can experience everything that life offers with a heart full of gratitude.

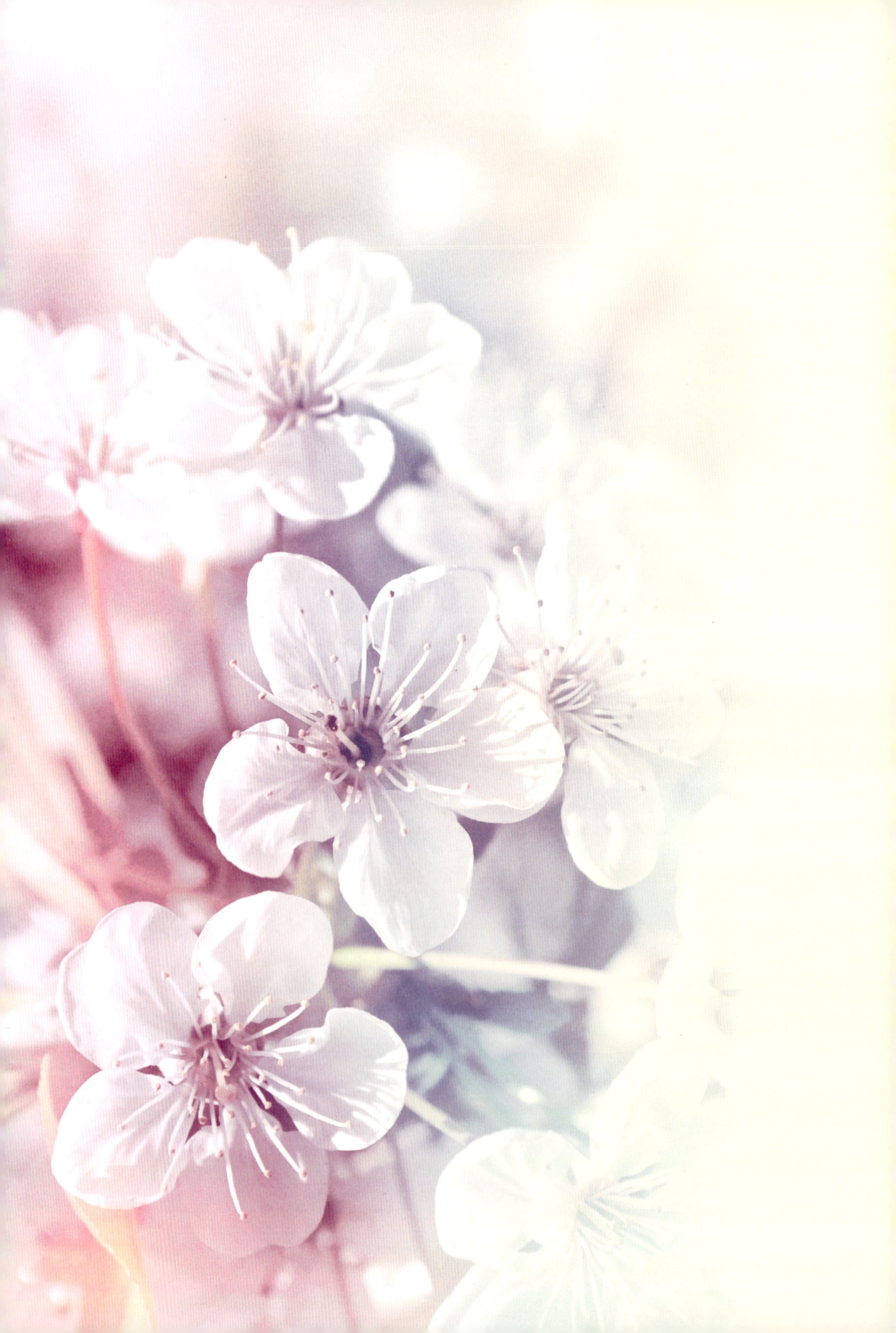

認識自己，提升內在

Knowing Yourself, Elevating the Inner Self

認識自己，不僅僅只是表層的瞭解個性，而是要更深入個性的根源和自我情緒好壞間的關連以及和周遭人互動的情緒反應，各種組合所產生的連結和結果。

Knowing oneself is not just about understanding one's surface personality traits. It's about digging deeper into the roots of these traits, understanding the emotional connections and reactions that arise in interactions with others, and recognizing how all of these elements come together to form outcomes.

伍、認識自己、提昇內在

　　認識自己？這似乎是很有趣的話題，幾乎每個人都覺得誰不認識自己呢？然而無論口中說的「認識」還是「不認識」，如果仔細想想、好好環顧四周（包括自己），有些人甚至每天都被大大小小的事情所淹沒、困擾，生氣、無助、爭鬥、情緒的反應，似乎負面多於正面。

　　誰不希望輕鬆、快樂？誰又喜歡負面情緒如影隨形？如果真的認識自己、瞭解自己，怎麼會讓自己陷入心情不佳、壓力重重的窘境呢？

　　我認識自己嗎？「我當然認識自己，我很清楚我的個性啊！」接著，我們會聽到下面的一些話：

- 「我知道我的個性很直，有時候講話會不小心傷到人，我是無心的。」

  （我瞭解我是心直口快、言語無心，所以別人應該要瞭解我和接受我無心的傷害？那麼，這是認識自己，卻可能傷到別人，蠻可惜的）

- 「我就是看不慣那種扭扭捏捏、拖泥帶水的個性，那種人很煩，很討人厭。」

  （我們都會有喜歡、討厭的人，然而把情緒表現出來的時候，同時也影響了自己的心情和行為，其實被討厭的人依然做他自己，那麼，何需讓自己有不好的感覺呢？）

- 「我做我喜歡的事，不喜歡的人或事情，就當做沒看到，我做我自己就好。」

  （我們可以排斥不喜歡的人、事、物，然而認識它與排斥它，是可以做出切割的，如果因為不喜歡而關閉這扇門，會讓自己失去很多客觀理解人、事、物的機會，盡量去認清世間萬物，更能認識完整的自己。）

　　上面那些存在於自己內在的思維，事實上並沒有讓自己的心境完全的自由、自在，因為，還是有某些的情境讓自己不喜歡、不快樂。

Part Five: Knowing Yourself, Elevating the Inner Self

Knowing oneself—this seems like an interesting topic. Most people would assume they know themselves, but if we pause to look around, including at ourselves, we might notice that many are still overwhelmed by daily challenges, anger, helplessness, conflict, and emotional turmoil. It seems negativity often outweighs positivity.

Who doesn't want to live a relaxed, joyful life? Who enjoys carrying negative emotions around all the time? If we truly understood and knew ourselves, how could we let ourselves fall into such states of stress and unhappiness?

Do I know myself? "Of course I do; I know my personality well!" Then we might hear statements like:

- "I know I'm blunt, and sometimes I accidentally hurt people with my words, but I don't mean to." (I understand that I am straightforward and don't mean harm, so others should understand and accept my unintentional hurts? This is knowing oneself, yet possibly hurting others—a shame.)

- "I just can't stand people who are indecisive or slow; they're so annoying!" (We all have people we like and dislike, but expressing such emotions also affects our own mood and behavior. The person we dislike will continue being themselves, so why let it disturb our own peace?)

- "I do what I like and ignore people or things I don't care for." (We can shut out people or things we dislike, but recognizing them and rejecting them are different. If we close the door on everything we dislike, we lose many opportunities to objectively understand the world and, in turn, ourselves.)

These internal thoughts and patterns don't necessarily lead to true freedom or peace of mind, as there will still be circumstances that upset us.

To truly know oneself is to be able to accept everything. For example, I might dislike someone and oppose their ideas, but I can understand why

真的認識自己，是可以接納一切的。例如：我討厭這個人、反對他的想法，然而我可以理解他為什麼會這麼想、這樣做。也就是說，我還是有喜怒哀樂，然而因為心境可以容納所有的不悅，也就能夠做出情緒和思想上的切割。

　　認識自己，不僅僅只是表層的瞭解個性而已，而是要更深入個性的根源和自我情緒好壞間的關連以及和周遭人互動的情緒反應，各種組合所產生的連結和結果，才是真正認識自己、瞭解自己，進一步讓自己的心境提昇到無為、平靜、自在、愉悅，那就是真正的認識自己、成長自己。

　　認識自己，從自我內在去深層探索，一層一層的深入根源，認清存在的意義和價值，瞭解生命的難能可貴，懂得珍惜自己又能夠盡量不妨礙他人，這樣的自己，才是真實的認識自己、接納自己。

they think or act that way. This means I still experience emotions, but I can compartmentalize my negative reactions and maintain emotional clarity.

Knowing oneself is not just about understanding one's surface personality traits. It's about digging deeper into the roots of these traits, understanding the emotional connections and reactions that arise in interactions with others, and recognizing how all of these elements come together to form outcomes. This deeper level of self-awareness can lead to a state of inner peace, calm, and contentment, which is the true understanding of oneself and the path to growth.

Knowing oneself involves an inward journey of exploration, digging down layer by layer to the roots of our existence and the value of life. It is about cherishing oneself without hindering others. In this way, we truly know, accept, and grow into ourselves.

52. 我是誰？

　　我是誰？因我有知覺，我知道我存在著、「活」著。無論現在是幾歲，看到這裡時，請靜心、放空思緒、慢慢的想一想，我，是什麼時候開始有知覺？知道「我活著」？在有知覺之前什麼都無所謂，都與我無關，因為，根本沒有「我」的存在，沒有「我」，任何意象都毫無意義。

　　我，是個獨立的生命體，從哪裡來？從有心跳的那一秒而來，往哪裡去？哪裡都不去，就在活著的時候，知道自己的存在，然後，那一秒停止後，永遠不再出現。當認真面對、看清這一事實之後會發現，原來，我，是如此的特別、唯一、無可取代。

　　生命創造了有知覺的我，我們把這樣的生命稱為人類，然後，我們用「名字」讓其他人知道我的存在，用名字與外界（人）交流、互動，其實，無論稱呼我是人類或什麼類，或我今天名叫A，明天改名叫做B，所有的變化都只是「我」的代名詞，那些代號怎麼變都不重要，重要的是，我因我的生命而存在，認清自我根源的本質，清楚明白我是誰，肯定「我存在」的價值。

　　我很清楚明白，因為我知覺的產生，讓我開始有了感覺，我知道了我的存在。這樣的存在感終有消失的時候，無論願意還是不願意，會在某時某刻某年停止，從消失的那一秒開始，我從此永遠失去「知覺」，我就永遠不復存在了，就是永恆無止盡的「無知覺」了。我們是否曾經想到，「我」的出現，就是這麼的「簡單」，這麼的不可思議，如此的「唯一的一次而已」。我們把這種感覺稱為生命，所以，我是誰？我，就是「生命」，我就是我的「知覺」！

52. Who Am I?

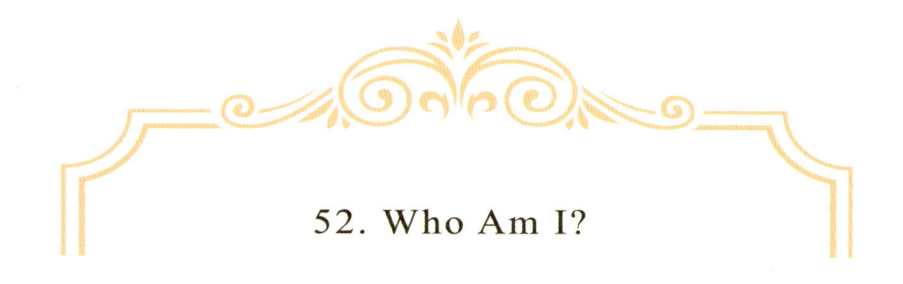

Who am I? I have consciousness, and I know that I exist and that I am "alive." Regardless of how old I am now, as I read this, I take a moment to clear my thoughts and slowly reflect: When did I first become aware of my existence? When did I first know, "I am alive"? Before having consciousness, nothing mattered. It had nothing to do with me, for there was no "me." Without "me," any image or thought was meaningless.

I am an independent living entity. Where did I come from? From the moment my heart first beat. Where am I going? Nowhere in particular, just living and being aware of my existence, until that moment when the heartbeat stops, and I will never appear again. When I face and fully grasp this fact, I realize that I am unique, special, and irreplaceable.

Life has created within me a consciousness, and we call such a life "human." We use names to let others know we exist, to interact and communicate with the world. But whether I am called a human or any other label, or whether today I am named "A" and tomorrow "B," all these are just symbols for "me." How these symbols change is irrelevant. The important thing is that I exist because of my life. Understanding the essence of my being allows me to clearly recognize who I am and affirm the value of my existence.

I understand very well that with the emergence of my consciousness came feelings. I became aware of my existence. But this sense of existence will one day vanish. Whether I wish it or not, at some point, in some year, it will stop. From the moment it ceases, I will lose all consciousness

這樣的想法會越想越清晰，會越認識內在原始的自己，知道自己是「誰」，真實探索了自己的「來源」，一種柔和、平順、靜心的感覺就油然而生，那是一種珍惜、自在、滿足的心境，顯現於外的就是情緒上的平穩、個性上的圓順，發之於內的就是自我心境上的自由自在、仁慈、善良，也就是完完整整的「做自己」了。

　　我就是生命，體會自我生命存在的真實感，用「心」去深層又深入的感覺真真實實的存在著，那是一種自我認同、接納與自信的溫暖感，而這樣的感覺，在我生命有知覺的那一秒開始就同時存在，也一直等待著外在的我去碰觸那內在的我，而一旦我與「我」的對話有了無時無刻的連結，也更清楚我是誰，生命（我）要的是什麼？可以肯定自我、不妨礙他人而無憂無慮的做自己。

　　體會生命（我）存在，我會輕輕閉上眼睛，雙手壓住雙耳（耳朵內折壓住耳洞），動作先輕壓然後停下來（可能幾秒或十幾秒，無妨，沒有任何時間規定，停多久全憑自己的感覺），此時，感覺到了什麼？聽到了什麼？看到了什麼？明明聽不到又看不見，好像「空」了！卻似乎有種聲音、有種影像，可以聽到、看到，又是確確實實存在著！是什麼意象讓我「聽到、看到」了呢？仔細感受一下那種奇妙的感覺。

　　之後，把雙手慢慢加重壓耳的力度，直到感覺雙手緊緊密密的壓住耳朵為止，同時可以增強閉眼的力氣，感覺雙眼緊緊的閉合。此時，一片寂靜的心靈傳來了一種規矩跳動的聲音！是心跳嗎？是生命跳動的呼喚！是如此的清晰、真實、令人感動，這是從何而來的什麼聲音呢？是生命訴說了我真實存在的事實！

　　慢慢的，緊閉的雙眼漸漸出現了亮光或明亮的影像！有層次、有變化，閉起眼睛看不見的世界，竟是如此的多采多姿、千變萬化，這表示了外在的看不見，不表示內在一片黑暗！此時此刻的「看不見」，更可以清楚、透澈的看清自己，徹底明白我的價值、我的存在！

　　上面的心靈探索旅程，可能會感覺到：全然放空一片空白、充滿喜悅、暗自啜泣、沉默不語、恐懼害怕……，無論產生什麼感覺，這樣的靜心動作，會反向迴盪內在深處，與內心的我反覆溝通、互動，會漸漸知道「我是誰」。

　　我就是生命，珍惜生命（我）就等於珍惜我（生命），完整的認識了自己，面對外在世界的千變萬化，也會用這種「珍惜」

forever, and I will cease to exist. It will be an endless, eternal state of "non-consciousness." Have we ever thought about how "I" came to be? It's so "simple," so mysterious, and yet such a "one-time-only" event. We call this experience life. So, who am I? I am "life," I am my "consciousness"!

This idea becomes clearer the more I contemplate it. I come to know the original, inner self, discovering who I truly am. When I explore my origins, a gentle, peaceful, and calm feeling arises—a sense of cherishing, contentment, and inner freedom. This emotional stability manifests outwardly as calmness and smoothness in my personality. Internally, it brings a sense of freedom, kindness, and benevolence, allowing me to be my true self.

I am life. I feel the reality of my existence by deeply and profoundly sensing my true being with my "heart." This brings about a warm feeling of self-recognition, acceptance, and confidence. From the very moment I gained consciousness, this feeling has always been present, waiting for the external me to connect with the inner me. Once I have established a constant connection between the two, I become even clearer about who I am and what life (I) wants. I can affirm myself, live without interfering with others, and be at peace doing so.

To experience the existence of life (me), I close my eyes gently, press both hands against my ears (folding the ears in to cover the ear canals), and begin by lightly pressing, then holding the pressure. It could be for a few seconds or longer—there's no set time limit; it's entirely up to how I feel. At this moment, what do I feel? What do I hear? What do I see? Although I can't hear or see anything, it feels like "nothingness"! Yet there seems to be a sound, an image. I can hear and see something, and it undoubtedly exists! What vision is allowing me to "hear and see"? Take a moment to carefully sense that peculiar feeling.

Then, gradually increase the pressure of my hands on my ears until they are tightly and firmly pressed against them. Simultaneously, strengthen the force with which I close my eyes, feeling the tight closure of my eyelids. At this point, a rhythmic beating sound emerges from the silent mind! Is it my heartbeat? Is it the pulse of life itself? It's so clear, so real, and so moving. Where does this sound come from? It is life affirming the truth of my existence!

（包容、體諒、深層同理心）的心去單純應對，因此，認識了自己，也就認識了外在世界，也就是說，每個人如果都以這樣的方式先認識自己，就會自然而然的認識、尊重了其他的「人」（生命）。

Slowly, as my tightly closed eyes remain shut, a bright light or luminous images begin to appear! They have layers and shifts. The invisible world behind closed eyes turns out to be so colorful, so ever-changing. This shows that what I can't see outwardly doesn't mean there's only darkness within! At this moment of "invisibility," I can clearly and thoroughly perceive myself, fully understanding my worth and my existence.

In this spiritual journey of exploration, one might feel: total emptiness, overwhelming joy, silent weeping, speechlessness, or even fear and trepidation. Whatever the feelings may be, these meditative actions reverberate deeply within, creating continuous communication and interaction with the inner self. Gradually, I will come to understand, "Who am I?"

I am life. To cherish life （me） is to cherish myself （life）. By fully understanding myself, I can face the ever-changing external world with a sense of "cherishing" （embracing, understanding, and deep empathy）. Therefore, recognizing myself also leads to recognizing the external world. In other words, if each person takes the time to first know themselves, they will naturally come to understand and respect other "people" （lives）.

53. 前世？今生！來世？

　　我們會對未知的事情充滿好奇，生命存在的時候，我們把這些現象稱為：過去、現在、未來；對於生命的出現與消失，則稱為：前世、今生、來世。活著的時候，似乎對於過去、未來、前世、來世特別感興趣，總希望瞭解現在自己的某些不如意，是否是因為前世（過去）的關聯而產生目前的狀況，也想知道未來的自己會是什麼樣貌，讓現在的自己知道如何調整、改變，而能夠有更美好的未來甚至是來世。

　　對於自己過去（前世）是什麼樣貌的探索，或許可以做為現在的我在面對人生時的參考；對於未來（來世）的自己，當然會充滿更美好的期待，然而當把現在（今生）的心思及解決自己發生困難的思緒，用在瞻前顧後、追尋過往及未來時，似乎忽略了最重要的根源：「就是現在（今生）」！

　　現在的我，才是扎扎實實、真實存在著，過去和未來的探尋，其實是比較虛幻飄渺的，認清現在（今生）的我才是真實、唯一的我，會讓自己心境感到篤定，會勇於面對外在的所有變化，而不會把現在（今生）不如意的種種解脫，寄託於過去或未來。

　　探尋自我「前世」所呈現出來的樣貌，其實多是自我知識認知範圍內的潛意識的投射。

　　無論生活在地球上什麼地方的人，幾乎都有前世的概念甚至際遇，我從周遭朋友的言談和跑了幾個不同洲別的國家後，把不同地區人們所說出的感覺，再全部融會在一起，發現了一些有趣的現象。

53. Past Life? Present Life! Future Life?

We are often filled with curiosity about the unknown. When life exists, we refer to phenomena as: past, present, and future; in relation to the emergence and disappearance of life, we call them: past life, present life, and future life. While we are alive, we seem particularly interested in the past, the future, past lives, and future lives. We often hope to understand whether certain dissatisfactions in our current lives stem from the past （or past lives）, and we also wonder what we will become in the future, hoping that such knowledge will guide us in adjusting and changing ourselves now to create a better future or even a better future life.

Exploring what our past （past life） was like may serve as a reference for how we face life today. Naturally, we have higher expectations for our future （future life）. However, when we spend our current （present life） thoughts and energy on looking backward or forward, seeking the past or the future, we tend to overlook the most important foundation: "the present （present life）!"

It is the current me that is tangibly and truly existent. The exploration of the past and the future is, in fact, more illusory and distant. Recognizing that the present （this life） is the real and only me will bring certainty to my mind, allowing me to face all external changes bravely and not attribute the dissatisfactions of the present to the past or future.

The exploration of what one's "past life" presents is often a projection of one's subconscious within the scope of one's knowledge.

No matter where people live on Earth, the concept of a past life is

為什麼前世的呈現，會是：知識認知範圍內的潛意識的投射呢？

在回到「過去世」的歷程，你會發現，一個人的視野和思想到什麼層面，他「前世」的模樣，就會呈現到什麼層面，不知道的層面，就不會呈現。例如：一位完全不知道、完全沒聽過馬雅文化的人，他所謂的「前世」樣貌或範圍，就不會有太陽神、鵰鳥、馬雅神話物象等等的前世樣態的選項。只是，「前世」是什麼，難道也會有範圍嗎？應該不是如此，所以，「前世」的呈現，其實只是自己知識認知範圍內的潛意識的一種投射罷了。

在封閉的原始部落，這些人們從出生開始，每天每天到一輩子，所看到的、所接觸的，不外乎就是族人、流傳下來的信仰對象、山、林、河、海、樹、草和一堆野生動物，例如：象、獅、豹、羚羊、馬、豬、狗、蟲……。

他們有前世的想法，當他們敘述著自己的前世是什麼的時候，幾乎都跳脫不出上面那些物象，例如：他們敘述自己的前世時，從來絕對沒有一位會說：我的前世是台灣人。如果真有前世，難道前世是台灣人，不可能是其中之一的可能嗎？不是不可能，而是他根本不知道台灣是什麼，所以，前世的呈現，其實是內在意念的投射而已。

前世的想法，如果把角度擴大到整個地球的人們，我發現了很有意思的事情。

歐美人士所敘述的前世的樣貌，幾乎都與他們的宗教信仰對象、古代文明物象、人物、神話等等有關，除非這位歐美人士曾經接觸過、瞭解過亞洲、非洲、大洋洲、中南美洲文化，否則前世對象只在他的認知範圍而已。

同樣的情況，我們周遭的朋友，不同的人說出自己前世是什麼的時候，我們仔細推敲一下，不難發現，其實和這個人的認知和意念有相當的關聯。

例如：某人對某宗教非常非常虔誠時，他的前世範圍，不會是另一類宗教的意象；某人對某種文化或認知非常非常強烈時，他的前世，幾乎都和那些物象脫離不了關係；一位在鄉下封閉社會生活一輩子的婆婆，問她前世是什麼時，絕對都和她的認知有關，絕不會說自己是十字軍東征的英勇武士或外星人這類的前世；

almost universal. Based on conversations with friends and my own travels across different continents, I've found some interesting phenomena when I merge the feelings people express in various regions.

Why is the presentation of past lives merely a projection of one's subconscious within the scope of knowledge?

When you retrace the journey to the "past life," you'll find that a person's view and thoughts determine the level at which their "past life" manifests. That which they don't know simply doesn't appear. For instance, someone completely unfamiliar with Mayan culture would not describe a past life involving sun gods, eagles, or Mayan mythological figures. But does this mean there are limits to what past lives can be? It shouldn't be so. Therefore, the manifestation of past lives is really just a projection of the subconscious within the bounds of one's knowledge.

In isolated primitive tribes, the people there, from birth until death, only encounter their fellow tribespeople, traditional deities, mountains, forests, rivers, seas, trees, grasses, and a host of wild animals, like elephants, lions, leopards, antelope, horses, pigs, dogs, and insects.

They have ideas of past lives, but when they describe them, they can't stray from the familiar images. For example, none of them would ever say, "In my past life, I was Taiwanese." If past lives are real, why wouldn't one of their past lives have been a Taiwanese person? It's not impossible; it's just that they don't know what Taiwan is. Thus, the past life manifestation is merely an inner projection of their subconscious.

If we broaden the concept of past lives to encompass all people on Earth, we find some fascinating insights.

Westerners' descriptions of their past lives are almost always related to their religious beliefs, ancient civilizations, historical figures, or myths, unless they've been exposed to and understood the cultures of Asia, Africa, Oceania, or Latin America. Otherwise, their past lives only exist within the scope of their knowledge.

Similarly, when our friends describe their past lives, we can see a clear connection between their past lives and their knowledge and awareness.

For example, if someone is deeply devout to a certain religion, their

告訴我們前世是什麼的這位人士，說出來的前世都和這位人士的認知範圍有關，例如：當這位人士完全不知道亞特蘭提斯是什麼時，就不會替別人「分析」出和亞特蘭提斯相關的前世，只是，難道就沒有人的前世可以和亞特蘭提斯有關嗎？當以更宏觀的視野去思索這類問題時，的確相當有趣。

　　如果真有前世，難道靈魂的漂移和轉世，會限定範圍嗎？前面舉例中特別強調「非常非常」，也就是說，如果沒有非常強烈受限的生活環境和思想，那麼，似乎前世的範圍就變廣了，怎麼會有這樣的差異呢？所以，這種現象，其實是自己潛意識的投射。

　　「來世」的探索，讓人們對不可知的未來充滿期待，尤其是在覺得今生有種種不如意、無奈、難以改變的現況時，對於未來的期待和美好，意念會更強烈。其實，「來世」，是一種心靈的寄託。對未來抱持希望，讓「現在」的自己，有一個持續生活下去的「目標」，即使這是個遙不可知的目標，在心裡卻似乎非常具體的存在，讓相信的人有種安定、歸屬的扎實感。

　　「前世」、「來世」的想法，有人深信不疑，有人不以為然。相信的人，會以此成為一個惕勵、參考、改變或努力的目標，是很好的一種心靈歸屬感。不相信的人，會以自己的思想和行為模式，去面對世間的所有人事物，由自己的判斷來記取過去和掌握未來，也是很好的方法。「前世」、「來世」用什麼角度去探索都好，任何想法，只要能因此讓自己的心境安定下來，中心思想有了目標，那就是對自己最好的方式。

　　我們都會為自己的思想和觀念，圓一個可以說服自己和合理的邏輯架構，而這個邏輯架構未必有絕對的是或非、好或壞，而是讓自己的感覺是「對」的，用自己認為「對」的方式生活下去，自己心中的「對」，只要能夠不妨礙別人，那就快樂做自己。

　　在探索前世、來世，寄託於過去、未來時，無論多麼悲慘或美好，畢竟還是會感到虛幻與不可知，或許可以當做今生自我認知的參考，如果過度相信、沉浸於期待而忽略現在，似乎有些可惜，其實，「今生」（現在），才是最重要、最務實的。

　　生命（我），只有現在！沒有前世、來世。與其摸索渺不可知的過去和來世，不如選擇把握今生，選擇相信現在正在呼吸的自己才是最真實的存在，唯有把握住生命活著的線段時光，認清我的「知」只有唯一一次的事實，才能激發內在無限潛能，摒棄

past life is unlikely to involve symbols of another religion. If someone is deeply immersed in a particular culture or belief, their past life will almost always be connected to those symbols. When asking an elderly woman who has lived her entire life in a rural, closed community about her past life, it will be related to her understanding of the world; she wouldn't claim to have been a heroic crusader or an alien. Someone analyzing another person's past life can only provide insights from their own scope of knowledge. For instance, someone unfamiliar with Atlantis wouldn't interpret someone's past life as being related to Atlantis. However, could someone's past life involve Atlantis? It's certainly possible, and when thinking about such issues from a broader perspective, it becomes quite intriguing.

If past lives are real, does the soul's migration and reincarnation have boundaries? In the examples given earlier, the repetition of "very, very" emphasizes that without very restrictive living environments and thoughts, the scope of past lives broadens. Why this difference? Because this phenomenon is essentially a projection of one's subconscious.

Exploring "future lives" fills people with expectations about the unknown future, especially when they feel dissatisfied, helpless, or unable to change their present circumstances. The hope for a better future becomes stronger. However, "future lives" are more of a spiritual solace. Having hope for the future gives us a "goal" to continue living, even if it's an unattainable goal; it feels tangible in the mind, providing a sense of stability and belonging.

The ideas of "past lives" and "future lives" are accepted by some and dismissed by others. Those who believe may take these concepts as reminders, guides, or goals for change or self-improvement, which can provide great spiritual comfort. Those who don't believe may face the world and all its people and events with their own thoughts and actions, learning from the past and controlling the future on their own terms, which is also an excellent approach. Whether one explores past lives or future lives, any perspective is valid as long as it helps calm one's mind and gives it a sense of purpose—that is the best approach for oneself.

We all create a logical framework that convinces and satisfies ourselves, and this framework may not have an absolute right or wrong, good or bad, as long as it feels "right" to us. As long as we don't harm

完全歸咎於前世、來世的宿命（如果相信而不沉迷，能夠激發自我、改變與成長，也是很好的），清晰、自主的掌握住自己的一生。

　　我，就是現在活著的「我」！自己的存在與價值，在此刻，已經越來越清楚、越來越明白，懂了自己、認識了自己，自然會懂周圍的「人」！

others, we should live freely in the way that we believe is "right."

In exploring past lives and future lives, we may feel both sorrow and joy, yet these experiences often seem illusory and unknowable. Perhaps they can serve as references for our current self-awareness. However, if we become overly immersed in these ideas and neglect the present, it seems a shame. In truth, "the present life" (now) is the most important and practical.

Life (I) only exists now! There are no past lives or future lives. Instead of seeking the unknowable past or future life, it's better to grasp the present, to believe that the me who is breathing right now is the most real existence. Only by holding onto the line of time in which life is lived, recognizing that "I" only have this one knowledge of life, can we awaken limitless potential within and abandon the belief in fate that ties everything to past or future lives. (If belief in these concepts leads to self-improvement, change, and growth, then that's a great thing as well). The key is to clearly and independently take hold of our own lives.

I am the "me" that is alive right now! My existence and value, in this moment, are becoming increasingly clear. Understanding myself will naturally lead to a better understanding of the people around me!

54. 我和人的關係

　　人，很難甚至無法離開人群自己一個人獨自生活一輩子，因此，周遭出現了一群與自己生命模式一樣的「人」，很自然覺得習以為常、理所當然。

　　和這些「人」的關係，有陌生、熟悉、陌生到熟悉、熟悉到陌生……。自己會把這些關係區分為：陌生人（例如：路人甲、永遠不知此人存在的人）、家人（例如：父母、兄弟姐妹）、親戚（例如：家族成員）、朋友（例如：同學、同事、事業夥伴）、好人（自己喜歡的）、壞人（自己討厭的）……。

　　和這些「關係人」的互動，似乎會因為自己心中感覺對那些「人」的：對象不同、喜好厭惡不同、情感情緒程度不同，而有了不一樣的關係和態度、應對和相處方法。於是，潛意識自然而然界定了一些不一樣的「心中模式」：

- 從出生那一刻，圍繞在身邊甚至無關血緣關係的人，會認定是「家人」，稱為「親情關係」。自己的下一代或領養的子女，稱是「親子關係」。

- 男女婚姻，稱做「夫妻關係」。未婚之前的男女相處，叫做「男女關係」。

- 沒有上面那些「關係」，會界定是「外人」，稱為「人際關係」。

　　自己的一生，因為心中界定出這些「關係」，所以和周遭這些人的互動模式就顯得不一樣，似乎就生活在這多變的「關係」裡打轉，也衍生出不同的脾氣和情緒反應，並且在那些錯綜複雜

54. My Relationship with People

It is difficult, if not impossible, for a person to live alone without interacting with others throughout their life. Therefore, we naturally find ourselves surrounded by a group of people who share similar life patterns. It seems normal, even taken for granted.

The relationships with these "people" can range from unfamiliar to familiar, from strangers to acquaintances, or from familiarity back to estrangement. We tend to categorize these relationships: strangers (e.g., passerby, people we may never know), family (e.g., parents, siblings), relatives (e.g., extended family), friends (e.g., classmates, colleagues, business partners), good people (those we like), and bad people (those we dislike).

Interactions with these "related people" seem to vary depending on how we feel about them in terms of relationship, preferences, and emotional intensity, leading to different attitudes, ways of handling, and methods of interaction. Naturally, we subconsciously define various "mental models":

From the moment we are born, those surrounding us, whether related by blood or not, are identified as "family," forming what we call "family relationships." Our offspring or adopted children create a "parent-child relationship."

Marriage between men and women is called a "spousal relationship." Before marriage, it's known as a "romantic relationship."

If none of the above relationships apply, they are considered "outsiders," forming what we call "interpersonal relationships."

Throughout our lives, because we define these "relationships" in our minds, our interaction patterns with the people around us naturally

的「關係」裡困擾著，感覺面對各種不同的「關係」和「人」，好像各有難度，所以必須懂得各種不同的技巧去跟不同的人相處。

例如：因為這個「人」是家人（父母、兄弟姐妹），所以有了：自家人是對的、胳臂要向內彎、天下無不是的父母……等等的想法和做法，也會用這樣的情感層次去和這些「人」互動。而這樣的互動深度，卻未必會發生在親戚、同事或自己喜歡的人身上，尤其是家人和外人有利益、衝突、糾紛的時候，此時情感深度有時會曚蔽是非判斷。

每個人的個性和行為，都有他獨特的一面，學習再多的技巧或模式，想和其他人一直保持「愉快」相處，似乎還是很難面面俱到，因此，有人會花很長的時間甚至一生的精力，去盡量圓滿與人的關係，然而不但辛苦也未必盡如人意，也可能因此感覺委曲、壓抑，所以會覺得與人的互動是不容易、困難的。

仔細想想，外在環境千變萬化，什麼樣的人都有，與其絞盡腦汁思索和什麼人要用什麼關係去相處，何妨單純的由自己的內在去探尋自己要的是什麼，只要做到瞭解自己是什麼樣的「人」，認清自己的想法，用自己一貫的態度去面對世界上所有的人，會覺得與人相處其實是可以很簡單的。

也就是說，用自己內心很清晰又篤定的「一個」態度，去面對外在「很多個」的「人們的關係」，會變得簡單而不複雜（用一顆簡單的心，去面對外在多變的世界），也不會有所謂「因人而異」的困擾或批評。我們很難，甚至不可能完全掌握與各式各樣的人的關係，至少，可以很確定的是，我，可以完全掌握我自己！

我完全認識了自己！知道我是誰！這唯一的一生要的是什麼！那會是自信、詳和、積極、正向，清楚的生命觀念，觀念決定了態度，態度決定了行為模式，用這樣的模式無論是面對家人、外人、什麼人，都會是一貫的，與人的關係，會變得單純，所謂的親情關係、夫妻關係、親子關係、人際關係……，也會成為自在的「簡單」關係。

我因為先懂「我」，所以懂得與「其他人」的簡單關係。

differ. We seem to live in a cycle of constantly navigating these varied relationships, resulting in different moods and emotional reactions. These complex relationships often leave us feeling troubled, as we face the various challenges of dealing with people, each interaction seeming uniquely difficult, requiring different skills for different individuals.

For example, because a person is a family member (such as a parent or sibling), there may be thoughts like "family is always right," or "blood is thicker than water," influencing how we interact with them on an emotional level. Such depth of interaction might not exist with relatives, colleagues, or people we like, especially when family and outsiders clash over interests, conflicts, or disputes. In such situations, emotional depth can sometimes cloud objective judgment.

Every person has their unique personality and behavior. No matter how many techniques or methods we learn to maintain "pleasant" relationships with others, it is still challenging to meet every expectation. As a result, some people spend a great deal of time, or even their entire lives, trying to perfect their relationships with others. However, it can be exhausting and may not always turn out as expected, often leading to feelings of frustration and repression, making human interactions seem difficult.

When we think about it carefully, the outside world is ever-changing, and there are all kinds of people. Rather than straining to figure out how to interact with each person based on their relationship, why not simply explore within ourselves to understand what we truly want? Once we understand who we are, we can approach everyone with a consistent attitude, and human relationships will no longer seem so complicated.

In other words, by facing the external "many" relationships with one clear and firm attitude from within, things can become simple rather than complex (using a simple heart to face a changing world). There will be no need to worry about adjusting to different people, nor will we be burdened by criticism. Although we cannot fully control our relationships with every kind of person, we can certainly control ourselves!

I fully understand myself! I know who I am and what I want in this one and only life! This will result in confidence, serenity, positivity, and a clear life perspective. Our perspective shapes our attitude, and our attitude shapes our behavior. With this mindset, whether dealing with family, strangers, or anyone else, we will act consistently. Relationships, whether familial, spousal, parent-child, or interpersonal, will become simple and natural.

By understanding "me," I can understand the simple relationship with "others."

55. 人和人的關係

　　有一次到新店碧潭逛逛，酷愛釣魚的我，目光當然會注意著在岸邊垂釣的人們，看到遠方有一位男士在釣魚，於是散步到他旁邊打招呼，好奇的詢問釣況。

　　這位先生看起來年約70多歲、一頭白髮，很平凡的穿著打扮，釣具設備也很簡單、陽春，感覺就好像是鄰居伯伯、歐吉桑，這是和這位陌生人第一次碰面時，從他的外表呈現出來的樣貌，所產生很直接的第一印象。如果就此和他擦身而過，可能對此人的印象，就只是停留在：很普通的一位陌生釣客。

　　和他從釣況、魚種、釣魚經歷開始閒聊，我發現他今天的釣魚裝備雖然很基本，其實是完全針對了他所在位置的魚種而來，垂釣什麼對象帶什麼裝備就行，不見得需要大包小包、全副武裝，是很有效率又可以很輕鬆的休閒方式，他，原來是一位很懂得釣魚的人！

　　這個階段，因為聊了這些事情，對他有了不一樣的觀感，與剛才那種鄰居阿伯、普通釣客的印象，又有了更多的瞭解，如果沒有剛才的對話，永遠無法知道他有這方面的內涵。

　　繼續閒聊下去，聊到彼此在國外釣魚的故事和經歷，原來這位外表看起來很平凡的老先生，常年旅居國外近30年，是從事國際進出口貿易的企業老闆，聊到這裡，因為他說出了他的工作類別和資歷，對他的觀感更不一樣了，從陌生釣魚老先生到學識豐富的釣魚人到國際企業老闆。

　　就在他細數當年如何打拼、如何風光時，我會不免慎重的想：

55. The Relationship Between People

Once, while visiting a new spot at Bitan, I, an avid fishing enthusiast, naturally noticed the people fishing along the shore. I saw a gentleman in the distance fishing, so I strolled over to greet him and curiously inquired about his catch.

This gentleman appeared to be in his seventies, with white hair, and dressed quite plainly. His fishing gear was also simple and basic, giving the impression that he was just an ordinary neighbor or uncle. This was my first encounter with this stranger, and his appearance left me with a straightforward first impression. Had I simply walked past him, my impression of him would have been limited to that of an average stranger fishing.

As we chatted about fishing conditions, fish species, and experiences, I realized that although his fishing equipment was basic, it was precisely tailored for the fish species in the area. The notion of bringing only the necessary gear instead of overloading oneself is an effective and relaxed way to fish. It turned out he was quite knowledgeable about fishing!

At this stage, having discussed these topics, my perception of him shifted significantly. He transitioned from being just an ordinary stranger to someone I felt had much more depth. Without that initial conversation, I would never have discovered his insights.

We continued our chat, sharing stories of fishing abroad. It turned out that this seemingly ordinary elderly gentleman had lived abroad for nearly 30 years and was an international trade business owner. When he mentioned his occupation and background, my impression of him evolved further, transforming from a fishing stranger to a well-educated angler and then to an

真的嗎？是不是吹噓呢？畢竟口沫橫飛、天花亂墜的例子也不少，當然，如果當做是一面之緣的吹牛聊天反正也無傷大雅，只是我的個性在與人相處上，會比較喜歡瞭解事情的真實性。

他所提到他去過的一些國家，有些我也正巧造訪過多次，因此我試著在他的話題裡找出共同點，用試探的方式來確認他「風光歲月」的真實性。

例如他提到在某某國家的某某城市碰過什麼有趣的事，這個地方我正好也很熟悉，我會說：對啊，這條街對面的那一家電器百貨去年才開幕，裡面的電腦居然比台灣貴了 3 倍多。如果他是吹牛的，話題一定接不下去，恐怕已經穿幫了。他接了我的話說：你說的電腦應該是 2 樓那台 IBM（當下我的反應：的確是 IBM 電腦沒錯），3 千多美金，我買了一台。

他聊到某個小國家時，我說：這個國家的機場有夠小。他說：過海關之前，左邊那間廁所又小又要排隊，出了海關向左邊走出去，再向左直直走那邊的廁所是這幾年新蓋的，還比較好一點。我心想：沒錯！連這些細節他都這麼熟悉，他是真的去過而且很熟。至此，我確信了他涉獵的廣闊，很愉快的和他天南地北的聊著彼此繞著地球跑的「釣魚吹牛經」。

從一開始剛剛見到他時，直覺只是一位釣魚的老先生，如果沒有閒聊，印象就會停在這裡，從此只會認定他是「普普通通的釣魚陌生人」而已。這是人與人相處的第一階段。

開聊後，發現他其實很懂得釣魚，話題也相當有內涵，從剛才普通陌生釣客的印象，成為感覺是一位學識豐富的人。如果只到這個階段，會認定他是「學識豐富的人」。

再聊下去時，他所敘述的豐富閱歷令人嚮往，然而真實性有多少？設法從自己的認知和判斷去確認真偽，會清楚知道這個人的真實性，這是人與人相處比較透徹又深入的階段。

人與人之間的關係，會因為對這個人瞭解程度的多寡，產生不同的觀感，例如：親屬關係、外表長相、服飾穿著、談吐舉止、頭銜職位、身份地位、認識深淺等等的一些「外在現象」做為第一印象，進而潛意識會顯現出「應對關係」的表現，而表現出不同的態度和相處模式，也衍生出各種所謂的相處方法和技巧，讓這些「關係」變得多樣、複雜、困難。

international entrepreneur.

As he recounted how he had thrived over the years, I couldn't help but think: Is this true? Is he bragging? After all, there are plenty of instances where people exaggerate. If it were just casual boasting during a fleeting encounter, it wouldn't really matter. However, I tend to prefer understanding the authenticity of matters when interacting with others.

He mentioned some countries he had visited, and I happened to have been there several times as well. So, I tried to find common ground in his stories to confirm the reality of his "glorious years."

For example, when he mentioned an interesting incident in a particular city in a certain country, I chimed in: "Yes, that electronics department store across the street just opened last year, and the computers there were three times more expensive than in Taiwan." If he were boasting, he wouldn't have been able to continue the conversation, but instead, he responded: "The computer you're talking about must be the IBM on the second floor （and my reaction was: yes, it definitely was an IBM）. It cost over three thousand dollars; I bought one."

When he spoke about a small country, I commented: "The airport in that country is really tiny." He replied: "Before going through customs, there's a restroom on the left that's small and often has a line. After customs, if you turn left and go straight, the restroom there was newly built in recent years and is much nicer." I thought: Exactly! He is so familiar with these details; he must have really been there.

At this point, I was convinced of the breadth of his experiences, and we enjoyed sharing our fishing stories as we traveled around the globe.

Initially, when I first saw him, my instinct told me he was just an old man fishing. Without our conversation, my impression would have remained stagnant, and I would have continued to think of him as an "ordinary fishing stranger." This is the first stage of interpersonal interaction.

After our chat, I discovered that he was quite knowledgeable about fishing, and our conversation revealed his depth. If I had only stopped there, I would have categorized him as a "knowledgeable person."

As our discussion progressed, his rich experiences became quite inspiring, yet how real were they? I sought to confirm the authenticity through my own understanding and judgment. This is a deeper and more thorough

例如：看到穿著平凡和全身名牌包包、服飾的人；沒有什麼職位和頂著高頭銜的人；口才平庸和能言善道、口沫橫飛的對象，相信多數人會直接表現出不一樣的態度，這是潛意識的直接反應，可能自己都不知道有這種行為，然而，人與人之間的關係真的可以如此判斷嗎？

就像前面那位釣魚老先生的例子，我們對一個人的感覺和評價，可能只是自己在認知程度下所下的定論而已，未必就是此人全部的呈現，因此，人與人的互動，如果沒有漸進而深層的交流，是難以知道此人真正的程度。

這個世界上，什麼樣的人都有，人與人之間與其絞盡腦汁思考如何和別人相處，何妨讓自己單純的保持著：一視同仁的接納態度。也就是人際的應對，每個人都可以用「簡單」的心，去面對外在所有看似複雜的人與人「關係」。

面對人際的關係，心情上保持著接納的心胸，不會有外表、頭銜、先入為主、狹隘判斷（自己確定已經很瞭解，然而真的嗎）等等的思維，對於「現階段」感到不怎麼樣甚至厭煩的人，可以把討厭和接納做出切割，也就是可以討厭甚至拒絕認識這個人或事或環境，然而在心態上要承認和接納存在的事實，如果可以的話，何妨去瞭解另一個自己不喜歡的「世界」，因瞭解而討厭和不瞭解而討厭，在人際關係領域絕對會有不一樣的視野和領悟。

我和人的關係，進而就是人和人的關係，每個人都單純的先懂自己，就會懂得與其他人的簡單關係！

stage of interpersonal relationships.

The relationships between people can create different impressions based on how well we understand them. For example: familial relationships, appearances, clothing, speech, titles, status, and the depth of acquaintance all contribute to the first impression, which then subconsciously shapes our interactions and attitudes, leading to various methods and techniques of communication, making these "relationships" diverse, complex, and challenging.

For instance: we may react differently to someone dressed plainly compared to someone adorned with designer brands; to someone with no official position versus someone with a lofty title; to someone who speaks poorly compared to a skilled orator. Most people will likely exhibit different attitudes based on these first impressions, which are subconscious reactions that we may not even realize we have. However, can we truly judge the relationships between people in this manner?

Just like the previous example of the fishing old man, our feelings and evaluations of a person might merely reflect our own limited understanding of them, and not necessarily encompass their entirety. Thus, without gradual and profound exchanges, it is difficult to know someone's true nature.

In this world, there are all kinds of people. Rather than exhausting ourselves thinking about how to interact with others, why not maintain a simple and accepting attitude towards everyone? In interpersonal interactions, everyone can face the seemingly complex relationships with a "simple" heart.

When facing relationships, we should keep an accepting mindset, avoiding judgments based on appearances, titles, preconceived notions, or narrow judgments （believing we already understand, but do we really?）. For those who seem unimpressive or even annoying at this stage, we can separate our dislike from acceptance. We can dislike or even refuse to know this person or situation, yet still acknowledge and accept their existence. If possible, why not seek to understand another "world" that we dislike? Understanding versus ignorance can lead to vastly different perspectives and insights in the realm of interpersonal relationships.

My relationship with others, in turn, reflects the relationship between people. If everyone simply understands themselves, they will grasp the simplicity of relationships with others!

56. 人和自然、宇宙的關係

　　自然是什麼？怎麼去認定、界定它呢？其實，小到眼睛張開看到的一切，大到我們生存的地球，都可以稱為「自然」，例如：原始象貌、山川流水、戶外野林、都市叢林、高科技環境，生命置身於何處，圍繞在自己身邊的一切景物，都可以稱為「自然」，而非只是直覺上的那種自然，人們對於「自然」的定義，或許只是心境上的感覺和對景物認知的差別而已。

　　人的一生，就是置身在「自然」的環境裡，如同和其他人們一起存在般難以切割，仔細想想，和自己朝夕相處、密不可分的自然，我們瞭解它多少？是什麼樣的依附關係？我們可曾去感覺、感受和體悟自己與自然的關係：生命的自然？生命的大自然？

　　生命的自然，是自我內在心靈的體悟。自然？「自」是表示，明白自己是自我、唯一、特別的生命存在現象。「然」是表示，內在心境平靜無波（無關外在的情緒起伏）、處之泰然。因此，自＋然＝自然，就是自我心靈內在的平衡、簡單、放鬆、自在、正向的生命價值感，是人與自然於內在潛意識的連結，是肯定自己真實存在、認清自己、無以為價的那份珍惜的互動關係。

　　發現生命的自然，其實，每個人都有屬於自己內心深處的心靈花園、美麗大地，等著自己去發掘、敲開，它可以無時無刻的修復著、洗滌著、滋潤著自我的心靈，徜徉在無憂無慮、陽光明亮的心境深處裡，一種放鬆、自在、愉悅的感覺隨時環繞著，這是專屬於自己修煉而得的「自然」。

　　生命的大自然，是對於外在所有所有一切事、物、環境的珍

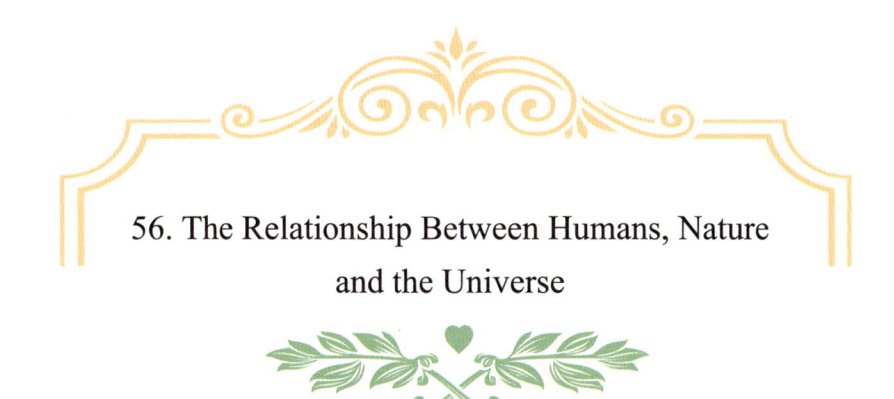

56. The Relationship Between Humans, Nature and the Universe

What is nature? How do we recognize and define it? In fact, everything from the small things we see when we open our eyes to the vast Earth we inhabit can be referred to as "nature." For example, primitive landscapes, rivers and mountains, wild forests, urban jungles, and high-tech environments—everything around us, where life exists, can be called "nature." It's not just the intuitive sense of nature; perhaps people's definitions of "nature" are merely differences in their mental state and their perception of their surroundings.

A person's life is lived in an environment of "nature," much like our existence alongside others, which is difficult to separate. If we reflect carefully, how much do we understand the nature we are intimately connected with? What kind of attachment do we have? Have we ever tried to feel, sense, and comprehend our relationship with nature: the nature of life? the great nature of life?

The nature of life is the inner realization of our own spirit. Nature? The "self" indicates an understanding that one is a unique, special phenomenon of existence. "Nature" indicates a state of inner peace (unrelated to external emotional fluctuations) and calmness. Thus, self + nature = nature is the balance, simplicity, relaxation, comfort, and positive sense of life value within our inner spirit. It represents the subconscious connection between humans and nature, affirming our real existence and cherishing that precious interactive relationship.

Discovering the nature of life, each person has a spiritual garden, a

惜、接納、擁抱。我們擁有了大自然，也是大自然擁有了我們！人，不會誕生在飄渺、無邊無際的空間裡，「自然」塑造了大自然，因這樣的環境，人（我們），奇妙的出現了，思索著這樣的依存關係，內心一股感動油然而生。

　　人與自然的關係，由內修體悟自我的「自然」，清楚明白自己真實存在的獨特與尊嚴；外煉而知道珍惜、接納、包容所見所聞的「所有自然」，感受自己心境中內外兼具的和諧，內在平靜的情緒，會讓自己更自然的和「自然」和諧共存。

　　仰望天空，靜靜的、盯著一個點、一直看一直看……，遠、再遠、更遠、無邊無際看似清晰卻又似乎是無止盡的遠，我們把這樣的感覺以及地球以外的環境稱為宇宙。因為在宇宙（大環境）的存在之下，出現了一個地球（小環境），很奇妙的是，竟然因此產生了一個短暫的、有感覺、有思想的我（小點）。

　　這種感覺，如同皮球（宇宙）裡面的一粒塵埃（地球），塵埃裡面的微小粒子（我）；也可以想像為母體（宇宙）裡面的子宮（地球），子宮裡面孕育的微小生命（我）。包容與接納生命的誕生和存在，都可以稱為「宇宙」，人在這樣環境下的依存關係，顯得原始又安定。

　　宇宙很神秘嗎？有多大呢？有盡頭嗎？有其他生命存在嗎？……？唯一可以確定的是，偌大宇宙的「壽命」比人們還長，人們只能在生命的接力之下持續的探索宇宙，然而，如果以自己有限的生命而言，對宇宙的瞭解只會是線段，也就是自己活著的時候，知道宇宙的現況，一旦自己的生命消失，宇宙是什麼，也毫無意義了。

　　人類瞭解宇宙多少？因為生命的有限，或許目前的一些知識可以知道過去和現在，而未來就不知道了，任何人都一樣，因為人都只存在於一個有限線段的「過去、現在、未來」而已。

　　有趣的是，當人們用心情在探索宇宙時，各種情緒反應湧上心頭，例如：寧靜、自在、無為、輕靈、飄渺、虛幻、無際……。

　　看似遙不可及、變幻深邃的宇宙，又給了人們身心靈的一種啟示和修煉，人可以無視它的存在也看似遙遠，然而，一種「宇宙觀」，卻是深深烙印在自己心裡。

　　因為宇宙，懂得自己的渺小，因為自然，知道珍惜身邊的一

beautiful earth deep within, waiting to be explored and opened up. It can continuously repair, cleanse, and nourish our spirit at any moment, allowing us to dwell in a carefree and bright state of mind. A feeling of relaxation, comfort, and joy surrounds us, which is the "nature" obtained through personal cultivation.

The great nature of life involves cherishing, accepting, and embracing everything in our external environment. When we have nature, nature also has us! Humans do not emerge in an ethereal, boundless space; "nature" shapes the great nature. In this environment, we (humans) emerge marvelously, pondering this interdependent relationship, and a surge of emotion arises within us.

The relationship between humans and nature starts with the internal realization of our "nature," clearly understanding our unique existence and dignity; externally, we learn to cherish, accept, and embrace everything we see and hear as "all nature," feeling the harmony of both the inner and outer aspects of our minds. The inner calm emotions allow us to coexist more naturally and harmoniously with "nature."

Gazing up at the sky, quietly focusing on a single point, looking and looking… far away, further, endlessly distant, appearing clear yet seemingly infinite, we refer to this feeling and the environment beyond Earth as the universe. Because, under the existence of the universe (the larger environment), there appears a planet (the smaller environment) —and intriguingly, this gives rise to a brief, feeling, and thinking "me" (a small point).

This feeling is like a speck of dust (Earth) inside a ball (the universe), with the tiny particles (me) within that dust; it can also be imagined as a uterus (Earth) within a mother (the universe), nurturing tiny lives (me). The acceptance and embrace of the birth and existence of life can be called the "universe." In such an environment, the interdependent relationship of humans appears primitive yet stable.

Is the universe mysterious? How vast is it? Does it have an end? Are there other forms of life? The only certainty is that the "lifespan" of the vast universe exceeds that of humans. Humans can only continue to explore the universe under the relay of life. However, when considering our limited

切，而這兩種物象，和人們沒有任何「交際關係」，語言不通？思想不同？行為模式互異？感受不到真實感？卻又如影隨形、分秒不離，這樣的關係，甚至比人的相處更緊密，面對孕育自己存在的自然和宇宙，如同慎終追遠、飲水思源般，有了它們的存在，才有我的出現，才有身邊的人。

　　有了這樣的心情，感恩、平靜、知足、喜樂之情油然而生。明白了自己的價值，知道了圍繞周圍人們的可貴，懂得自然環境的珍惜，瞭解宇宙的啟示，這樣的自己，會清楚認識自己、愛自己，每個人如果都能深刻體會出其中的真義，人與人、自然、宇宙的關係，會因此過得簡單而自在。

lives, our understanding of the universe is merely a segment; that is, while we are alive, we know the current state of the universe, and once our lives cease, the universe holds no meaning.

How much do humans understand the universe? Due to the limitations of life, perhaps we can know some past and present knowledge, but the future remains unknown. Everyone exists within a limited segment of "past, present, and future."

Interestingly, when people explore the universe with emotions, various emotional responses arise, such as tranquility, ease, nonchalance, lightness, ethereality, illusion, and boundlessness.

The seemingly unreachable and profound universe provides an insight and cultivation for the body, mind, and spirit. While it may appear distant, a sense of "cosmology" is deeply imprinted in our hearts.

Because of the universe, we understand our insignificance; because of nature, we learn to cherish everything around us. These two aspects have no "communication relationship" —are our languages incompatible? Are our thoughts different? Do our behavior patterns vary? Is the reality unperceived? Yet, they follow us closely, inseparably. This relationship may even be closer than human interactions. Facing the nature and universe that nurture our existence, it's like remembering our roots and being grateful for the source; only through their existence do we appear, and only through them do we have those around us.

With this sentiment, feelings of gratitude, tranquility, contentment, and joy naturally arise. Understanding our value, appreciating the preciousness of the people surrounding us, cherishing our natural environment, and realizing the insights of the universe will lead us to clearly know and love ourselves. If everyone could deeply experience the true meaning of this, the relationship among humans, nature, and the universe would lead to a simpler and more effortless life.

57. 如何愛人、愛我？

懂得愛自己，才會真實的愛別人。怎麼愛自己呢？在這本書的〈愛自己〉、〈愛的表達〉和其他章節裡，提出了一些我個人的想法和作法，或許可以提供彼此參考和交流，任何一些愛自己的方法，沒有絕對的模式可循，只要能因此確實的愛自己，其實都很好。

我們都明白，對於一件事，沒有實際經驗、親身經歷過的人，即使說的頭頭是道、口沫橫飛、煞有其事，當他實際去做之後，才會發現跟現實狀況有差距，甚至根本不是所想、所說的，相同的道理，沒有先做到愛自己之前，所有愛別人的行為，都會產生困難、阻礙、不切實際和難以持久。

懂得愛自己之後，再用愛自己的方式去愛別人？我們聽過這樣的抱怨：「他（她）都感受不到我的付出」；「為什麼愛（包含：愛情、親情、友情、關懷……等等的付出）總是被拒絕？」，愛自己之後去愛別人，絕對不是複製愛自己的愛，而是因為自己感受了愛自己的所有心路歷程，懂得對別人付出同理心的愛，知道不同的人需要哪一些的愛與關懷，讓對方感受到我們的愛，就是真實的愛。

在自我修煉、體驗愛自己的歷程中，會漸漸認清自己的個性和優缺點，也知道自己喜歡或不喜歡什麼樣的人事物，而最終無論喜歡或不喜歡，會因為珍惜自己、明白自我價值，在情緒厭惡與接納間做出切割，也就是說，即使內心非常厭惡某人、事、物，那樣的情緒也不會顯露出來，這與壓抑情緒而表面鎮定不同，是看穿、看透後的淡然處之，因此更懂得包容與接納他人。

57. How to Love Others, Love Myself?

Understanding how to love oneself is the first step to truly loving others. How do we love ourselves? In this book's sections on "Loving Oneself," "Expressions of Love," and other chapters, I present some personal thoughts and practices that may provide references and insights for each other. Any method of loving oneself doesn't follow an absolute pattern; as long as it genuinely leads to self-love, that's perfectly fine.

We all understand that for any matter, those without practical experience or personal encounters may speak eloquently and convincingly, but when they actually try it, they often find a gap between their expectations and reality. Similarly, if one has not learned to love oneself first, all attempts to love others will face difficulties, obstacles, impracticality, and a lack of sustainability.

After understanding how to love oneself, should we love others in the same way? We have heard complaints like: "He（she）doesn't feel my contributions" or "Why is my love（including romantic love, familial love, friendship, care, etc.）always rejected?" Loving others after learning to love oneself does not mean simply replicating self-love. Instead, it means understanding the entire journey of self-love and applying that empathy to others. It's about recognizing what different individuals need in terms of love and care, allowing them to feel our love—that is true love.

In the process of self-cultivation and experiencing self-love, one gradually becomes aware of their personality, strengths, and weaknesses, and learns what they like or dislike. Ultimately, regardless of likes or dislikes, one learns to cherish themselves and understand their self-worth, allowing for a clear distinction between emotional aversion and acceptance. This means

每個人都有屬於自己的喜好厭惡，懂得愛自己的人，是因為充分接觸與理解所有層面之後，選擇了在盡量不妨礙他人的前題下最喜歡的方式，這樣的自己去關愛別人時，會理解別人的喜好厭惡，用別人喜愛的方式去愛對方，這就是同理心的愛，也就是前面提到：「懂得愛自己，才會真實的愛別人」的真諦，而非盲目的用愛自己的方式去付出，這樣可能適得其反、不被接受或讓對方感到壓力，這就不是愛別人了。

　　「愛別人，是給他所需，而非給他我想」。那麼，有人會以為，是不是就是有求必應？予取予求？他如果喜歡吃喝嫖賭也同意嗎？就是給他所需嗎？當然不是！

　　以喜歡吃喝嫖賭為例，雖然我不喜歡吃喝嫖賭，然而在自我成長的歷練中，我仍然願意去瞭解吃喝嫖賭是怎麼一回事，明白為什麼有人樂此不疲的原因，因此，當我關愛這些人時，話題接得上，不會是講道理和一堆訓斥或教訓，會讓此人充分感到認同與同理心。

　　試著理解此人為什麼喜歡吃喝嫖賭，接納並附和他的想法，讓他盡情說出他的喜歡，之後再從他的生活現況試著連結出吃喝嫖賭與他衝突或在乎的地方（例如：健康、財力、家人、子女……等等），只要有一個與他衝突或在乎的話題連結上吃喝嫖賭時，我們不必講什麼意見或道理，相信他自己也會發現問題並且自己找答案，而我們頂多只要給予選擇性建議或參考就好，不給如果是我會怎麼做的答案，如此循循善誘，他自然會漸漸擺脫吃喝嫖賭。這樣的愛別人，會是真正的愛。

　　愛別人如同愛自己，愛自己就會愛別人。自己心中有了愛，人生視野無限寬廣。

that even if one internally detests someone, something, or some situation, that emotion will not be outwardly expressed. This differs from suppressing emotions while appearing calm; it's a state of tranquility that comes from seeing through and understanding, allowing for greater tolerance and acceptance of others.

Everyone has their own preferences and aversions. Those who understand how to love themselves do so after fully engaging with and understanding all aspects of their being, choosing to express their favorite ways without disturbing others. When such individuals care for others, they understand others' preferences and aversions and love them in ways that resonate with them. This is empathy in love—aligning with the earlier notion that "to understand how to love oneself is to genuinely love others." It is not about blindly giving love in the way one loves oneself, as this could backfire, be unaccepted, or create pressure on the other person, which would not constitute loving others.

"To love others is to provide what they need, not what I think they need." Some might think this means catering to every request or giving in to every demand. Does this mean we agree with someone who indulges in vices like gambling or drinking? Of course not!

Using the example of vices, even though I don't indulge in them, I am still willing to understand what they are about through my personal growth journey. I seek to comprehend why some people find joy in them, which allows me to engage in conversations that resonate without preaching or reprimanding. I can try to understand why a person is drawn to such activities, accept their thoughts, and let them express their preferences fully. From there, I can connect their vices to aspects of their life that may conflict with or concern them (like health, finances, family, children, etc.). If we can find even one topic that relates vices to their concerns, we don't need to impose opinions or lessons. They will likely recognize the issues themselves and seek their own solutions. Our role is merely to offer selective suggestions or references rather than prescribing what we would do. Gradually, they may find their way away from their vices. This is what true love for others looks like.

Loving others is like loving oneself. When we love ourselves, we can love others. When our hearts are filled with love, the horizons of our lives become infinitely broad.

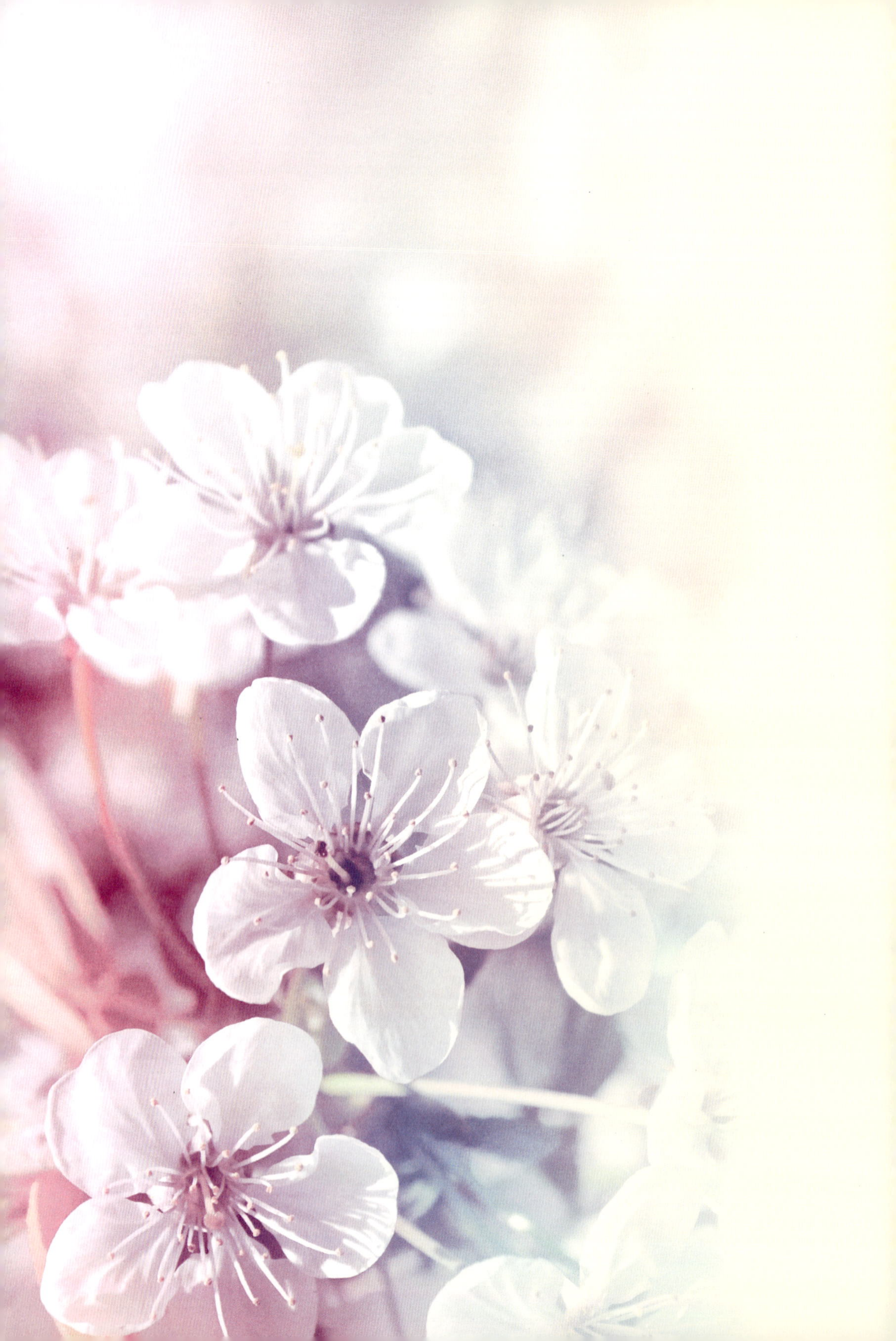

大自然心靈之旅

A Journey of the Spirit in Nature

認識自己,情緒是成長的絆腳石,感動是成長的潤滑劑。

Emotions can be stumbling blocks to growth, while inspiration acts as a lubricant for growth.

陸、大自然心靈之旅

　　人類來自於大自然，再回到大自然的懷抱，就好像回到胎兒期在腹中的感覺般的安全、滿足、感動、溫暖，這樣的感覺會讓外表冰封的心重新柔軟起來。

　　有形的大自然是眼睛所見的一切，徜徉其間，愉快輕鬆而自在；無形的大自然是內在的心靈淨土，那是一種無時無刻、形影不離的陪伴，讓心靈滿足而溫馨。置身在有形或無形的大自然環境裡，讓整個心完全的放空而融入其中，細細的、靜靜的去體會徜徉大自然的心靈之旅，神遊其間，有形的愉悅和無形的寧靜，會充滿無限的滿足，發現大自然之美，心情會變得平和，會更加的珍惜自己所擁有的那種心滿意足的感動。

　　情緒是成長的絆腳石，感動是成長的潤滑劑，經由大自然的洗禮，讓自己的生命因此陽光而正向。用感動的心來溶化自己的情緒，打開心門投入大自然的懷抱，感受和體會大自然單純、寧靜的愉快。

　　我喜歡用「心」去感受、體會、欣賞大自然微妙的變化，同樣的一景一物，每次造訪，都能呈現出不同的樣貌，總是一次次、一次次吸引我的目光，似乎在敘述著各種的心靈故事，讓我們去發掘、去品味，擁抱大自然，來趟心靈豐盛的饗宴，以下的心靈之旅，每個人有不同的意會，期待你的感受，能彼此分享，讓我們一同發掘似是隱藏又乍現、無限寬廣的大自然之美！

Part Six: A Journey of the Spirit in Nature

Humans come from nature and return to its embrace, feeling the safety, satisfaction, emotion, and warmth reminiscent of the fetal stage in the womb. Such feelings can soften a heart that has been frozen on the outside.

The tangible aspects of nature are everything we see with our eyes; wandering amidst them brings joy, ease, and freedom. The intangible aspects of nature are the inner sanctuaries of the mind, offering constant companionship that satisfies and warms the soul. Being in both the tangible and intangible environments of nature allows our minds to completely empty and integrate with the surroundings, enabling us to experience a spiritual journey through nature, filled with both the joy of tangible experiences and the tranquility of intangible feelings. This can lead to infinite satisfaction as we discover the beauty of nature, making us more appreciative of the feelings of contentment we already possess.

Emotions can be stumbling blocks to growth, while feelings of connection can serve as lubricants for development. Through the cleansing influence of nature, our lives can shine positively. We should melt our emotions with a heart full of gratitude, opening ourselves to embrace nature and experience its pure and peaceful joy.

I enjoy using my "heart" to feel, appreciate, and understand the subtle changes in nature. Each time I visit the same scenery, it presents a different aspect that continuously draws my attention, as if narrating various stories of the soul for us to explore and savor. Embracing nature becomes a rich spiritual feast, and the following spiritual journey will resonate differently for everyone. I look forward to hearing your feelings and sharing them, allowing us to discover the seemingly hidden yet vast beauty of nature together!

58. 煙靄繚繞的湖泊

　　晨曦微亮、似暗似明，來到了煙靄繚繞、湖面如鏡的湖泊。

　　遼闊的水面，太陽初綻光芒，水波不興、無風無浪，湖泊平靜的像一面大鏡子，飄落的落葉聲音如此清晰；一顆小小的石頭泛起了層層擴散的漣漪，沒想到這麼微小的東西也有這麼大的力量，只有破曉的清晨，我發現了它的存在。

　　陣陣輕煙，一種朦朧、飄渺、似幻似真的感覺，在平靜如鏡的水面上舞動著千變萬化的煙雲，像極了一幅山水國畫，更像飄逸的仙女。

　　一條小魚躍出水面，偶而傳來清脆的鳥叫蟲鳴聲點綴著寧靜的湖泊，似乎要喚醒沉睡的大地；陣陣清香的空氣，忍不住深呼吸，全身頓時心曠神怡、神清氣爽。

　　不忍離開，在輕煙飄渺的湖畔，與大地一起迎接漸漸昇起的朝陽，向美好、喜悅的一天快樂招手。

58. The Misty Lake

As dawn breaks, dim yet bright, I arrive at a lake enveloped in mist, its surface as smooth as a mirror.

The expansive water reflects the sun's first rays; the waves are still, with no wind or ripples, making the lake calm like a giant mirror. The sound of falling leaves is strikingly clear; a small stone causes ripples to spread outward. I hadn't expected such a tiny object to possess such power. It's only in the early morning light that I discover its existence.

Waves of light mist create a hazy, ethereal feeling, dancing on the calm surface of the water, transforming into ever-changing clouds, resembling a beautiful landscape painting, almost like a fairy in the air.

A small fish leaps from the water, and the occasional chirping of birds and the calls of insects punctuate the tranquil lake, as if awakening the sleeping earth. The air carries a fresh fragrance, and I can't help but take a deep breath, feeling instantly uplifted and invigorated.

Reluctant to leave, I stand by the misty lake, welcoming the gradually rising sun alongside the earth, happily waving goodbye to a beautiful, joyful day ahead.

59. 溪谷的迴響

　　小溪潺潺、滾滾長流、瀑布飛奔,溪水在不同的地方譜出了截然不同的樂曲,只是水,也擁有很美的音樂旋律,就像一首豐富的心靈音樂從耳邊不斷的流入,靜靜的聆聽,特別舒服。

　　透明、清澈的溪水不停的沖刷石頭,越顯得光亮、潔淨,就好像陽光、喜悅的想法,不斷流過心靈深處,越顯得乾淨、明亮。

　　水如果只有一滴不會流動,一滴接著一滴,一滴推著另一滴,就成為溪流奔向大海,一滴水的重要,就像小螺絲成就大飛機,如同聚沙成塔、積少成多的道理,小小的自我是無比重要的。

　　一片落葉順著溪水向下游流動,碰到石頭轉個彎繼續流去,無論碰撞多少次,它都會轉彎。

　　似乎告訴我,事情沒有絕對的困難,轉個彎繼續往目標前進一定會抵達目的地。葉子卡在石縫不動了,怎麼辦?沒問題,等大雨來臨,會幫助它繼續漂往目的地。這也提醒我,碰到困難沒關係,等一下、靜一下,一定有解的。

59. Echoes of the Stream

The stream flows gently, continuously, rushing in waterfalls, creating a unique melody in each place it passes. Water alone holds a beautiful rhythm, like a rich piece of music for the soul that flows quietly into our ears, bringing a profound sense of peace as we listen. The transparent, clear water polishes stones as it flows, making them shine brighter and cleaner, much like joyful, sunny thoughts that cleanse and brighten the depths of the mind.

If there's only a single drop, it won't move, but one drop after another, pushing each other forward, creates a stream that rushes toward the sea. The importance of a single drop is like that of a tiny screw in a great airplane—just as sand grains build a tower, small efforts combine to create greatness, showing how every individual contribution matters.

A fallen leaf drifts downstream, turning whenever it encounters a rock, always continuing its journey. This seems to tell me that obstacles aren't absolute barriers; by taking a new path, we can still reach our goals. What if the leaf gets stuck in a crevice? No problem; the coming rain will help it move again, reminding me that when facing challenges, it's okay to pause and wait patiently—there is always a way forward.

60. 雲的變幻

喜歡低頭望雲、追逐雲的感覺。

從飛機往外看，雲就在腳下、眼前、遠方、頭頂上，彷彿置身雲的懷抱裡，似棉花、像毛毯、又像小孩子喜歡的棉花糖。

好像看到了群山峻嶺，又可以變幻出各種樣貌，總是讓我的目光不忍離開，注視著每一秒的變化。

想像躺在雲朵上柔軟舒服的感覺，欣賞天際間飄遊的變化，一股隨著它飄往世界各地的心情，多麼喜悅、遼闊。

雲，時而稀疏飄渺，又可以呈現多種風貌和顏色，整個心境飄向了雲，目光的凝望讓思緒完全放空，讓雲的感覺飄進心靈深處，就像雲一樣的四處遨遊、海闊天空。

此時來個深呼吸，感覺好像把雲整個吸入了內心世界，一片潔白、寬廣、寧靜，感覺真的舒服極了。

60. The Transformation of Clouds

I love the feeling of looking down at the clouds and chasing after them.

From the airplane, clouds are beneath my feet, before my eyes, far away, and above my head, as if enveloped in their embrace, resembling cotton, blankets, and the cotton candy beloved by children.

It seems to reveal towering mountains, morphing into various shapes that continually captivate my gaze, making me unable to look away as I observe every second of their transformation.

Imagining lying on the clouds feels soft and comfortable, admiring the changes in the sky, experiencing emotions that drift with them around the world—how joyful and vast it feels!

Clouds can be sparse and ethereal, yet they present numerous appearances and colors. My heart drifts along with the clouds; the intensity of my gaze completely empties my thoughts, allowing the feeling of clouds to penetrate deep into my soul, akin to roaming freely in a boundless sky.

At this moment, taking a deep breath feels like inhaling the entire essence of clouds into my inner world—pure, expansive, and tranquil. It's truly a delightful experience.

61. 石頭

　　石頭多采多姿的樣貌總吸引我的目光，因為心中永遠有著「下一顆一定不一樣」的想像空間。

　　因為地質的不同和水的洗禮，石頭的形狀、紋路和顏色變化，讓人驚嘆！圓、長、扁、方、弧形……奇特形狀；山川、人物、動物……抽象想像；綠、橙、金、灰、紫、藍……各種顏色！

　　拿一顆石頭在手中賞玩，有時候竟像一幅潑墨畫、抽象畫，看著看著，感覺石頭好像在敘述它的故事，心情被帶往石頭神遊。

　　金黃色好像陽光普照大地、藍白色好像藍天白沙、綠色好像翠綠森林、黑色好像岩壁山洞、紫色好像薰衣草花海，每一顆的小石頭，有著太多太多令人神往的故事，難怪會看著、看著發呆了。

61. Stones

The vibrant forms of stones always capture my attention because my heart is filled with the imagination that "the next one will surely be different."

Due to geological variations and the washing of water, the shapes, patterns, and colors of stones change, leaving people in awe! Round, long, flat, square, curved... unique shapes; mountains, figures, animals... abstract imaginations; green, orange, gold, gray, purple, blue... all kinds of colors!

Holding a stone in my hand, sometimes it resembles an ink-wash painting or abstract art. The longer I look, the more I feel that the stone seems to narrate its own story, and my mood is transported into its world.

Golden hues evoke the sunlight shining upon the earth; blue and white reflect the blue sky and white sands; green resembles the lush forest; black reminds me of rocky caves; purple evokes lavender fields. Each little stone holds countless enchanting stories, making it no wonder I could stare and lose track of time.

62. 遠眺的感動

遠眺的感覺，有種高處遠望、心情寬闊的感動。

站在高處，越高越好，可以看到地平線上見不到的景象，那種遠可以更遠、遠想要再遠、可以一望無際的想像，整個人好像跟著遠景而飄遊四方。

日出、夕陽、遼闊草原、無際大海、碧海白沙、城市景象、萬家燈火，眼前一覽無遺的景象伴隨著晴天、陰天、雨天、颱風天、白天、夜晚的變化，每一種感覺都很特別。

一陣風從山谷吹過，芒草如波浪般舞動；汪洋大海中的一艘貨輪，竟像沙土般渺小；高樓林立的都市叢林，好像堆疊的積木而已；萬家燈火的城市，有如點點繁星閃爍；居高臨下遠眺夕陽西下的大海，金黃色的落日餘暉，伴著點點銀色的反照，景緻之美，讓我感動。

在馬雅神殿的最高處，眼前呈現的是讓我驚奇的大片雨林，站在獨立而高聳的神殿中，頭頂上是湛藍的天空，神殿下是一大片只有風聲、遙望無際的森林，神殿裡的風聲，似乎告訴我馬雅王朝的故事，沒有登上神殿遠眺，永遠無法體會馬雅王朝的偉大。

遠眺，爬的越高，望的越遠，越遠越渺小，越微不足道。

62. The Emotion of a Distant View

The feeling of gazing into the distance evokes a sense of vast openness and awe, like standing on high ground and looking far and wide. The higher you stand, the more you can see beyond the horizon, with a view that seems to stretch endlessly, filling you with boundless imagination and a sense of drifting along with the distant scenes.

Sunrises, sunsets, expansive grasslands, endless seas, turquoise waters and white sands, cityscapes, and the myriad lights of homes—all unfold before you, changing with sunny skies, cloudy days, rain, typhoons, day and night. Each brings a unique feeling.

A gust of wind sweeps through the valley, making silvergrass wave like ocean waves; a cargo ship in the vast ocean looks as small as a speck of sand; the skyscrapers of the urban jungle resemble stacked building blocks; the city lights sparkle like stars. From a high vantage point, watching the sun set over the ocean with its golden glow and shimmering silver reflections is a scene of breathtaking beauty.

Standing atop a Mayan temple, I was stunned by the vast rainforest stretching out before me. Surrounded by the clear blue sky above and an endless forest below, the wind blowing through the temple seemed to tell the stories of the Mayan civilization. Only by climbing this temple and looking out could I truly grasp the grandeur of the Mayan world.

The higher we climb, the farther we can see. The farther we see, the smaller and more insignificant everything appears.

63. 大海的聲音

　　在海灘，海浪一波波推向沙灘。澎澎的拍打著軟沙；唰唰的推攪著細石；喀啦喀啦的滾動著鵝卵石，漲潮時，聲音顯得持續有力，退潮後，雖然一波波推向岸邊，聲音卻是漸弱的，就好像音樂一樣，節奏時而快、時而慢，旋律時而鏗鏘有力、時而低沉，隨著潮起潮落，伴奏出了海的旋律。

　　在礁岩，海浪拍向了千奇百怪的岩石，有時海浪從岩縫中竄出，碰撞出碰碰碰的聲音，海浪退回時，岩縫裡傳來嘩嘩嘩的聲音；一陣急浪拍向礁石掀起高高白浪，是一陣啪啪啪的海浪墜地聲，那些聲音，一直周而復始的循環著。

　　無論是海灘還是礁岩，靜靜聆聽海的聲音，享受它各種旋律的變化，一種聲音牽引著一種心情，海的聲音與心靈的聲音產生共鳴，經由潮起潮落的拍打和洗滌，也沖刷出了平靜的心情。

63. The Sound of the Ocean

On the beach, the waves push toward the shore in rhythmic pulses. They crash against the soft sand; swirl and stir the fine stones; roll the pebbles in a clattering sound. During high tide, the sounds resonate powerfully, while during low tide, the waves gently retreat with diminishing sounds, almost like music—its rhythm alternating between fast and slow, the melody at times resounding and at other times soft, accompanied by the ebb and flow of the tides, creating the symphony of the sea.

On the rocks, waves crash against oddly shaped stones. Sometimes, the waves surge from the crevices, creating a series of splashes, and as they retreat, they produce a murmuring sound. A surge of waves against the rocks raises high white foams, resembling the sound of applause. These sounds echo in a perpetual cycle.

Whether on the beach or the rocky shore, listening quietly to the ocean's voice allows me to enjoy its varied melodies. One sound leads to a particular mood, resonating with the heart, and through the relentless ebb and flow of the tides, it washes away my worries and brings peace.

64. 雪

　　天空飄下棉絮般的白點，大地披上了一片的銀白，冰冷的感覺、冷冽的空氣，第一次碰到下雪，是在北京的街道上。

　　台北不會下雪，10來度的氣溫就叫人直打哆嗦；日本零下氣溫的雪，卻感覺沒有台北那麼寒冷，即使緯度相同，中美洲和東南亞氣溫30度的感覺，就是不一樣，不同地區溫度變化所呈現出來的感覺，未必溫度越高越熱、越低越冷。

　　這似乎告訴我，不能以自己的感覺，去判斷其他人的感覺。

　　小雪就像小雨，大風雪有如大雨，雪是白的、雨是透的，氣溫的變化，讓它呈現不一樣的樣貌。

　　氣溫高，只是飄散空氣中的水氣；氣溫適中，成為了水；氣溫低，它變成雪；極地氣溫，成為堅硬的冰石。

　　這似乎告訴我，我的喜怒哀樂會像氣溫變化一般，對周遭的人有很大的影響，情緒的抒發和修為，真的很重要。

　　雪的來臨，「溫暖」了我的思維。

64. Snow

White flakes, like cotton, drift from the sky, blanketing the earth in a silver sheen. The icy sensation and crisp air—my first experience of snowfall was on the streets of Beijing.

It never snows in Taipei; a temperature of around ten degrees sends shivers down my spine. Yet, snow at sub-zero temperatures in Japan doesn't feel as cold as in Taipei. Even at the same latitude, the 30-degree heat in Central America and Southeast Asia feels different. The sensations presented by temperature changes in different regions show that higher temperatures don't necessarily mean more heat, nor do lower temperatures always equal cold.

This seems to tell me that I cannot use my own feelings to judge the feelings of others.

Light snow resembles light rain, while heavy snow is like a torrential downpour. Snow is white; rain is transparent. The variation in temperature presents different appearances.

When the temperature is high, it simply disperses moisture in the air; at moderate temperatures, it becomes water; at low temperatures, it transforms into snow; at polar temperatures, it solidifies into ice.

This seems to indicate that my emotions—joy, anger, sorrow, and happiness—will affect those around me, much like temperature changes, highlighting the importance of expressing and cultivating emotions.

The arrival of snow has "warmed" my thoughts.

65. 世界輕旅行

一次次的 Departure，一次次的 Arrival，
無數次的 Airport，無數次的 Shuttle，
數不盡的 Transfer，數不盡的 Transit，
道不盡的 Nice to meet you，說不完的 See you again，
反覆著飯店的 Check in、Check out，
航空公司櫃台，習慣的一句：Aisle seat，please，
機場經常廣播著：Attention please，……
飛機上習慣聽著 Tea or coffee；Beef or fish；Noddle or rice，
不同的各國海關，相同的一句：Next。
很自然的把 passport/boarding pass/immigration form 夾在一起，
簡單行囊，一只背包，一支全球漫遊手機，一瓶寶特瓶，
就這樣，
輕鬆自在，簡單愉快，環遊世界五大洲七大洋。

65. Light Travel Around the World

Departure after departure, arrival after arrival.

Countless airports, countless shuttles.

Endless transfers, endless transits.

Countless "Nice to meet you," and never-ending "See you again."

Repeated check-ins and check-outs at hotels.

At the airline counter, the familiar request: "Aisle seat, please."

Airports often announce: "Attention please…"

On the plane, I'm accustomed to hearing "Tea or coffee? Beef or fish? Noodles or rice?"

Different customs in various countries greet me with the same prompt: "Next."

Naturally, I keep my passport, boarding pass, and immigration form together.

With a simple backpack, a globally roaming phone, and a bottle of water, I set off.

Just like this,

Easygoing, simple, and joyful, I travel around the five continents and seven oceans.

國家圖書館出版品預行編目資料

愛自己的力量 = The power of loving yourself / 許立田(Raymond)
著 . -- 初版 . -- 臺北市：博客思出版事業網, 2025.02
面； 公分 中英對照
ISBN 978-626-7607-05-3(平裝)
1.CST: 自我實現 2.CST: 生活指導
177.2　113020092

心靈勵志 63

愛自己的力量（中英文對照）

作　　者：許立田
主　　編：楊容容
編　　輯：陳勁宏
美　　編：陳勁宏
校　　對：楊容容　古佳雯
封面設計：陳勁宏
出　　版：博客思出版事業網
地　　址：臺北市中正區重慶南路 1 段 121 號 8 樓之 14
電　　話：(02) 2331-1675 或 (02) 2331-1691
傳　　真：(02) 2382-6225
E - MAIL：books5w@gmail.com 或 books5w@yahoo.com.tw
網路書店：http://bookstv.com.tw/
　　　　　https://www.pcstore.com.tw/yesbooks/
　　　　　https://shopee.tw/books5w
　　　　　博客來網路書店、博客思網路書店
　　　　　三民書局、金石堂書店
經　　銷：聯合發行股份有限公司
電　　話：(02) 2917-8022　　傳真：(02) 2915-7212
劃撥戶名：蘭臺出版社　　　　帳號：18995335
香港代理：香港聯合零售有限公司
電　　話：(852) 2150-2100　　傳真：(852) 2356-0735
出版日期：2025 年 2 月 初版
定　　價：新臺幣 350 元整（平裝）
I S B N： 978-626-7607-05-3

Preliminary Cataloging Data for National Central Library Publications

> The Power of Loving Yourself / Hsu Li-Tien (Raymond). -- 1st ed. --
> Taipei City : BlogThink Publishing, 2025.02
> Pages ; cm   Chinese and English bilingual
> ISBN 978-626-7607-05-3 (Paperback)
> CST:1. Self-actualization 2. CST: Life guidance
> 177.2 113020092

Spiritual Inspiration 63

The Power of Loving Yourself
(Chinese and English Bilingual Edition)

Author: Hsu Li-Tien
Editor-in-Chief: Yang Rong-Rong
Editor: Chen Jin-Hong
Graphic Designer: Chen Jin-Hong
Proofreaders: Yang Rong-Rong, Gu Jia-Wen
Cover Design: Chen Jin-Hong
Publisher: Books5W Publishing
Address: 8F-14, No. 121, Section 1, Chongqing South Road, Zhongzheng District, Taipei City, Taiwan
Phone: (02) 2331-1675 or (02) 2331-1691
Fax: (02) 2382-6225
E-mail: books5w@gmail.com or books5w@yahoo.com.tw
Online Bookstores:
http://bookstv.com.tw/
https://www.pcstore.com.tw/yesbooks/
https://shopee.tw/books5w
Books.com.tw, Books5W Online Store
Sanmin Bookstore, Kingstone Bookstore
Distribution: United Publishing Company
Phone: (02) 2917-8022
Fax: (02) 2915-7212
Bank Transfer Payee: Latai Publishing
Account Number: 18995335
Hong Kong Agent: Hong Kong United Retail Co., Ltd.
Phone: (852) 2150-2100
Fax: (852) 2356-0735
Publication: 2025.2 (First Edition)
Price: 350 NTD (Paperback)
ISBN: 978-626-7607-05-3